PERCY ROGERS

Taking Action:
A GP's lifetime of learning, love & labour

First published in Australia 2021 by
Stories to Keep Pty Ltd
PO Box 5012
Brunswick Victoria 3056
www.storiestokeep.com.au

Hardbook ISBN 978-0-6452457-0-7
eBook ISBN 978-0-6452457-1-4

Printed and bound in Australia by Ingram Spark.

Foreword

I started writing this memoir in Papua New Guinea in 1976 while cooling in the evening after the swelter of the day. I was working as a medical officer at the PNG University of Technology in Lae. Uninterested in the clubbing scene there, which amounted to alcoholic socialising into the night, I sat at the kitchen table and began what I thought would be a list of the jobs I had done in my life. My then-wife had lost count of just how many there had been.

That was 44 years ago. Now, at the age of 93, with the world in the grip of a pandemic, I find I need to update my book on the second half of my life – arguably the more interesting part of my life.

A book of my career exists, *Active Labour: Memoirs of a Working-Class Doctor* (Black Inc, 2018), but these are my more personal and political writings. They speak of a time when a boy of 14 had to leave his family in an outback town in Western Australia just to finish high school.

They talk of social upheaval, success and challenge, and their impact on me for better or worse. In this life, I have found myself a willing participant in some of the greatest and most divisive political periods and events of Australia's history. My father instilled in me the moral judgement to recognise injustice, and this later burst from me like a flame. I railed against injustices and snobbery by whatever means I had at my disposal. This came at a personal and emotional cost, but it makes me the man I am. Just as the sculptor cannot create without making deep cuts into a wooden block, so too have I come to realise that personal change is painful, and losses are inevitable. There can be no pruning or cutting without some sap running out of the trunk.

Chapter 1
Early days

On August 12, 1927, I, Percival Stanley Rogers, became the second-born son of Olive Adelaide (nee Powers) and John "Jack" Alfred Rogers, of Busselton. My elder brother Jack had been born 18 months before me.

We were not a political family, but my father had a strong sense of working-class attitudes. A train driver by trade, Dad knew life's wisdom, but he was not a schooled man.

There were just five books in our house: *The Bible*; *The Gorilla Hunters*; *The Last Days of Pompeii*; a catch-all book on how to treat common ailments called *Rubbing Heals Pain*; and *The First-Class Engine Drivers' Manual*. Dad studied that manual, and I was always proud to say he was "an engine driver – First-Class," for he had his driver's ticket. In Western Australia, railwaymen were transferred every few years from one small country town to another, and we went with Dad. He was often away working a railway line for stretches at a time.

At the age of six, I briefly went to a convent school. So began a life-long educational journey.

In 1933, with my baby sister Rona added to the family, we moved up the coast to Geraldton – population 2559 at the time. I remember getting there by train late at night. The streets were deserted and we had no place to stay. Dad's fireman, Mr Kerridge, who worked with Dad keeping the steam engine fires burning, was given the job of booking our family's accommodation on the first night, and he forgot. I vividly remember Dad running up and down Marine Terrace, Geraldton, knocking on one boarding house after another. Finally, Dad negotiated for us to sleep on the big back lawn of a boarding house. The boarding house rented us mattresses and threw in the bugs for free.

It was exciting for us kids, but my mother was reduced. Not to tears or rages, but diminished. To have married a railwayman was a bearable enough comedown but to sleep under the stars was too much.

5

My mother came from a proud Victorian family. The Powers family was led by her father, who ruled with a rod he kept at the kitchen table. He would lash it down on anyone who opened their mouth to speak at mealtime.

The Powers family migrated to Western Australia in the gold rush days of the late 1890s, settling in Perth. There, my maternal grandfather declared he had worked enough and that his family of eight daughters and twin sons could support him. He was the ripe old age of 40, but his children obliged him. They were all successful, particularly the boys, Andy and Stanley, who were pampered and spoilt rotten. They both became accountants and then captains in the army.

My mother Olive was especially close to her sisters, but bearing children transformed those bonds into competitive tethers. Their ties were strong ,but they were often spiteful about their nieces and nephews. This provoked deep and bitter anger that lasted until they died.

The Powers girls left school for work at 14. My mother was a dressmaker's apprentice for 2/6 per week. She gave 2/4 to her mother and "kept tuppence for ribbons". By the time she was 30, she was running her own business, employing 30 girls in Hay Street, Perth.

Around this time, my mother fell in love with a divorced man called Adrian. Her father, with all the moral rigidity of the time, refused to let his daughter see a divorcee. When Adrian pressed his suit with Olive he was warned off by her brothers, we think with a beating.

Heartbroken, my mother abandoned her dressmaking shop and ended up in the wheatbelt town of Brookton. It was there that she met a young engine fireman called Jack, and he married her on the rebound. She was, undoubtably, still a virgin when she married, but the loss of that first love cost her. In her later years when her mind became confused, she would often recall Adrian. It was only after her death that I pieced together her story, for she was a proud, narrow and busy woman who held to her prejudices. Throughout her married life she kept her glory box of embroidered lace tablecloths in the bottom drawer of the dresser, only brought out for guests or "good" as she described it. This continued even when near poverty had diminished our family.

So that first night in Geraldton was not an easy one for my mother, who just a decade earlier was a successful Perth businesswoman, an employer of 30 seamstresses. Now she was sleeping under the stars. Reduced indeed.

But soon my father had built a family home at the base of Geraldton's Sanford Street sandhills. It was a timber house with a tin roof and fibro cement sleepout. I still remember putting my foot through the sleepout's asbestos sheeting as I aimed for my big brother Jack's head. Forty years later, I returned to find it mended, more easily repaired than the emotional scars of brothers.

My sense of that house was that we never had a sixpence to take to school. My mother once gave me a shilling to buy a present for a school friend's birthday. The quest was impossible, so I bought some lollies, ate them, and didn't go to the party.

My nickname was "Mutts". It started as "Mutton Chops," a loving reference to my chubby cheeks, but Jack turned it into an insult. I was fat, and stayed that way until I left Geraldton, living mainly off bread, rabbits and the occasional crayfish. The nickname remained.

My elder brother blotted my life and dominated the household as my parents pandered to him. He was vicious, cruel and physically stronger than me. He felt entitled to coerce me by brute force. This sparked a powerful maniacal rage in me which became my only defence. It was the only thing I knew frightened him.

My father was aware of his older son's physical brutality and tried to side with me. After one of Jack's savage beatings, I showed the bruises to my father. When big brother arrived home, Dad asked: "Did you do that to Perce?"

Truculent as ever, Jack replied: "Well, he bloody well deserved it."

Dad took off his coat, slowly turned around and punched Jack so hard I thought he had killed him. After that, Dad got us each a pair of boxing gloves and taught us to box in the kitchen. I can still hear his instructions: "Cover your face, protect your chin, watch your stomach, never drop your guard, lead with the left, lead with the right, lead with the right again." This went on night after night. While I was still mercilessly belted, I never stopped coming back and covering up.

I was not my big brother's only target. He viciously taunted my youngest brother, Alec, and my little sister, Rona. He was an absolute sadist to us, yet maintained friendships outside the family. Later, as a father, he kept a length of plastic-coated wire which he called his "persuader". His poor children.

I never stopped fighting him, even now he is long dead. Now it is an internal battle to suppress the "highly critical" influence he had on my personality. This trait has made me unfairly critical of others and has hurt my relationships.

Dad learnt to box from his father, a professional fighter who also spent time in jail for larceny. This may not be my family's only prison link. I have long believed I am related to the Irish convict Thomas Hassett. "Tommy" was one of 62 Fenians and Irish Republican Army dissidents transported on the last convict ship to Australia, the *Hougoumont*, which docked in Western Australia in 1868. Hassett is a relatively rare name in Ireland and both Tommy and my dad's grandmother, Ellen, hailed from Cork and shared the surname, although a direct genealogical link has not yet been found. Still, the Fenians' journey to Fremantle is a wild story of rebellion and escape, and well worth seeking out. I am proud to say, in 2018, I was included among the Fenian descendants commemorating the 150th anniversary of the *Hougoumont's* landing.

Dad came from convict stock but he had a moral code and he ensured we knew it. He would have local tales to explain right from wrong. Truth, and knowing the truth, was vital. He told us how a bloke on the railways had stolen a fish down on the wharf. When he was found out, he lost his job and could no longer feed his children. He could not get another job in Geraldton because he was a known thief. Dad taught decency and loyalty, and explained the working man's struggle to get a decent wage so he could have a decent life for himself and his family.

Because my mother was quite the snob, I was not allowed to make friends with the children of Sanford Street. They were the children of itinerant workers, widows and "sussos" – as people on "sustenance", or the dole, were called. They were "not the sorts to take tea with," as my mother would say. My only brush with "poor table manners" was when Mr Kerridge brought his family for Sunday tea.

Our oval table seated up to 14. We would sit wide-eyed as the Kerridge kids snatched food and yelled that "he's had more pieces than me". They were never "quiet at the table". Surely, Mr Kerridge belted them silly when they got home?

Dad and Mr Kerridge would be away working the railway lines for days at a time – Three Springs was two days away, Yarloop was three days away, Meekatharra was four days away.

When Dad arrived home, my mother would sit down next to him and see that he ate. He was as starved of food as she was of his company. She always made him jam tarts. My earliest memory of them together is of him, tired out, sitting at the head of the table and my mother replacing each dish as he finished the last, and her talking to him the whole time. If we ventured into the kitchen, we would hear: "You kids get out and let me talk to your father." We got out and somehow never resented it.

After school, we would ask if Dad was asleep. The answer determined whether we would play outside. When he was asleep, I indulged in my passion for the sea – fishing, canoeing and swimming. Late at night, we would go to Railway Jetty to catch crayfish. A bloodied sheep head was wired to the bottom of a drop net and thrown over the side of the jetty. Every 15 minutes we would draw it up to reveal our haul of fish, crayfish and the occasional octopus.

During summer, Geraldton was hot by day, but the cold sea breeze on that jetty blew through us at night. We sheltered behind piles of ropes, small sheds and pieces of timber. When I look back, the reason we were so cold was we simply didn't have the clothes to put on.

I was once asked to leave the classroom at Geraldton High School because I didn't have a coat. The newly built school was establishing standards and insisted that every pupil wear a coat.

My mother wrote a note to say that I did not own a coat, and would they wait till payday? Feeling very tiny, I returned to school clutching my note. I was barred at the entrance by the headmaster and his assistant. I was told to stay home until I had a coat. My mother gave me the housekeeping money to buy a blazer and that was sufficient. I only ever draped it over my shoulder or wrapped my football boots in it, but it satisfied the standards.

Geraldton High was an exciting but dual world. When I read my books the classes seemed thrilling, but at other times the classroom was a place of utter boredom. The drone of the teachers competed with the moan of the south-easterly trade winds blowing in from the equator.

I was good at mathematics and languages and was either top of the class or second. My father promised 5 shillings to Jack and me if we came within the first five in the class. We rarely missed. In 1941, we both topped our respective classes. My father complained about the double payout – but I knew it was to hide his pride at our success.

Like most intelligent, uneducated men, my father was idealistic and enthusiastic about "education". It was the answer, he said. The advantages were obvious – good jobs, clothes, no shift work, good salaries and, if you kept at it, you might well become a teacher. '

The shadow of war

Just before World War II broke out, a Japanese submarine had berthed at Railway Jetty. The boys raced down on their bikes. The girls hung back because we had all heard stories about what the Japs did to young girls. We watched as these small, strange men jabbered and tied up ropes, took photographs, loaded our food and water onto their sub and then disappeared beneath the sea. It was clear to us they were doing their reconnaissance.

Coming home that day from school with my friend Eddie Nelson, we discussed the international position. One Australian was equal to four Germans, 20 Japs, 10 Yanks and two Englishmen. The English had the best navy, Germany had the best army and Russia, we whispered, had the best air force. The Turks didn't like cold steel, the Germans didn't mind it, and any Australian loved it. With the war looming, our learnt prejudices were comforting.

When the war started, we had air-raid drills at school. No one was to panic. We had to crawl under our desks and stay there. Glasses made a boy look weak, so Eddie and I decided the bespectacled Peter Farrington was the most likely to panic. As soon as a siren sounded, we agreed to knock Peter on the head so his panic would not infect the rest of the class.

We were given knapsacks and a water bottle and were told to keep them at the end of the bed, in case we had to evacuate to the sandhills where a train was supposed to be waiting. We were convinced Geraldton would be a target.

Three times we headed for the sandhills when unidentified aircraft flew over Geraldton. The Japanese invasion felt very real then. And it was. Unbeknownst to the Allied powers, let alone us, there was a big conflict in the Japanese armed forces as to whether they should invade Australia. The Japanese navy felt they had stretched their supply lines to the limit. The army wanted to conquer everything in its path, starting with walking through South-East Asia. Thankfully, the navy had its way. Little did they know that in 1941, when Singapore fell, there were just six Wirraway training planes left to defend Australia. The sycophantic Prime Minister Robert Menzies had sent the 7th, 8th and 9th divisions to the Middle East – to defend Britain.

Each time the air raid sirens went off it was early morning. While we scampered up the sandhills, Dad remained at the house, exhausted from his shiftwork. Crouching with us behind a bush, my mother said: "My life is down there with him, not with you kids." I felt unease at that, but my worries that she might abandon us on the sandhills were outweighed by the comforting thought that she wanted to remain with Dad. It was a sign of how much she relied on being with him, and also a hint of what was to come.

My first schoolboy romance was flagged by a girl called Heather Schloss. I was kicking a football on the oval with friends when Heather told me Fay Farley liked me. In typical Geraldton boy fashion, I snorted and feigned indifference, then desperately set about discovering Fay Farley's identity.

Fay was a freckled, brown-haired girl and we went about for a long time. She took me through the local cathedral and, being a Catholic, knelt before the altar. I could hardly believe this pagan practice existed in sunny Australia. Once, on the Chapman River, when I was 14, she was determined to kiss me. She followed me around a Geraldton wax bush, putting flowers on my lapel until she was close enough that I kissed her. She wrapped her arms around my neck. Later, all I could think to do was squeeze her hand.

Riding home on our bikes, I was elated. I pedalled hard up the hills and felt so flushed I could have taken on "Pud" Green, the school's best fighter.

My parents learnt of Fay's existence when I was selected for the Geraldton High School Under 16s team to play against Perth Modern School. There was quite a send-off as the team boarded the Perth-bound train. My family crowded at the window with instructions to see aunties Eileen and Violet. My father, proudly, was standing back with a grin on his face. Through all the bustle, Fay made her way to the window, where brother Jack promptly introduced her to my father as "Mutt's girlfriend".

Aw, shit! Blushing and tongue-tied, I was too mortified to say another word to my family, Fay or anyone else until the train left the station.

That journey was a taste of freedom. Once we had exhausted our smutty jokes, the conversation turned to our opinions on every teacher. We unanimously agreed we would kill Modern School. At every stop, I filled up on a pie and coffee. When we reached Perth, at my stomach's limit, those same pies and coffees came back up again.

I stayed with my father's mother. Note that I don't call her my grandmother. Far from grandmotherly, she was a small, chippy Irish biddy. Mean, narrow-minded and very Catholic, she was constantly finding fault. She did, however, seem to miss the finer details regarding a cousin of mine who came to keep me company. Annette was young and well-developed, and soon we were holding hands and kissing. If the cousin or I had known anything else we would have done a bit more.

The football was a disaster. In typical sportsman style, our team agreed the score didn't matter. The game was the thing. I hated Perth Modern School for a long time afterwards.

In early 1942, under threat of actual Japanese air raids, my mother, Rona and Alec were evacuated to Meekatharra for four weeks. My father, Jack and I were left to bach. Dad immediately told us to put away every tablecloth, doily and mat – no unnecessary washing for him. We lived on rice and rice and rice. Dad was no cook. Lacking time and inclination, the most he could stretch to was a blob of tomato sauce on top.

It was during this time that an old bachelor, Mr Young, parked his camper truck beside our house and moved in. He convinced me that ants would take over the world. He gave me the worst nightmares of my life.

After four weeks our family was briefly reunited. Within a fortnight I was packed off with Mum, Alec and Rona to stay with Dad's sister in Pinjarra, south of Perth. Jack stayed back with Dad to complete his Leaving Certificate. My greatest wrench was leaving Fay Farley. My mother felt a wrench too, as the family ties were beginning to unravel.

While World War II upended my life, as a schoolboy in remote Geraldton and even remoter Pinjarra, I didn't give a stuff about the war itself. They were just foreigners fighting over there. How insular we were in Western Australia.

Pinjarra was a small, sleepy town. My mother, Rona and Alec boarded with one of my aunts. With a full house, as the eldest, I lived in a room in a brick house that opened up to an apple orchard on the Murray River.

While in Pinjarra two of my father's railway friends offered to take me fishing outside of town. One dinked me on his bike, and when we arrived at the riverbank, the two fell into a slumber. Just along from us was an Aboriginal man with white hair. He told me he liked to fish, but this was a "sorry" place where many Aboriginal people had been killed by white men. I later discovered he was speaking of 1834 when Governor James Stirling led a group of men in a massacre of up to 100 Bindjareb Nyungars. This story, the sadness and injustice of it, made a lasting impression on me.

Fishing aside, there was nothing to do in Pinjarra and all day to do it. Like the town, the school was small and sleepy, and I learnt nothing in the eight months we were there. No one cared. I did not attend classes but was instead set work by teachers to prepare me for the Junior Examination.

In Pinjarra, I felt the stirrings of adulthood. I could have coped with these feelings in a united family, but my father was in Geraldton and my mother barely noticed I was alive. Her time was taken up with relatives, her distant husband, and my younger brother and sister. In Pinjarra, I could see myself slowly dying.

Miserable and bored at school, I did woodwork for months. Towards the end of the year, my cousin Hetty Fawkner offered me a place at Northam High School, where her teacher-husband Freddy worked. I pleaded to go to Northam, which was less than 100km north-east of Perth. With my parents' blessing, I stayed there with Hetty for two weeks, then boarded with a local woman, Mrs Reid, for about four weeks. I caught up with an entire year's study within six weeks and sat exams for six subjects in my Junior Certificate. I passed.

After finishing school, I returned to my family, at Dad's new posting – the town of Narrogin, south-east of Perth. Our fortunes had taken a hit. The house in Narrogin was small and cold. There was no money except for my father's weekly wage. Once rent was taken out, there was little left. I began working at Mowday's grocery store – bagging potatoes, serving at the counter and weighing out sugar – for 10 shillings a week. I wrote a short story out of this experience: *The Town that Started to Laugh*. The story involved Narrogin shopkeepers who harboured a strong animosity towards customers, and a joke.

I saved up to buy a pair of "long-uns" pants and a coat. I was at a crossroads. I could see myself having a pleasant, aimless life, passing the time, enjoying a swim, tennis and dancing. Ahead I could see a wife, children, a house and a "name" in the district. Yet I railed against this conformity, itching to get the hell out of there. I needed to break this circuit of leisure and pleasure. My overriding fear was that the school year would start in Perth without me.

Fear is a great motivator, and so, in 1943, aged 15, I bought my rail ticket to start the school year at Perth Technical College.

Making my way in Perth

At 2.30am in late January, I closed my cardboard suitcase on all my worldly possessions and said goodbye to my mother. It was bitterly cold – Narrogin is in a hollow and the clouds hang low – as I carried that suitcase to Narrogin Station to catch the Albany Express to Perth.

With a lonely expectation I looked out for my father at the station. He had left home hours earlier to shunt trains. Passengers stood on the platform eating railway pies and drinking milky coffee. When the train arrived, I found an empty carriage and got settled. Suddenly, the door opened and there was Dad in his engine driver's garb – a jumper and greasy, soot-stricken overalls. He wore his engine driver's badge pinned to his chest. Relief washed over me.

It was a momentous departure for Dad and me. I have thought about it often. I felt he wanted to hug me. I was leaving home to make my way in the world, but he couldn't embrace me because men didn't do such things. It was agonising. I knew he longed to tell me something from his heart. Instead, with manly stoicism, he shook my hand and gave me 10 bob. He said he would be in touch. As the train departed, I vowed to keep Dad's parting gift as a valued possession. I was forced to spend it within a week.

I had no doubt I would get a job in Perth. An aptitude test had showed my mathematical ability was near genius level. Surely, I just had to mention this and I could name my price. I was wrong.

I had a vague notion of being a chemist. I found an advertisement for an apprentice to Mr Steel, an analytical chemist. He was a small and paunchy man with frontal baldness and steel-rimmed glasses.

He offered me 15 shillings a week to wash analysis equipment, sweep floors and keep the chemicals in order. The next morning, I turned up in my clean shirt, my pale green long-uns, and Narrogin blazer. I met the boy I was replacing, "Horsey" Rogers – no relation. Horsey wanted to introduce me to the world of jazz and sex in Perth. He told me the line to use on the girls at the Trocadero dance hall. I had to get a suit and learn the Charleston. We started lessons immediately, clearing the chemistry bottles off the floor and pushing aside boxes of acids. While Horsey jived, I whistled *The Darktown Strutters' Ball,* the words of which were "I'll be down to get you in a taxi, honey." Whatever the line was, I never used it as I never had any money to go to the Trocadero.

Horsey's ambition was to be Perth's most advanced dresser, and he suffered for it. Years later, Horsey turned up in his sharp gear to my university and the conservative students threw him and his sharp clothes into a pond. Perth men had strong notions of conformity even back then.

While I needed to work to live, I aimed to get my Leaving Certificate at Perth Technical School (later Curtin University). I couldn't go to school during the day so I arranged to attend four night school classes a week. I studied maths, physics, chemistry and English from 6.30pm to 9.30pm.

It was a good mile from the chemist in William Street to the college in St Georges Terrace. I needed to be closer. Near to the college I noticed the building of Elders Smith, the agricultural giant now known as Elders. It was a grand building made of huge stone blocks with long narrow windows. Inside the main office was a flight of wide polished stairs, which led up to even bigger windows.

The Elders Smith head manager, a Mr Foreman, threw me a glare when I first asked for a job. Hierarchical snobbery was imbued in Elders Smith's very being. Mr Foreman gave me the impression that he only employed the best boys from higher-grade private schools – boys from Hale School. To hear Mr Foreman tell it, there was something truly refined about selling sheep, pigs and farming stations. Imperiously, he said he would consider my application.

My prospects looked bleak until I told my namesake, Uncle Percy Burton. He told me to mention to Mr Foreman the Freemason Lodge where my uncle sang. I was hired. It was my first experience of secret societies and the value of brotherhood.

With the single-mindedness of youth, I told my chemist boss Mr Steel of my ingenious plan. Mr Steel did not share my delight. Instead, he became furious, describing me as ungrateful.

"Don't you know there is a war on?" he demanded.

Of course, I knew there was a war on, but what did that have to do with my Leaving Certificate?

Mr Steel refused to pay me. I was shocked. I gathered up all the bravery my union-man father had instilled in me. With the full authority of a squeaky 15-year-old boy, I went white and trembled that it "wasn't fair". I must have looked pretty upset or angry, for he pulled 6 shillings out of his pocket and told me to close the door on my way out.

Ever mindful of being polite, I said: "Goodbye, Mr Steel," but never made myself known to him again.

On Monday morning, I entered the huge hall of Elders Smith. I felt and looked like a schoolboy wearing a blue double-breasted suit coat. It was a bit big, so I shortened the sleeves and changed the buttons *á la mode*, even if it did hang too far over my bum.

No one noticed me or my coat until a typist directed me to the correspondence room in the dungeon. The correspondence room was long and marked by huge stone pillars. Along one wall was a table with a sorting bench for a dozen boys. Letters from all over the building would come down a chute at one end of the table. These letters were distributed in piles to each boy. Our job was to fold each letter, stick it in an envelope, and/or glue the flap down. The sour taste of envelope glue sat on my tongue all day. The letters were then sorted by whether they would be hand-delivered or sent via post. Boys used suitcases to hand-deliver letters to and from station owners and station solicitors. Returned letters were given to the correspondence manager, David Marychurch Jenkins – a more pompous name you could not find.

The pecking order was everywhere, even in the pissoir. If a junior wanted to take a widdle, he had to wait until the senior had shaken off the last drops of urine and buttoned up his fly. Only then could the junior seek relief. As the most junior in the building, lunchtimes could be a strain, especially after I'd had two or three cups of tea. Some of the other stamp lickers were countryside flotsam like me. Others were either stock agents' sons getting "stock experience" or failed Hale School students whose parents saw banks, insurance offices and stock firms as places for solid career advancement.

Most of the day the boys talked about the typists. This one would be good for "a root", that one had a good pair, this one was hot. Jesus! Most of their talk was masturbation fantasy. I didn't say anything for fear that someone would know I masturbated. At 15, I thought I was the only one in the world with that secret.

The jig was up when David Marychurch Jenkins, aged about 24, announced: "When you masturbate you get hairs on your palms." Three of us fell for it, looking straight at our palms to pluck any offending hairs out.

I couldn't talk about typists the way the other boys did. All the more as I regularly struck up a conversation with one beautiful typist in particular. After work, while I waited for night school to start, we spoke about Banjo Paterson, country and city life, and when the war would end. It felt like a betrayal to describe her as a "good root". Although she did appear in my fantasies.

This desire-and-respect contradiction remained perplexing, until years later when I learnt the true significance of loyalty in an intimate relationship. The risk of intimacy is vulnerability. I was green back then, but I got the sense that it was simpler to talk to a beautiful typist without leering at her in my mind.

The intention of night school was to try to cover two years' work in one and so, the Leaving Certificate workload was enormous. Studying was impossible by the time I had walked the mile from the station to eat my dried-out tea at Aunt Irene's, who was my mother's sister.

Classes were held in old brick buildings in a lane. The air in the classrooms was stale from all day use. I tried to concentrate, but the teacher's voice would drift away and my head would topple from my hand supporting it.

I tried everything I could. I tried eating sausages and mash before the classes. When fuel failed, I tried hunger, leaving my meal until after class. I also tried deliberate yawning, bending down and listening intensely, but after a full day's work my body demanded a short sleep spell, and I took it.

The only time I stayed fully awake throughout the three-hour class was when fellow student Joe Pickles climbed out the window behind our teacher, old Jock Hetherington. I was so nervous for daredevil Joe that for once, I couldn't possibly snooze.

My older brother Jack was already established at Aunt Irene's house when I arrived. We shared a room for 25 shillings a week. Life was barren at Aunt Irene's.

Like my mother, Irene had left Perth to live in the little wheatbelt town of Brookton. Pregnant and abandoned by her lover, Irene's unmarried shame was so great that she stayed behind a trellised verandah for the full nine months until her baby girl was born. Years later, my mother's competitive nature would have her whisper that my cousin, also Irene, was born "a bastard," even though my aunt later married her father, Ivan Wittington.

As if trying to atone for her shame, Aunt Irene maintained a spotlessly clean house in Perth. The lounge room was not to be used. There was no sitting on my bed. I was to sit in the kitchen, as long as I wasn't in the way. Studying was not allowed inside. Jack was unfazed. He was at teachers' college and didn't need to study. My only refuge was the garage, where I rigged up a table by placing a board across two boxes.

It was bitterly cold. The garage was wooden with a cement floor. Lake Monger was just 50 yards away and the double wooden doors were no match for the wind that cut through them. At the back of the garage was a sliding door that also let in a nasty draught.

One Sunday, my father walked into the garage on a surprise visit. It was so cold I was nearly frozen. He was speechless. I jumped to greet him. He was almost crying, so I made a joke and told him the icy air kept me from nodding off. Then I added that after I graduated, these digs were exactly the kind of thing I wanted. Two days later, he sent me a warm grey overcoat with white checks on it. I treasured that coat until it fell apart.

By the time I had moved in with my aunt, my uncle Ivan was absent from the house and my cousin, Irene was married. My aunt's sons, Ivan and Stanley, were away at war. Little wonder they joined. In 1938, towards the end of the Great Depression, Ivan turned 21. By rights, he should have begun earning an adult wage but was instead sacked and replaced by a junior. Unemployed for a year when the war broke out, Ivan jumped at the prospect of 6 bob a day, free clothes, food and a trip overseas. He joined the 2nd Australian Imperial Forces as a private. Stanley had absorbed his mother's lower-middle-class snobbery and applied for an officer's course. He went overseas as a lieutenant.

Occasionally, the brothers came home and invited girls over for a party as they enjoyed different house rules to me. On these occasions I was no more than a spectator. I desperately wanted a girlfriend, but I had no money, and no girl wanted to talk to a serious 15-year-old whose passions were study and reading. Yet I longed to be friends with just one girl. I wasn't exactly sure how you did *it*, but I dreamed of "accidental" encounters. These all ended in vaguely erotic experiences. In these dreams, we were always friends long before we took our clothes off.

As 1943 rolled on, my only interest in World War II was in the street fights between American and Australian soldiers. They constantly sprawled and brawled from Perth's pubs. The Australians would give chase, but the Americans would often escape on trams, as the tram drivers slowed to help them escape.

In August of that year, the University of Western Australia advertised for a cadet in the chemistry department. It gave two half days off a week for studying – heaven.

The university office had rows of books and papers, and a desk with two deep leather armchairs. Sitting in them sparked a life-long affection for club chairs. Awaiting my interview, I overheard university types talking about a trip to London, via Los Angeles and New York. It was a world away from my most expensive journey – the railway concession to Narrogin. Surely nobody could have enough money to pay their own way to America or England. "Scholarships," I thought. The conversation went on, with gossip about who was shifting laboratories and who was working on "calcium". I was in a foreign land.

Sir Noel Stanley Bayliss, noted calcium professor, summoned me and fixed me with a stare. I thought it was rude. Smart he might be, but his manners were poor. Like Mr Steel, the professor did not share my ambition for completing my Leaving Certificate. Sir Noel was decidedly cool on allowing me the full two afternoons off to study.

Still, I got the job and carted acids, filled bottles for medical and science students, cleared up after practical classes and was a general roustabout for the whole department.

The job lasted three weeks, and I believe would have continued had I not reached the end of my tether with Aunt Irene. Late home one night, I was getting my tea out of the oven when she came into the kitchen complaining that I had left the cushions untidy when I had sat in the lounge room. She then described the Banjo Paterson's poems I had hidden in a drawer as "trash" and a "waste of money".

That "trash" was the first book I had ever bought. Irene's words stung. She had no idea how much I missed the freedom of the country. I missed the bush, which, to me, was both a challenge and security. The Western Australian landscape of my boyhood was both an identity and an affinity for me. Banjo Paterson carried all the swing of the bush right into the middle of the noisy streets of Perth. My aunt's attack on Paterson was more than I could bear.

Rising from my chair, I pushed the tea dishes away and asked her outright what rights I had in her house.

"None," she said.

"Right," I said, "I'll pack my bags."

Throughout this enormous row, Jack just sat there, mute. "You shit," I thought. He didn't help me, and offered no support. I have often wondered why Irene treated Jack better than me. I suspect she was afraid of him. He had a meanness to his face.

I packed my heavy bag and lugged it from one lamp post to the next. It was so heavy I counted my steps and rested every 50 steps. I made for the tram, not knowing where to go. The YMCA? A boarding house? But then I remembered another of my mother's sisters – Aunt Kate.

When I got to Kate's, everything was dark. Her husband thought I was a burglar. Seeing it was me lurking at his door, he thought there must have been a death in the family. I didn't realise it, but there had been a feud between my two aunts, and my falling out with Irene was just grist to the mill. I was given a room at the end of a verandah. It was a temporary measure and, after two days, I realised there was no room for me and I had to move.

Back to the bush

I had saved nearly £5. I made 19 shillings a week at Elders Smith, but my board was 22 shillings and sixpence a week. I made up the difference by working on Wednesdays from 3am to 8am as a stock boy for Elders Smith at Midland Junction, where sheep, cattle and pigs were unloaded. A stock boy's job was to smack the stock on the snout to get them moving quickly. We earned no pay but instead received a rail pass to Midland Junction, money for three meals during the day, and our fare home. By using my rail season ticket and having cups of tea, I could pocket the 10 shillings and sixpence reimbursement and save about eight shillings. This, plus odd jobs I had done, gave me some savings.

I wrote to my mother asking her if she would lend me about £5 until the end of November as I intended to abandon Perth Tech and return full-time to Northam High School.

In Northam, many townsfolk supplemented their income by taking in school boarders, often developing strong friendships between the families involved. Sometimes boarders were kept better there than at home. The usual cost for full board was 22 shillings and sixpence. I allowed myself 25 shillings a week, with 2 shillings and sixpence pocket money. I estimated I could survive for one term.

On the train going up to Northam, I don't know that I had ever felt happier in my life. I would be able to study when I was fresh, and the Northam teachers were more helpful than old Jock Hetherington.

I stepped out of, Northam Station to see a dense fog hanging low over the Avon River. Swans were gliding beneath the bridge. The place smelled so friendly I was able to carry my case up to 70 steps before having a rest.

I stayed for a few nights with a Mrs Reid before moving to Mrs O'Loughlin's. At Mrs O'Loughlin's, three of us studied and slept in one room.

My roommates were Boyd Anderson and John Spurling. Boyd was the lanky son of a farmer. Like many farmers' children, he was going to teach. John was the son of a widow, and was going to be a doctor. I had no idea what I wanted to do, except get to school and get my Leaving Certificate.

To catch up on the schoolwork I had missed, I studied through until 2am or 3am, although one night I worked through to the next school day. Despite my determination, by November my money had run out. I couldn't sit for the exams. Although I was forced back to work, I was not despondent, as I could see my clear path back to Northam High and my elusive Leaving Certificate.

The Western Australian grain growers' cooperative, Co-operative Bulk Handling, offered well-paid tally clerk jobs to high school and university students. Students camped at the various railway line sidings for the harvest season, tasked with keeping accurate accounts of the weight of each farmer's wheat harvest.

To get an adult wage, I bumped up my age by four years and earned £5 to £7 a week. Starting in November or December, over six weeks I could earn nearly enough to pay for an entire year's schooling. It was my lifeline for the next six years.

The cooperative sent me to Lyons Camp, a small siding at the end of the Miling branch line, 160km north-east of Perth.

Before going, I had to explain to the headmaster why I could not sit the exams. To my astonishment, he arranged for me to stay and have a meal at the local police sergeant's house at Toodyay, 31km from Northam. Toodyay was on the Miling line. The headmaster wished me luck and urged me to return the following year. I must have appeared quite jaunty for I did not recognise this as kindness and did not know how to respond. All I knew was I dared not relax or lose spirit.

As I was the only passenger, the train guard invited me to sit with him in the van, to drink tea and share his wife's sandwiches. The guard was a friendly chap and I told him my dad was a First-Class engine driver. I described my battle to get my Leaving Certificate. As I rocked along for hours, looking out over the desolate bush, I became despondent. The only landmarks were a railway shed, a wheat bin and a weighbridge hut. The guard saw my face sinking.

"Look, son," he said, finally, "wherever you are, make it your home and make it a good one."

It is still a piece of emotional furniture that I use today – and I needed it badly then.

Lyons Camp was in darkness when we arrived on a Friday night – not a light, a house or a person to be seen. The train stopped for as long as it could. The guard waved goodbye, and I was alone.

I would never forget that night. I dragged my gear over in a couple of trips to the weighbridge hut and lit the kerosene hurricane lamp. I hunted around for some wheat bags to make a bed and to add warmth to my one blanket. For a pillow, I stuffed my boots in a jumper, wrapped in a towel. Sleep was nearly impossible. I heard every scratch, chirp, hoot, call and thump. Long before dawn came the most pitiful wail I had ever heard. It kept up for about 30 minutes, shattering any last chance of slumber. I later discovered it was a curlew bird.

With no meat supplies at Lyons Camp, my diet was spuds, onions and carrots. Once I caught a parrot, boiled it and drank the soup. For sweets, I became a dab hand at making thick pancakes smeared with treacle.

At first, my only companion at the camp was "Matey" Brown. A bin attendant, he was an evil, unshaven character who could talk the leg off an iron pot. Matey had been batman, or personal servant, to General Sir Edmund Allenby – commander of the Egyptian Expeditionary Forces in World War I. To hear Matey tell it, the 1st Australian Imperial Force would still be in the desert if Matey had not told Allenby to set off on the Charge of the 4th Light Horse Brigade.

Matey taught me his morning coffee ceremony. First, he put salt into the coffee to make the grounds settle, then he thrust a burning wood branch into it. After that, you couldn't see any coffee grounds, mainly because of the floating dirt and charcoal. Occasionally, there was another ingredient. If the fire wouldn't light, Matey would throw a cup of diesoline (diesel-gasoline) on the fire to get it started. On those mornings we would have coffee grains, dirt, charcoal and a film of diesoline.

All but alone at Lyons Camp, I was 16 and naive. I didn't know how Australia was governed. I was nescient of Australian culture. My beloved Banjo Paterson was all I knew of literature. Schools and newspapers taught prejudices, so I knew how I felt towards those I didn't understand – Aboriginal people, Asians, the Hun, and the eastern states of Australia. From personal experience, I saw all railwaymen as kind, decent and generous because they were the aristocracy of labour. You couldn't say the same about anyone else. Hitler, the international Jews and the Russians caused the war. We were, and always would be, on Britain's side. These were my "truths" back then.

One truth has stuck fast to me: If you read textbooks and "did" the right plays and novels, you would become educated. You could only do this if you had enough money to support yourself, and that meant work. Money equalled education. Camp Lyons was funding my education. My emphasis changed over the years, slightly, so that I believed education or cultural development must be paid for by the state or other means. A student needs to eat and buy books. Without them, there can be no tuition, and education becomes confined to the wealthy elite.

At Lyons Camp, I also discovered that the bush could be a refuge for those who sought unusual lifestyles. There I found a house-cum-post office run by a brother and sister, who lived as husband and wife. They made no effort to conceal their tenderness to each other. They never welcomed me in and they never had any mail for me from my family.

I tried not to dwell on the lack of contact. Many years would pass before I truly understood the pressures of family life and the effort required to retain relations.

By night, my right hand solaced the loneliness of the place. Always in my mind, I created a mythical relationship storyline before progressing to my erotic fantasies. By day, I took comfort in the money I was making, and saving.

After seven weeks, during which I would walk six miles into town for supplies and meet the train twice a week, my time was up. I cleaned my frying pan, billy and hurricane lamp and packed them into an old fruit case along with my enamel plates and mug. Then I set off on the train home.

Cheerier times

With Christmas just round the corner, I dared hope it would be a cheerier family affair than the previous year, when there was no money in the house and the festive season was anything but. Everyone had felt contracted and mean. The few gifts and special foods we could manage had done nothing to ease the tension. Jack was particular dissenting and I did not resile from him. I have no doubt this friction had my parents ill at east. We compared our dismal Christmas to what we saw others enjoy, and we felt joyless.

As it turned out, Christmas of 1943 was a big improvement on previous years. Never had I realised the influence money could have on relationships. My father had bought a big stone house with huge fireplaces in Errol Street, Narrogin. Two sons were home, both with cheques in their pockets. Jack was on leave and cashed up, courtesy of the Royal Australian Air Force. My cheque from the Lyons Camp work could support me for nearly an entire year. I had taken my place in the workforce as a man. Thrilled, my father took us down to the Railway Institute to play billiards.

"Meet my two sons," he said to a fellow railwayman.

"Gawd Jack, they're taller than you," said the man. "How do you control them?"

My father just chalked his cue and smiled his proud smile. "Come on, break 'em up," he said to us. "And I'll give you 20 start."

Neither my brother nor I took the 20 points head-start in billiards, as we knew we would be beaten every time. My father was a superb billiard player. He played this like he played bowls and bridge: "You must master it. It's no good just fooling around. Take it up and master it." We took his advice but could never beat him at billiards.

At night we played bridge. My mother was a good player. My father partnered me because I was considered the weakest player. The games were serious, but I could never be serious long without joking. The losers always got supper. As this consisted of a cup of tea and cheese on toast, the preparation was not elaborate. But at least with my brother and I helping out, we had more than enough food to go round. My younger brother and sister loved this short period of our life.

In 1944, I went back to Northam High School with a new pair of pants but no footy boots. My mother held my money. She sent 25 shillings every week with 2 shillings and sixpence for incidentals. I resolved to live within my means, but this proved to be the source of my greatest humiliation.

When I returned to Northam High, I suddenly found I was popular, and to this day I cannot answer why. My budget had not taken this into account, nor had my personality. I had been a lonely person up to this point and had built up a strong imaginative life that fed on books and mathematics. I had no idea how to cope with this new-found popularity.

Every afternoon, about six senior boys walked down the main street. Someone might have a health magazine with pictures of nude women, or someone would know a smutty joke, but the walk always ended at a milk bar. The milkshakes cost sixpence, or 7 pence with ice-cream. Try as I did, I couldn't make my incidentals fund last beyond Tuesday or Wednesday at the latest. I would try to skive off, but the group were insistent: "I can only come if you lend me sixpence."

I don't know why those milkshakes tasted so good but, combined with the companionship, it was all too alluring. I could never borrow money without feeling reduced in the asking, not unlike my mother when we arrived in Geraldton. Yet I asked week after week until I could ask no longer.

Every penny was paid back, but this only got worse as I was mortgaging my allotted 2 shillings and sixpence. In the end, I stopped, because it brought home again the lesson that everyday relations depended on money.

I was an average footballer but, in my dreams, I could do a 70-yard dash and goal with tremendous flourish. The only dash I ever did ended with me smacking into a goal post and breaking my nose. Aged 12, I had been prescribed glasses for myopia, yet I hardly wore them. I played by sound rather than sight, but I didn't miss a Thursday afternoon game. I played centre halfback. When I hired Noel Fitzpatrick's footy books for threepence a game, I was often one of the best on the field. The boots didn't fit, but they stopped me slipping. I was included in the school's first under 18s, and used my fists to bulk out my biceps for the team photo.

Without the distraction of work, I had the freedom to study full-time, and my school marks soared. In the first term, I was competing with the best in the class. By the second term, another boy and I were competing for the best in the class. Mathematical concepts were so transparent to me that I can, even now, feel the pleasure of solving some of the problems in applied maths.

The year passed quickly, and I passed my Leaving Certificate. Although I needed to take a supplementary exam in English, this hardly touched me as I never thought this an important subject.

Western Australia awarded 11 distinctions in mathematics that year, and three classmates and I made up four of the 11. This extraordinary feat at Northam High School was largely due to Mr Walker – a brilliant maths teacher. Unfortunately, he was later promoted to become a dreadful school principal at Narrogin.

Based on my maths score, I was assured of a place in the quota at a university. During the war, the competition was fierce for places and you had to make it into the quota. With my score, my place, a scholarship and a living wage were assured.

Was the war still going on? I hadn't noticed.

CHAPTER 2
Lumping it and leaving it

The day after finishing my exams, I headed home. But not for long. I loaded up my fruit crate of cooking supplies once more and set out for South Kumminin siding. About 300km east of Perth, South Kumminin was slightly bigger than Lyons Camp. It had a tally clerk, an attendant and a "black gang" or roofing gang – whose job it was to build roofs over the wheat to protect it from rain. This was a dirty job where even with a hat you got sunburnt and your skin grew darker, and the men liked the rugged esprit de corps the name gave.

Australia had a bumper wheat harvest in 1944, but buyers had dried up as a result of World War II. The only thing the grain growers' cooperative could do was bag the wheat, lump it into a wheat stack – as it did at South Kumminin – and hope the market would pick up in later years.

We camped about 100 yards from the stacks. Every evening, about dusk, I could hear rustling in the trees. It wasn't the cool breeze, but millions of weevils pouring out of the wheat stacks and moving towards the lights of our camp. (They could convert a healthy pile of wheat into a heavy mass of stinking necrotic filth within a year.) Soon every inch of my body was covered in weevils. There was no alternative but to turn out the lights and go to bed, lest these airborne pests make it into my ears.

We started work at 8am, bagging wheat until lunchtime. After lunch, we would stack the wheat or load it into trucks at the siding.

Bagging wheat is one of the most irritating jobs I have ever undertaken. For a start, the bags came open-topped, and we used twine to sew them shut once they were full. We would stand on a raised platform, called "the table", where bags of wheat would be loaded onto our backs, then we would cart them up a plank and lump it onto the pile. The wheat was manhandled into a hopper using an ingenious device called a Clarke shovel. Basically a huge piece of tin, the shovel was attached to a pulley on an elevator. Men needed to keep pressure on the rope, pulling it back, to stop the ratchet from taking off and hauling the wheat to the mouth of the elevator. The wheat then went through a series of buckets, spilling over into the chute. Men then fed it into bags. As each bag filled we had to jigger it between our knees to ensure the wheat settled down to reach the 180-pound (about 82-kilogram) capacity. The insides of my thighs were raw. Wheat also sprayed everywhere, covering my shins in a fine, bran-like dust that itched every pore.

Across one scorching week, the temperature cleared 100 degrees (38 degrees Celsius) every day. The dust, the heavy bags and the heat magnified petty irritations into major hates. We worked in anger and could fly off about anything or anyone. When a chap on a motorbike dared ride by shirtless, with a girl as a pillion passenger, that really set us off. He was soft, a bludger, a pervert – God, how we hated him.

The foreman, Dick, set us the work for each day. He would retire to a small tin humpy on wheels that we called The Beetle. We were polite enough to his face, but as soon as he retired, he became a lazy, lying bludger.

At 17, I wasn't the youngest of the crew. We had a boy of 14 on hand who lit our fires, made the tea and threaded the string on our bagging needles. He had a harelip, one of the many unrepaired congenital abnormalities in the country back then. Once, while fooling around, he flicked a grain of wheat at me, stinging my face. Without a thought, I wheeled around and kicked him fair up the arse and nearly off the table.

Lumping the wheat entailed backing up to the table with a bag hook, which we used to sling the 180-pound bags of wheat across our shoulders. We then slung the bags into a railway truck or onto a wheat stack. After a half-day of this, my shoulders were raw, so I cut the sleeves off my shirt and stitched them as padding across the back of my shirt. Even my throat muscles ached from where the bag pushed my head too far forward. After a week or two of this, I could lump for a full day without trouble.

On Saturday afternoons, with a half-day free, we'd pile into the back of a truck and head 50km to the nearest settlement of Kondinin. We'd spruce ourselves up too, put on clean socks and iron our shirts with flatirons heated on the campfire.

Kondinin was a single street town with a café and two pubs. My money was too hard-earned, and I didn't want to piss it up against a lamp post. So, while my fellow gang men hit the pubs, I would spend several dismal hours browsing the windows of the drapery store, the general store and the farm equipment showrooms. For added entertainment I'd order a tea, coffee or even a full meal at the café.

One night in Kondinin, we went to a dance. I knew no one and, being short-sighted, could barely make out the features of any of the girls. As mentioned before I rarely wore my glasses. My only glory came when a group of boys my age looked around at me and said, with obvious respect: "He's with the black gang at South Kumminin, lumping."

At 10 o'clock closing time, the gang would spill out of the pub and we would weave and sing our way back to camp. They would be ravenous, having eaten only a few well-salted beer nuts. With the fire lit and the frying pan covered with fat, we'd sit around eating fried eggs, bacon and toast, smothered with tomato sauce. No food ever tasted better to me.

Sundays were grim at South Kumminin. While the men slept off hangovers, I spent the morning cleaning up my tent and washing my clothes. The afternoons were long as the men would pile into a ute and head off somewhere. Reading never filled the void as I stayed behind. I walked through the bush but longed to find someone to talk to at the other end. I felt that while I was working in such isolation, life was passing me by.

Years later, I read a short story by Lyndall Hadow called *Sunday Afternoon*. A boy packed his bags and ran away from the farm. Sunday afternoons are like that.

After five weeks, a letter came telling me I had been given a position in the highly competitive science quota at the University of Western Australia. I read the letter while standing in the blazing heat on the table, and almost fainted.

After I recovered, it was back to business as usual. We began arguing about the number of grain bags a man could sew in a day. A fellow by the name of Jack Miller insisted the record number was 600, while "Snowy" Baker chimed in to say that the bloke who claimed that record used only the minimum 10 stitches to the bag and had an assistant to thread his needles. I worked out we were doing about 250 bags a day, to which Jack Miller said: "And that's all we're fuckin' well gonna do."

Jack had seemed pleased enough with my news of the university offer – he announced he was going to have a "skin-full" on my behalf. But while he and the others were outwardly happy for me, it was a reminder that I was not one of them. For many years afterwards, the fact that I went to university was something I tended to hide from working men. They could not cope with the contradiction of an average, decent bloke studying in such a way. University was for the privileged few. Out at South Kumminin, men like Jack Miller, Snowy Baker and Foreman Dick soon joined ranks against my privilege, and I left on the train to Narrogin two days later.

A tumultuous first year of university

Coming home was a happy-sad event. Everyone was pleased to see me, but the family was splitting apart. My younger sister and brother were quiet and sullen. My mother had developed a mania for fighting with townsfolk. She would row with anyone, from neighbours to tradesmen to members of the local golf or racing club. She reserved special resentment towards bank managers and "that crowd". The family disintegration that began with Pinjarra was nearly complete. My mother was clearly unsettled at losing her sons to war and work. This was not helped by the family's reliance on my father's wages, even though he sometimes worked 17-hour shifts or overnight on the railways.

Amid the gloom, it felt vital for me and my siblings that I return to my role as the family clown. It didn't help that our home was still devoid of cultural touchstones. Except for the mantel wireless, there was only my copy of Banjo Paterson's works. But that was enough for me to work with. I read Paterson's *Saltbush Bill*, which even got my parents laughing. I cheered young Rona and Alec with my comic songs, which were the only ones I ever knew. In my spirit-lifting endeavours I was ably assisted by "Steamboat Bill", a dog I had brought home with me. His name rapidly changed to "Mr William Steamboat", and then to other names, until the poor mutt didn't know what his name was. Yet, he amused my family as easily as I had calculated he would. As Charles Dickens' Mr Pickwick says of how easily an odd name can entertain people: "It is calculated to afford them the highest gratification, I should conceive."

While clowning at home came easily, I never saw myself taking advantage of the lighter moments of university life. From my first day at the University of Western Australia, I wanted to be part of the place. But I brought with me my working-class prejudices against the "sort" that went to universities. Besides, even with my allowance, I was poor.

With my university friends from Northam High School all taking rooms at St George's College, I joined them, as I didn't know any other residential colleges. The oldest residential college at the University of Western Australia, St George's is a relic of the best and the worst of British colonial educational institutions. It provided excellent facilities for studying, a separate library, and separate tutorial fees. Each student had a study with a combined bathroom, a common room, sporting facilities and a chapel.

After the bagging tables and my galvanised iron tent at South Kumminin – this was heaven. I shared rooms with my old Northam High friend Brian Le Lievre. He was studying engineering and took not the slightest interest in anything outside this course. When I met him 25 years later, he was a professor of engineering in Toronto and was hellbent on stopping Canadian uranium plants from polluting that country's waterways. The University of Waterloo in Ontario now has an engineering scholarship in his name.

At St George's, we had to ask tutors for permission to go out, giving them a semblance of control over our study. I always resented this. I went out frequently because I had met the most interesting young woman, Marie Healy. Until then, I had thought girls were only concerned with domestic chores, but Marie was the editor of the university newspaper. She would be my love for two years, until – unable to afford to join her on a holiday to Rottnest Island – I lost her to a student named Bruce Penny. Marie later became an editor of a daily newspaper in Adelaide.

Keeping up appearance wasn't always easy at St George's, and being poor was no excuse for being slovenly. I once left my room to walk over to the university when the janitor yelled out that I had something white sticking out of my trousers. It was my shirttail. My trousers had worn so thin that the cotton parted on both sides of my pants, leaving my shirt flapping from the arse of my pants. I missed my lecture as the janitor's wife patched the seat of my pants.

The dress code at St George's was such that we residents were expected to don gowns in the dining hall for dinner. The college warden, Josh Reynolds, intoned some Latin before we could start slurping our soup. The masters sat at the high table and occasionally a student was invited to join them.

At 10 o'clock every night, we assembled in the common room for supper. We talked, played billiards or got into fights. I was amused by it but, having worked with real men, I was well aware that these were boys playing at the game.

One evening in the common room, I was pouring out the tea and coffee. This was an accepted part of being a "fresher", or "scum", as the first years were known. One chap, "Tracker" Towey, came in and said: "Black tea." I had poured milk in a cup so I just tipped the milk out and poured tea in it.

"I said black tea," Towey said.

"That's what you've got," I said.

"Right," Towey said, marching around behind the servery, grabbing the teapot and pouring himself a fresh cup of tea.

I thought no more about it until Towey came marching up to me in the hall.

"You're pretty big for a scum, do you want a smack?" Towey said.

"Listen, Towey," I said, "for every hit you give me, I'll give you one back."

"Right, get the gloves," Towey replied.

Towey was captain of the rowing crew, and a hefty character. But I was unafraid. I knew I was still fit and strong from wheat lumping, not to mention all those fights with brother Jack. My Northam High mates weren't so confident. One friend, Harry, bravely stepped between me and Towey, saying I was too young to fight. Towey just lifted Harry off the ground and swung him around like a feather.

My blood was up and I demanded he put Harry down. After all, he was a polio cripple. Losing interest in the fight, Towey and his mates decided I should be thrown in the pond instead, which I duly was.

Weeks later, when Towey was leaving to work at an oil company in the Middle East, he made a point of shaking my hand. I don't quite know what that meant, but he got no change out of me.

I initially studied chemistry, physics, maths and geology. Still finding my way, I tended to play and socialise more than I worked. I did very poorly in the term exams with the exception of my old faithful, maths.

Around Easter of 1945, I went home to Narrogin. While there, I went to see my father at the rail yards – this trip would be the last time when I would see him fit and well. I caught up with his engine and I sat in the driver's seat while he did some shunting. I was still fit and brown from lumping wheat. My father introduced me to his fireman as his second "fool's head" – a reference to me being the second son and the joker of the family. He never mentioned my university place, though I could tell his heart was filled with pride. I waited for Dad to finish work and we walked home together, me carrying his tuckerbox. I felt so close to him that day. If ever he was recompensed for supporting his children, I felt it was that day.

Returning to university, I realised that if I didn't knuckle down I would fail. I would lose the very thing I had worked so hard to get. And so I studied harder than ever, never retiring to bed before 2am.

Physics was my first August exam, and I did very well. I felt sure I would breeze through chemistry the next day. It wasn't to be. Around 4am, the college hallway phone shattered my sleep. I wished to God someone would answer it as I had a chemistry exam in a few hours. Warden Josh Reynolds came to my door 20 minutes later. My father had had a heart attack. Even now, I can recall the numbness I felt and the distracted way I packed a case, went into the station, and caught the 7am to Narrogin.

Dad died within three days of my reaching home, on August 8, 1945. My 18th birthday was on August 12 and the war ended on August 15. What did I care? I had lost my father as I reached manhood.

The Narrogin household just collapsed. When I was a child my mother seemed strong, but I now I knew just how dependent she was upon my father. She unravelled.

When Dad's brother, Uncle Jim, arrived we assumed he was offering brotherly sympathy. Only later did we realise he was casing the place to put in a claim on what little our family had.

The post-exam break passed and I returned to St George's. My studies were a disaster. Every time I started to read, the tears welled up in my eyes. University lost its relevance. I went to lectures mechanically. This lasted for nearly a month.

I was just starting to regain some interest in studying when Dad's mother – the mean old biddy I had stayed with years earlier – accused my mother of poisoning my father, with help from my brother and I. She claimed it was to collect the insurance money to pay for my university education. She was an ignorant Irishwoman who had more fears than facts. She contacted the Perth CIB, and detectives arrived at our house. We were interviewed. Studying was impossible during the investigation. I failed every subject.

The biddy knew nothing of my family's financial status, as I was under the Commonwealth Financial Assistance Scheme, a government scholarship, so there was no need for insurance money to pay for my tuition.

Mourning my father, rattled by police and failing my studies, I had a fresh problem: how to keep my place at university and scholarship after World War II. In 1945, there were about 600 students at the University of Western Australia. We all knew each other. By 1946, there would be 2500 students, drawn mostly from the ranks of war veterans, courtesy of the Curtin government's Commonwealth Reconstruction and Training Scheme for returned servicemen and women carried out by Chifley's government. For hundreds of thousands who would ordinarily have missed out on a tertiary education, it was the chance of a lifetime. For me, it was a rude awakening – competition would be even fiercer now and I needed that living wage scholarship to stay at uni.

I went to see the educational officer about re-entry and he readmitted me. He restored my scholarship and asked me how I felt. Years later, my Australian Security Intelligence Organisation file would detail how my family doctor in Narrogin, Dr Jacobs, pushed my case for a return to university and for my scholarship to be reinstated. Dr Jacobs described how I was forced to work through high school and the impact of my dad's death. The officer apparently told Dr Jacobs: "I'll be buggered if I am going to make him work through university as well."

With my place at university assured, I left Perth to meet Jack at the wheat bins near Mullewa, about 100km east of Geraldton, to work through the summer break – him as a tally clerk and me as the bin attendant.

I felt more reconciled to Jack after my father's death, partly due to his conduct at Dad's funeral. Wearing his air force uniform, Jack saluted my father's coffin as it was lowered. Seeing him standing there that day, I realised he might have a softer side.

For seven weeks, Jack and I worked side by side. It was so hot that for most of the down time we lay on our bunks. Jack constructed a hessian Coolgardie cooler, which we hung in the shade. One day, a swarm of bees settled on the damp hessian. At lunchtime, Jack tried to drive the bees away with a fire under the cooler. The bees dispersed just as the butter melted into a custard, the milk turned smoky and the tomatoes burst.

One another occasion we were visited by a scruffy man with a posh English accent. We gave him a cup of tea out of the billy lid. He claimed to have come to the west during the 1890s gold rush with a Lord Perceval, who had bought land in the district. The good lord then apparently returned to Britain, leaving this scruff with the land, and an incredible story. The man added he was the only sane man in the district, and had the paperwork from a Perth psychiatrist to prove it. The vastness of Australia's outback makes for some odd characters.

On another day, a farmer pulled up in his truck and unloaded two wild goats as a gift. I wanted to train them, but Jack wanted to let them go. We had a terrible fight. Jack thought my year at St George's College had made me a snob, while he had been radicalised and democratised by the air force.

I felt I was his equal now, and was not prepared to accept such patronising, big-brother talk. I have since realised that even if I live to be 100, Jack will always be the older brother, and I will always be the younger.

To his credit, while we were both still in the sullen glowering stage of the argument, Jack came over and put out his hand: "I think we were the biggest goats." I wish I had been more gracious, but I agreed, and we shook hands.

After that, we played poker nearly all day. Our fortunes would oscillate from four matchsticks up to 28 down. They were big stakes.

On Saturdays, we would take the train the 18km into the town proper of Mullewa. From there we would head straight for the café, downing one meal of soup, fish and dessert, only to order a second. Even so, we lost so much weight from not eating enough at the siding that I could not walk more than 20 metres without my heart pounding. To save money, we used to ride without paying a fare. One day we were caught, and I felt so ashamed I never did it again.

That year, after years in the air force, Jack decided to go back to high school. He wanted to study medicine and felt he needed to improve his knowledge of maths, chemistry and physics. In the meantime, I would begin my second year of university, having decided to live at the University Hostel. So began four of the fullest, most exciting years of my life.

A whole new world at University Hostel

The University Hostel was a tin and timber structure built during the war to house Americans. A large building with four long corridors and cabins on either side, it had a shower block between each corridor and a wide verandah at the other end. There was also a mess hall with a common room. Most importantly, it had a separate women's block across from the common room, and it was surrounded by Kings Park bushland.

I had a small room in B corridor. It consisted of a bed, a small desk, bookshelves and a cupboard. Most of the other hostel residents were ex-servicemen taking advantage of the aforementioned Commonwealth Reconstruction and Training Scheme, now under the auspices of the Chifley government.

At the hostel, we had pilots who had flown in the battle of Britain, army men who had fought in New Guinea – men from every theatre of war. These ex-servicemen were grown men, not swollen up St George's schoolboys. I had been working in a man's job for years and these men had ideas. They did not adhere to any artificial hierarchy. I fitted into all this as though it was home.

Most of the men at the hostel had experienced firsthand the politics of war, and were bitterly opposed to the early Menzies government (from 1939 to 1941), which had launched Australia into World War II. While full of songs, jokes and stories, they were also committed to their studies. They were, in short, grabbing their educational gift with both hands.

Entering this realm, I realised just how unworldly I had been. I had known next to nothing about culture, literature, political thought or government. At The University Hostel, I became a sponge for experiences and knowledge. I began to wear army disposal clothes, partly because they were cheap and allowed me to blend in, but also it aligned me with the men I admired so much. My mother shortened a blue air force coat for me, turning it into a battle-type jacket. I became friends with nearly everyone in the hostel. Comradeship was easy. Ex-servicemen returned from the war with an enthusiasm for ideas, making the hostel a heady post-war atmosphere.

Women too were opening up my mind. A fellow student by the name of Grecian Snooks asked me into her room to listen to some records. She played Beethoven's Violin Concerto and I was in raptures.

On Friday nights, a group of us would head for the Captain Stirling Hotel, just up the highway. We would play darts, talk, walk home singing, then find out where the next party or dance was happening. On these nights, someone would organise a "niner" – a nine-gallon keg. This needed to be drunk as a point of honour before the night was through.

I was studying psychology, philosophy, physics and mathematics. I had come to realise I was more interested in people than the physical sciences. And to say I studied with joy would be understating it. I took pleasure in the fact that I could understand things quicker than those who had spent years away from study.

It was in this year that I became interested in politics. Before this, I shared the usual conspiracy theory of international politics common among the workers: decisions made by a small group of men had caused the Great Depression and the Second World War. These men varied from Geneva gnomes to Jewish financiers to oil company magnates.

Wandering one day through St George Terrace, to the London Court Arcade with its Tudor-style clock, I noticed a little jeweller's shop that sold pamphlets. I browsed through and found one called *The State and Revolution*, by a bloke called Vladimir Lenin. I had heard of Lenin, but now his words almost leapt at me. I saw the shopkeeper size me up. I paid him for the pamphlet and took it home. The next day I bought Engels' *The Origin of the Family, Private Property and the State*, then Emile Burns, *What is Marxism?*

Marx's analysis of class, particularly in emerging capitalist economies, was so simple but so true. When factory workers' wages drop, their purchasing power drops and they can no longer afford as much of what their factory makes. Responding to a drop in demand, the factory owners' cut production, which leads to fewer shifts and lower wages, and the economic spiral ensues. This situation was played out with devastating effect during the Great Depression. In 2020's pandemic, the Federal Government feared the workers would lose their purchasing power and the impact it would have on shops, so they subsidised their wages. But in 1945, I imagined everyone must have heard about this economic genius, and I was the only ignorant one who had stumbled across it.

Enthusiastically, I joined the university's Labor Club. It was a broad church of left-leaning individuals – communists, socialists, humanists and Australian Labor Party members. It was affiliated with the ALP, so I was asked to be a Labor Club representative to the ALP metropolitan meetings. The first ALP meeting saw one member take the entire meeting to explain why he was more suited to federal than state politics. He struck me as an arrogant oaf who had nothing in common with workers. I never went again.

By the middle of the year, it was necessary to study almost every night. The blokes I used to go down to the pub with on a Friday decided they wanted to go on a Wednesday as well. This move was instigated by an engineering student by the name of Ken Knowles, who had been known as a consistent drinker in the air force. He was failing university and his condition suggested he had a war neurosis. The pressure to go down and drink mid-week was very strong. I was worried I was offending my friends by refusing to go. Until one of those friends, Jim Connelly, said one day on his way out, "Jesus, I wish I had your willpower, Perce." I didn't regard it as willpower – I just said no.

Every holiday I would throw a few clothes in a bag and hitchhike on the Albany Highway to Narrogin. With Dad gone, life at home was worse than ever. Rona and Alec were both at school but most unhappy. Rona was daydreaming and had no schoolmates. Alec had his dogs and almost no one else. Mum was oscillating from manic activity to aggressive, defensive depression. She had a series of boarders who never lasted more than a few weeks.

One time, travelling back to Perth by diesel train, I sat next to a girl who was going to Perth for her holidays. She told me where she lived and I promised to visit her. When I arrived, her sister told me she was out. I waited for an hour. As soon as she returned, she took me by the hand and led me away from the house. Then she turned around and kissed me.

She then unbuttoned my jacket, slipped her hand onto my chest, and put my hand on her breast. Not a word was said. We walked like that in the park. I think she decided we had no place to go, so she arranged to see me at the hostel the next day.

Turning up in my room at 2pm, she repeated much the same manoeuvre, and lay down on the bed. I unbuttoned her shirt and started to touch her breasts. I don't know who got more scared, but we stopped, got up and went for a milkshake. It was not a very successful first encounter.

The year ended and I finished all my subjects. The day after exams ended I collected my bunk, hurricane lamp, frying pan and billy, and set off for Bulyee siding – about 190km east of Perth – where I was to work on and off for the next four years. There, I was the tally clerk and bin attendant. It meant more work, but also more pay.

Hostel comrades Les and Jim Gibbney were working on sidings just up the line, so we met every weekend and spent our time in the nearby town of Corrigin. The Gibbney brothers were Australian to the back teeth, but they had a strong interest in history, biology and literature from any country. They introduced me to Robert Graves, Shakespeare, Ibsen, chess, choir singing and poetry. Jim would end up at the National Archives in Canberra, where he produced 80 biographical entries for the *Australian Dictionary of Biography*. Les would become an Antarctic explorer, with an island named for him.

At the Corrigin pub, the Gibbney brothers and I met an ex-Navy bloke who insisted we share a bottle of whisky with him in his room. He started to sing Navy songs. He went through *The Ballad of Eskimo Nell*, *Good Ship Venus* and *Abdul the Bulbul Emir*. This started my abiding interest in underground songs and poems.

While I was working at Bulyee I became a tennis player. The Bulyee siding was little more than a wheat bin, a small store and a weighbridge – but it did have four tennis courts. The Bulyee Tennis Club would stage an open tournament every Saturday.

At the club, I started hearing the name Joan Ryan. She was a state tennis champion and the eldest daughter of an old local, George Ryan. George had survived the Depression with the help of the brandy bottle. As a young man he had spent 11 years clearing his land, living alone in a tent, before taking a wife. Then the real work started. They built a farm of bitterness and a family of seven children.

Joan came home from teachers' college after Christmas. She was a year older than me, rather plump and very fit. We clicked from the start and played a lot of tennis. My serve and backhand picked up with her. I found that if I wore my glasses, I could play quite well.

I used to stay at the Ryan farm on weekends. It was assumed that Joan was mine but she was older, and I was still a student. We were only ever firm friends that year.

I found myself won over by the district's salt-of-the-earth farmers in the Christmas of 1946 – a view only partially shattered when they became affluent 30 years later. Back then, the desolation of farming during the Great Depression was still fresh in their minds. Some survived with religion, some with the bottle, most had survived with hard work and an ironic sense of humour. To make a general point or describe a man, they would tell a story.

Jim Sandycock (pronounced "Sandy-co") was acknowledged as the biggest character of the district. Like the time he lost his finger in the harvester, only to find it a week later, sticking out of a wheat bag. "Gawd, it looked funny," he quipped.

Then there was the time a fire broke out on the Sandycock farm. We were harvesting at George Ryan's place to help him out when we saw smoke. We raced over to find about 20 men slapping the fire with wet hessian bags, and stamping out the flames. The alternative was to burn a low-level fire break further away to tackle it. One of those fighting the fire, Jim Poultney, said: "Look, fellows, what do you want to vote on doing? Burn a break down here or just bash away?"

One of the Corey boys shouted out: "You say, Jim, whatever you reckon."

"No," said Jim. "We ought to vote on this."

In the middle of a bushfire, we voted to continue to bash. This sort of democracy was grassroots stuff for me.

Jim Sandycock sprayed a section of the fence with his spray pack, but this caused a new fire to erupt: "Gawd, I had to laugh," said Jim Sandycock. "Young Arthur [his son] must've put kero in instead of water."

With the harvest over and the wheat received at the siding, large piles of wheat were left in what was known as "pig pens". These bulkheads were designed so one man could pile hundreds of tons of wheat. The drawback was that if it rained, the first half-inch of the pile would be ruined. This was where the "black gang" came in.

I joined the local black gang. We travelled from one siding to another on the back of a huge truck. We threw up our tents at the siding, always started with a cup of tea, and then began roofing.

In the full sun, the wheat not only became intolerably hot, it also reflected heat. By the middle of the day, it was impossible to stand in it. To overcome this, foreman Bert French would wake us at 4.30am. We would work with a short break until about 10am, then rest in our tents, away from the worst of the heat, until 4.30pm, when we would work for another two hours.

Friendly banter flew, continuing from the moment Bert woke us. Every morning it was a variant of: "Gawd, look at the time," "The bastard's gone mad this time," and "Jump him and certify the bastard." Bert left smiling. He knew we worked hard, and apart from a few instructions, he left us to it.

Throwing myself into everything

In the mid-summer of 1947, I returned to university, changing my room for a bigger one down the corridor. I was prepared to work hard studying pure mathematics II, statistical maths and social psychology. That year I found the work easy and felt I could express my deepest-held beliefs through investigations into my subjects, particularly psychology.

The hostel had developed a distinct "esprit de corps". We supported each other in university elections, recognised each other as friends at parties and dances, and were assured of a welcome no matter where we sat.

By this time, aged 19, I was a convinced socialist. I recognised that wars and depressions were the economic consequences of the capitalist model. Any tinkering with the economy only delayed the crisis, I thought. I had seen the effects of the Great Depression, and now I was absorbing every detail of the war. Such horrors had to be prevented from ever recurring. Comradeship could be encouraged and developed in a socialist society.

An ex-Spitfire pilot, Hugh Sanderson, convinced me of socialism's necessity.

"Of course, you must be a dialectical materialist," Hugh had observed.

"Yes, of course," I replied, thinking, "What in the hell is that?" I knew the term but had no idea of its meaning. In philosophy, we spent all our time in Plato's dialogues and the various theories of truth but never got around to dialectical materialism. I read Marxist philosophy and argued with the religious, the unconvinced and even the politically committed.

That year, I was selected as captain of the university's A-grade seniors hockey team. I also captained the hostel's basketball and hockey teams. I swam and ran for the hostel, running the mile in the inter-college competitions and participating in the hostel cross-country run.

In 1947, my brother Jack began his pre-medicine course, joining me at the University of Western Australia. He soon carved out a position of respect among a small circle of medical students. Intent on broadening my knowledge and experience, I sought my acquaintances from as wide a field as possible.

At one of the hostel parties, a young woman started dancing on the table where I was sitting. The room rapidly filled up when it was discovered she had overlooked her underpants. She later married into a well-respected Perth family and has denied strenuously any recollection of this dance. I was still a virgin, afraid that a pregnancy would derail my academic life.

Only two hostel students were married, a couple from Hungary known to all as "the Count and Countess Radovensky". They lived in a caravan on the hostel's grounds and complained bitterly to all who would listen that the advancing Russians had smashed their family crockery. To my regret, I never asked their full story and certainly never discussed Lenin with them.

I continued to throw myself into everything. I dramatised the song *Klondike Kate* for a hostel concert – it brought the house down. My cast included a man who would become Chief Magistrate of Papua New Guinea, a Dutchman who could hardly speak a word of English and the girl of my heart, Marie Healy.

We put out a magazine and I submitted two poems; one was published. It was a spoof of the British abstract poet Edith Sitwell – staccato nonsense – but it got taken seriously. I was asked to explain the poem to people who should have known better.

When elections for the University Hostel committee were held, I was nominated for secretary. The election went to three ballots. Jack was of the opinion that my electoral fate weighed on whether anyone could vote for "that communist". The other chap, Roley Farrant, won on the third count by one vote. My brother was right, and I hadn't read the straws in the wind.

The hostel took priority over university activities, but I entered various debates for the university. I once argued that the state should take over the care of children from birth, as most parents were incapable of rearing them. Bill Snedden told me I had presented the best argument. Billy – who became the federal Liberal Party leader and Speaker of the House of Representatives – was cultivating the art of saying the right thing at the right time.

Late in 1947, I joined the Communist Party. It seemed to carry the policies and attitudes of true humanitarianism. Its causes, like Indonesian independence from the Netherlands, seemed so reasonable that they barely needed arguing. Even Prime Minister Chifley agreed, referring the armed Dutch conflict to the United National Security Council in July that year. Australia became the first country to ask the UN council to resolve a conflict.

The misery of Western Australia's Aboriginal people was well known to me, and the Communist Party advocated the only correct humane policy – recognising through internationalism the equality of all nations and peoples. Meanwhile, Australia did not even recognise Aboriginal people in the Constitution until 1967. The Communist Party supported civil rights and Aboriginal workers' strikes. We were in fierce agreement on these matters.

My first party branch meeting was in North Perth, with about 10 present. It worried me that there were no workers present, only one other Australian and six anti-fascist Jewish refugees, along with other migrants. I was frustrated that the Jewish refugees spoke in generalities, which had little to do with what was happening in Australia. Australia's Aboriginal people and workers were suffering right in front of us, and here people from overseas were talking about the bigger picture.

The meeting started with a report that I thought a piece of fantasy, but people took it seriously. It referred to the Communist Party as "leading the working class". I knew this not to be true. The trade unions were affiliated to the ALP and, when required, the ALP "led" the trade unions and the working classes. Up until that time, no communist had ever led my father's union, although other unions could lay claim to communist leadership. Their second falsehood was when WA's Liberal Premier Ross McLarty was described as a "fascist leading a fascist government". I also knew Ross McLarty from my time in Pinjarra. He had a large holding down there and gave prizes away at the primary school. He was short, bluff and stupid but as removed from a fascist as I was from that first Communist Party meeting.

I expressed my opinions. Everyone was a little embarrassed. Then a Jewish couple – he an engineer, she a teacher – explained that the party had the "theory" to lead the working class down the revolutionary path to socialism. I argued that the working class needed to accept the "theory" of socialism before the Community Party could claim to lead the working class. The discussion bogged down.

I agreed to sell *The Workers' Star*, a weekly socialist newspaper, the following Sunday morning. By being pleasant and talking to people, I sold 17 copies. This was hailed as though a real revolutionary had joined the ranks. Hardly much to lay a revolutionary hat on, but the following week my efforts were reported in the *Star*.

Shortly after I joined the branch, exams ended and it was time to celebrate. We adjourned to the Captain Stirling Hotel, then to the university boat club for a dance. Marie Healy had left me for Bruce Penny. I was pretty upset about it.

I spent the next day clearing my headache before getting on the road to hitchhike to Narrogin. That Christmas I was again working at Bulyee, with Jack about 14km down the line at the next siding, at Kweda.

Everyone in Bulyee was glad to see me back. On my first day, I went to the store and post office to see "Old Bill". He had a shock of white hair, a ruddy complexion, walked with a limp, and had a habit of repeating the last two words of a sentence. Our conversation would follow a pattern:

"G'day, Bill."

"Good day, good day, good day, good day."

"Bit warm."

"Yes, it's warm, it's warm, it's warm, it's warm."

And so on.

As the post office operator, Bill's livelihood depended on a steady stream of farmers and wheat deliveries. He was also the official rain recorder. Rainfall had an impact on wheat collection. If more than 10 points of rain fell on a wheat paddock, and it was then harvested and stored, it became mouldy. It was my job to shut down the silo if more than 10 points fell. It could teem buckets, but Bill only ever recorded up to eight points.

After opening the silo, I began getting invited over to farm homesteads at weekends. I went out to Jim Poultney's. He was trying to educate himself by reading *Hansard*, the official record of Federal Parliament. He had hundreds of editions lining his dining room, but the speeches poured out faster than his eyes could take them in. He ended up tying a string through the corner and using them as toilet paper.

Jim Poultney lived with his mother, wife and three children in a house with a long kitchen, a huge stove, and cupboards crammed with food. They had a quiet working harmony. Everyone had a job, and after that, they rested. Any variance in work was met with long, loud laughter, particularly among the kids.

Jim had a quiet sense of humour. One day, I was driving a truck when the brakes failed. I crashed through the gates. When the truck finally stopped, Jim drawled: "Got a new way to open gates, Perce?"

Jack too was getting invited to homesteads at weekends. One night, we were invited to stay with a farmer, his wife and two daughters. He wanted us to go out to a dance that night, but we opted to stay at home. He asked us to mind the two Italian prisoners of war he had working for him to ensure they did not run away. It was common for farmers to employ POWs from the internment camp at Kalgoorlie. It ended up being a hilarious night. Us with no Italian, them with little English. Each of us shouting to be understood in the time-honoured translation method of raising your voice when you cannot speak the lingo. They taught us an Italian card game, I think called Scorpa. It was well worth missing the dancing.

But it was Joan and the Ryan family who monopolised most of my spare time. The Ryans were keen for me to marry their eldest daughter, and went to some lengths to encourage me. They went on holiday after the harvest and left Joan at home. I was asked to look after her. I would go down to the wheat bin at 8am, then pedal the bike back to the farm each night.

Joan would wear the most provocative gear. One night she had on her younger sister's shirt, so that her breasts stretched the buttons. If I so much as brushed by, the buttons popped.

We would sit in the big chair after tea, and kiss. I would caress her breasts, but between us we had no idea about sex – she had been brought up in a convent, and I knew nothing apart from the gauche stick-it-in-get-it-out-and-wipe-it instruction. This did not seem appropriate for Joan.

I did suggest I might creep into her bed one night, but she said she would be disappointed in me if I did. From that moment on, I started to withdraw from her emotionally. I thought it odd that she would not welcome the idea.

In 1948 the political limitations of farmers became apparent with the introduction of the Wheat Industry Stabilisation Act. The act brought back the centralised Australian Wheat Board. The board was introduced initially during wartime to established a single desk for export and to create a monopoly. Between the war and 1948, each farmer would get the best price he could from the agents at each siding. At Bulyee, I had about six agents, including Goldsborough Mort and my old friends at Elder Smith. The agents would offer a price per bushel and the farmer could take it or try elsewhere. It doesn't take much to imagine the collusion that went on to depress the price paid to the farmer. A farmer could end up with 1 shilling per bushel below his production cost.

The new act abolished all private bargaining. Instead, the Commonwealth Government negotiated the price on an international level and made advances to the farmers. It guaranteed a farmer's income and made wheat farming the least hazardous type of farming in Australia.

Initially, farmers were actively opposed to it, calling it socialism. I spent hours leaning over the weighbridge counter telling them socialism was not a menace to farmers.

Australia had one more year under Ben Chifley, and the country was still politically free. My enthusiasm for the obvious advantages of socialism meant I was blind to gathering anti-labour, anti-communist forces.

After this period, I went to Yealering for three weeks until the university year started. Here I did the same work with two other men, both permanent Yealering residents.

During this time, I heard about a motor mechanic who was a socialist, living in Wickepin, about 30km to the south. I called him up and expressed an interest in chatting about socialism and politics. Within an hour he was there in a car. We had a picnic of cold chops and bread beside Lake Yealering – a huge lake, cold and clear – and talked about politics all day.

The motor mechanic, Karl Bailey, along with his brother Harold, had been brought up on a farm by their educated mother. Karl stayed and learnt his trade, while Harold taught himself to read languages from translated Bible passages. He went to the University of Western Australia and, by the time he left Perth, was familiar with up to 40 languages. He became Professor of Sanskrit at Cambridge University.

Karl was a brilliant, immensely well-read man. He was a polymath with no training, but he had knowledge. What he lacked was a formal understanding of science and how it impacted on life. His passion, and later livelihood, was as a water diviner.

According to Karl, there was no need to study medicine because he knew a chap in Kalamunda, near Perth, who could diagnose disease using a plumb bob. When we went to see this phenomenon, the man gathered a few coloured pieces of cotton and suspended a plumb bob by a short string. His "diagnosis" – and a similarly quackish "antidote" – led him to pull a few leaves off a tree to cure his wife's diabetes. I looked for her name in the death notices for a few days, but she survived the cure.

After working for about three weeks at Yealering, Marie Healy sent me a telegram. I had got First-Class Honours in pure mathematics, Second-Class Honours in statistical mathematics and a pass in social psychology. Jack had passed all his subjects too, so we celebrated with a meal and a few beers at Corrigin.

Coming home in an old car, we hit and stunned a chicken crossing the road near a farm. Jack was all for potting it, but I noticed two "General Grant" tanks on the farm. I thought the farmer must have had a standing army on his land and insisted we move on hastily. I later found out the farmer slung a huge chain between the two tanks for "scrub bashing", or clearing scrub.

After the wheat bins closed down that year, Jack and I camped a few sidings further down the line and loaded the bulk wheat into trucks. We soon realised that we were both fit and strong enough to load our quota of 50 tonnes by midday. Besides, we could not stand in the wheat in the impossibly hot afternoon sun longer than a few minutes.

In a nearby paddock were some very tempting watermelons, grown by the husband of the local shopkeeper. They were the love of this man's life. He was forever telling us: "The young fella, he nearly got it in the arse," referring to his aim with the shotgun at watermelon pilferers. Undeterred, Jack or I managed a watermelon every day or so.

One day when the watermelon man offered us a swig from his water bag, Jack, in deference, went to pour a mouthful into a cup. The water oozed out a white mud. Jack couldn't drink it, and I wasn't thirsty. Jim drank it, saying it contained "the good hearth, the good hearth". This became our catchcry for dirt on the bread, dust in the stew and flies in the tea.

After this period, I went to Yealering for three weeks until the university year started. The two permanent Yealering residents I worked with went to the pub every lunchtime. I went once, had a couple of beers, and then returned alone to start the Clarke shovel engine. The beers had muddied my head. I felt dizzy and started to feel myself fainting. I managed to turn the engine off before flopping into the shade. Had I not laid down, I may have fallen into the wheat. Not a problem in itself, except if I landed face down and suffocated. It was the last time I ever had any grog in the middle of the day.

With work finished at Yealering, I spent a relaxing couple of weeks by the lake before returning home. While waiting for the train to leave with my gear in my fruit box, a woman pulled up in a utility to pick up a parcel. She was headed for Narrogin and offered me a lift in the back. It was the first time I had ever been driven by a woman. She drove carefully over the 70km journey, but I felt uneasy. It shook my sense of maleness to accept the lift, and I felt my prejudices were justified when I had to change her car tyre.

In my homecoming excitement, I was oblivious to the ever-worsening household tension, which Rona would describe to me years later. My mother had begun disappearing, leaving my young siblings to fend for themselves. Throughout my university life, I felt unease and guilt when thinking of Rona and Alec at home, but I was in no position to help.

Daphne and other discoveries

In 1948, in the third year of my degree, I enrolled for two psychology subjects. I began studying on the first day and didn't stop until the exams were over. At the same time, I was busy re-establishing my friendships. I was soon elected president of the Psychological Society, became hostel secretary, and remained captain of the A-grade hockey team. I was also the hostel committee member for my corridor. This mainly entailed ensuring noise levels were low if anyone wanted to study – except on Friday night, which was the recognised party night. If a student wanted to study on a Friday, they went to the library.

Anxious that my university degree was nearly complete, I was determined to make the most of my time. So it was often me who was at the library on Friday nights. It was on one such Friday evening, air heavy with the sensuous scent of pittosporum, that I first noticed Daphne Bennett.

She was freckled and had long hair and a diffident manner. She was doing psychology but was bonded to the Education Department and had to spend time at the Teachers' Training College. All this I found out when we went over to the café for coffee. She was an artist and liked dancing. She explained that she was a twin. Her sister, Rose, was the dominant twin and led in all areas. Both were very clever, but Rose somehow stole the spotlight. I had a natural sympathy for the suppressed and so felt sympathetic and attracted to Daphne. She asked me over to meet her family that Sunday for dinner. My company was secured when she mentioned she was a socialist.

Sunday afternoon I felt nervous. The house looked too grand and there seemed to be dozens of people there. Mrs Bennett narrowed her eyes at me while she assessed my suitability as a husband. The father was an editor at the *Sunday Times*, and a more emasculated product of suburbia I have never met.

We all sat around the tea table while the father told jokes. No one else said much except for the twins, who poured scorn on their father's attempts at humour. The mother continued to assess my prospects: Was I going to be a teacher? No. Didn't I like the Education Department? No. Did I know what I was going to do? No. What did I have in mind for a job? Nothing. I could see she had second thoughts about me, and that attitude would not shift until it was all over between Daphne and me.

After tea, the parents stayed in the dining room. Rose took the room to the left with her boyfriend. Daphne and I took the room to the right. Mrs Bennett seemed to be under the impression that we would spend our time chatting before returning for supper at 9.30pm. Both boyfriends were to start for home at 10pm.

As soon as the door closed we were upon each other. I was hesitant, but Daphne encouraged my hand to creep up her legs. Her pants were soon off after she showed me what she liked most – and she liked it frequently. She unbuttoned my fly. My trousers stayed on, in case of an emergency, but her hand did the job, and a wet stain on my underpants showed we had had a very successful chat.

Daphne and I soon established a favourite spot under a stage at an outdoor theatre. The climate in Perth was made for such "outdoor loving", and we quickly worked out an effective means of contraception. A blanket, a contraceptive pessary, and we were lost to the world for an hour.

With Daphne I could see a life reduced to a respectable job, a wife and family, mortgages. In short, the kind of slow death I had escaped in Narrogin. Slow death was not on my agenda. I had not even started to see Australia or to explore the ideas of the world. I had barely begun and could not stop now. Daphne made stopping very attractive, but the world seemed so alive and active – I needed to be a part of it. Daphne would have gone with me, but I would have been held back as I advocated for ideas.

Eventually, her response would be: Why you? Why not someone else? You must think of your wife and children.

My enthusiasm for Daphne conflicted with my fervour for the strong Communist Party branch I found at university. The university communists ran the branch as if it was a secret society. While I enjoyed good relations with everyone on campus, branch members were isolated from students and seemed to me to pick unnecessary fights. When the university branch members talked about the working class, I almost laughed. None of them had ever worked for a living. Some had "industrial experience" but went home after work, had a good bath and relaxed in a comfortable home with a whisky and soda. Most of them didn't know a worker outside the very few who were in the party. I found it uncomfortable, but this was the Marxist Party. The ideas were sound and inspiring, so I stuck with it.

Back then, you could be a socialist supporter of the Labor Party, a general humanist and a supporter of the Labor Club – you didn't have to confine yourself to one persuasion. I felt the Labor Club espoused humanist values, while humanism taken to its natural conclusion was socialism.

When Audrey Blake, a prominent communist and Eureka Youth League, came back to Australia from a communist youth conference in Budapest, she said that all socialist youth must honestly declare themselves as Marxist-Leninists to establish a political position of independence from the Labor Party. She said that labor clubs at universities should be exclusively for Marxist-Leninists. This move was designed to attract Australia's socialist youth to the party rather than the Labor Party.

To carry the word to Perth, Melbourne University activist Ian Turner came over and met the socialist students. I couldn't understand half of what he said, but at a meeting, I questioned whether cutting ourselves off from other left-leaning students was wise. I explained that I had a wide circle of left-leaning friends who did not declare themselves as Marxist-Leninists, and under these changes they would be excluded as members. Such a move, I felt, was too sectarian and limiting. My approach was to talk to and work with these people, not cut them off.

Turner's response suggested he regarded me as an enemy. Talking to others after the meeting, I was suspected of having suspiciously right-wing deviations. I considered this to be bullshit. This I made clear to the leader of the university branch of the Communist Party, Brian Carey. We fought, and slowly I drifted from the Communist Party. I made a basic mistake in those days of believing that unless you were in the party you could not champion the ideas of Marx and Lenin.

My studies during 1948 delved into every branch of psychology. It was four years later that I realised how superficial and eclectic these studies were.

During this time, I did a final-year project where I surveyed Indigenous orphans at New Norcia, the old Benedictine mission about 130km north of Perth. Also on the project were three other final-year psychology students, two women and a man.

Back then, it was said that Aboriginal children were incapable of absorbing much education and that from the age of about 14, their intelligence deteriorated. This kept Aboriginal boys suppressed in manual farm work and girls in household servitude. They were unable to continue any education.

Although I later realised how superficial this study was, we dined out on that project for months, as it captured the imagination of the psychology department. I discovered that I could convince people as a public speaker – my principle being that I never said anything I did not believe, and I said it with sincerity.

That year my work never fell below First-Class Honours. And it was over all too soon. I was back on the road again to Narrogin to unpack my billy, frying pan, bed and hurricane lamp.

An English migrant I met at the hostel, Alan Richardson, was going to join me at the wheat bins as my tally clerk. He had been in the Communist Party of Great Britain and was rather bewildered by the narrow, aggressive and isolationist stance taken by Australia's local party members. Alan and I became friends. He was a person outside my experience. While politically alert, he combined this with such things as acting, reading plays and reciting poetry aloud. Alan invited me to his family's home in Perth's bayside suburbs, and his father insisted I read Charles Dickens and a little-known author A Neil Lyons. I enjoyed *The Pickwick Papers* so much I could recall whole paragraphs. His father could recite pages of Dickens.

Alan was keen to see the country, so we went off together. I found I had to translate the farmers for Alan, and Alan for the farmers. We enjoyed our camp, and even more so when the results came through. I had gained First-Class Honours in both my psychology subjects.

After the wheat bins had finished I spent very little time at home. The head of the psychology department wrote to me, asking if I would conduct an intelligence and educational ability survey of the Aboriginal children of the north-west coast of Western Australia. I hitchhiked to Perth to see the state's Commissioner of Public Health, Dr Cecil Cook, who was funding the survey.

The educational theory that Aboriginal children's intellect diminished from after their 14th year was so prevalent by the late 1940s that the annual report by the Commissioner of Native Affairs, Auber Octavius Neville, stated as much. The Department of Native Affairs and the Department of Education would do nothing to rock the boat. Both were sitting on an explosive situation, and with an active United Nations organisation and a Federal Labor Government, the old policy of absolute suppression had to be held tight.

Only the Department of Health and its enlightened commissioner Dr Cook would do anything to disprove this theory. As Chief Protector of Aborigines for Northern Australia, Cook had already famously fought battles for Indigenous health up north and was not about to take a backward step.

An interview with Cecil Cook went well until the last question.

"I must ask you, are you a communist?" Cook asked.

I had been expecting the question. The chill winds of anti-communism had been blowing in the newspapers, and those winds had picked up a bit. I looked him straight in the face and said: "I am a scientist."

"Yes, good answer," he said.

Technically, I had resigned from the party, but I am sure he knew my political attitudes. When asked what salary I wanted, I said £10 a week. Cook thought my price too low, but I said I wasn't doing it for the money. Besides, I would earn that if I worked elsewhere.

When I told Daphne, she became scared that my communist status might be checked, but federally the Labor government remained in power, with the secret police kept at bay.

Flying north

I left Perth in February of 1949, on my first aeroplane flight. I was worried I would get airsick, as I knew I got very seasick. As the plane rumbled, I could feel myself getting more and more nauseated. "This is where I chunder," I thought. I looked out the window and saw the plane was stationary. Since then, I have never had the slightest hint of aircraft nausea.

That flight opened up a new world as we passed over the most desolate country I have ever seen.

The characters I met on that trip felt like they were all in a play called *Outback*, so fictional did it feel. We picked up two men at Hammersley who told me they were on the run and were heading north. They told me about bashing up a "Jew boy". I'd never heard the expression before and felt their story seemed false.

At Port Hedland, the local paymaster drove me to The Esplanade Hotel. I soon found that the taps here ran with seawater – so the showers ironed, rather than combed, your hair – and my room above the bar allowed me to hear all the brawls and arguments that flowed until 3am.

The bar was filled with locals and stockmen drinking away their farming station cheques. They were usually dressed in leather chaps, wide-brimmed hats, boots and spurs. I never saw one ride a horse, but saw plenty dressed for a western movie.

Locals quickly became hostile towards both the survey and me. A few years earlier, the local Aboriginal people had gone on strike, seeking 30 shillings a week for station work, along with better conditions and treatment all round. This challenge to slave labour signalled profit losses or ruin to the squatters. The chief negotiator for the Aboriginal people, a white prospector called Don McLeod, had been jailed in Port Hedland, as had Indigenous leaders Clancy McKenna and Dooley "Winyirin" Bin Bin, who were both sentenced to three months hard labour.

By the time I arrived, tensions had simmered down, but the dispute bubbled until 1949, when the Seamen's Union refused to load wool onto the *SS Kybra* at Port Hedland in support of the Indigenous workers' industrial action.

White locals were guarded and suspicious of me as it was seen that I was out to prove the Aboriginal people were as good as the whites – of course, that was my premise. For the entire time I was there, only two white people spoke to me, the Inspector of Native Affairs, Laurie O'Neill, who was checking up on me, and the inspirational local physician Dr Eric Saint.

Dr Saint was an Englishman with the Royal Flying Doctor Service. I believe he instigated the survey. He was delighted when I told him I had read Engels' *Origin of the Family, Private Property and the State*, and he lent me a few other books.

We went to Marble Bar one morning, with the temperature beyond 100 degrees Fahrenheit (38 degrees Celsius) by 8am. Marble Bar's teacher told me she believed the Aboriginal people had close rhythms with nature, and so had a much better artistic feel than white children. Nothing I had seen contradicted this.

Originally, I planned to survey several north-west coastal towns, but the Department of Native Affairs succeeded in limiting the survey to Port Hedland, and only the primary school and convent children at that.

The Port Hedland primary school teacher was a Catholic who regarded Aboriginal people as the hewers of wood and the carriers of water. One day, he barred me from visiting his home, fearing I was contaminating his timid wife with my ideas of equality.

Once the primary school survey was complete, I moved onto the convent, where I found the sisters to be charming, very fresh and convinced they were being persecuted for their Catholic beliefs.

The upshot of the survey was that Aboriginal children performed as well as white children where they had equivalent exposure to education. They performed equally on culturally neutral tests but poorly on tests based on Western culture. In both schools, the most intelligent child was Aboriginal.

These were hardly world-shattering findings, but within a week of my submitting the report I received a call from the WA Native Affairs Minister, Ross McDonald. He questioned my qualifications and asked me to suppress the results from the public. I refused the censorship as the Health Department, not his department, had funded the survey.

I was interviewed on radio and invited to speak at an Aboriginal rights meeting at Narrogin. Dr Jacobs, who had long supported my education, chaired the meeting. After I spoke, the Aboriginal people present were urged to leave the hall as Narrogin had a curfew of 8pm for Aboriginal people. They returned home to an Aboriginal reserve with one tap to serve up to a dozen families. Coincidentally, the reserve was also the local tip. This was in March, 1949.

The chill of the Cold War

Returning to studying psychology at university, I felt a growing sense of dissatisfaction. Psychology felt inconclusive and, in an odd way, wrong. I thought perhaps it would come alive through its application and enrolled to do an honours year in educational psychology.

I knew very little about education, so enrolled in a Bachelor of Education and was granted permission to do Education I, Education II, English I plus my honours course in psychology.

I was interested in the conditions under which children learn and the social relations that promoted and retarded learning. To study this, I set up three groups of children to teach. I taught them using three methods – the democratic discussion method, a didactic method and a laissez-faire method.

Still, I felt a vague uneasiness. My studies were becoming too removed from what was happening. I found the newspapers' strident anti-communist flavour and the hardening of attitudes towards communists disturbing.

Upon my return to university, I was immediately called up before a Student Representative Council committee. A left-wing witch hunt was running.

It was sparked in late 1948 by Brian Carey, the head of the university branch of the Communist Party, and my old political sparring partner. He had published an atypical undergraduate leaflet criticising an economics lecture. The right-wing SRC committee of inquiry seized upon the leaflet and my study as "scandals" that had to be investigated. The committee was stacked by mainly Catholic anti-communists.

Long before Joseph McCarthy, Roy Cohn and Richard Nixon began their anti-communist witch-hunts in the US, this form of political intimidation was under way in Western Australia.

I was called up before the committee, chaired by the SRC president, Bruce Rosier. He was later a Rhodes Scholar and an Anglican bishop. A Catholic student lawyer conducted the cross-examination. His first question irked me as much as his manner, so I told them that I thought this method of inquisition was the most undemocratic thing I had ever heard of, and furthermore I had no intention of taking any further part in it. I carried on for about five minutes. When I paused, Rosier said: "You are not doing yourself much good by this sort of thing."

That set me off again. Grecian Snooks – who would later become a historian and marry fellow student Ross Day, Professor of Psychology at Monash University – started applauding my outburst for all she was worth. The inquisition was a shambles. But for me, it had kicked off the Cold War at the University of Western Australia.

Throughout the year I concentrated on studying. Politically, the right-wing campaign against the Federal Labor Government was in full throat. The banks were campaigning against bank nationalisation, so everyone wanted to argue this out.

In mid-1949, after forgoing pay increases during the war, the coal miners union went on strike. I supported the strike, believing their grievances to be genuine. Years later, I learnt the Communist Party-led union had used the strike to expose the social democrat members of the Chifley government as traitors to the working class. The Chifley social democrats limited themselves to the payrise issue. The Communist Party believed the strike was an opportunity to nationalise the coal industry and take the first steps towards the socialist revolution in Australia. This was orchestrated by Jack Blake, then a Communist Party central committee member. The miners' economic issues were secondary. As expected, Chifley put the troops into the mines. After defending the Labor Party in so many arguments, I couldn't resolve the contradiction that posed without condemning the party.

It had become an anti-Australian stance to support the only known socialist country, Russia. I was becoming alienated from my friends. Despite positive Russian sentiment during the war, the press campaign had now turned Russia into a dirty word.

The bright spot of this year was the People's Liberation Army's victory on October 1, 1949, in China, which prompted the founding of the People's Republic of China. The local press and anti-communists at the university tried to portray this as a local skirmish to be resolved, but the People's Army was so strong and popular it endured.

The more the right-wing forces buffeted me, the more they pushed me into the bosom of communism. The left-wing members of the Labor Party fell silent. No one was saying anything except the communists and a few brave souls. This was Perth in 1949, even before the long Cold War years of Menzies.

The trouble was I could see the mistakes and downright stupidities of local communists, and I made this plain to them. Still, I felt guilty when a group of local party members were bashed up at the speakers' corner on The Esplanade, the site of public speeches in Perth every Sunday since the 1890s. I made it my business to be there to help bulk out the crowd and protect the speakers from harm. A small group of young bloods would turn up week after week with a skinful of booze, supplied by the local publican who hated communists. They tried to prevent the communists from speaking. The rowdy roughs had the protection of the police, and nearly every Sunday there was a brawl.

As the Cold War began, Daphne's mother stepped up her own cold war against me. She told Daphne it was time I settled down to a job if I was going to make anything of my life and marry her.

The whole Perth socialist scene was slowly being strangled. Coupled with this were the obvious pleasures of living in Perth – the beaches, the sun, the surf, the beautiful parks. All together or singly, they were capable of seducing me away from any political involvement.

Chapter 3
Beyond Perth

I had little difficulty in passing my exams at the end of 1949, although I had to do a supplementary examination in Education II. After I got my results I applied for a position as a psychology tutor at the University of Melbourne. The application asked for my academic record and, not wanting to boast, I wrote that "I have some mathematics". The department was chasing someone with my maths background, but as I kept a low profile, my psychology graduate colleague Cecily Ryan, who had no maths, was chosen. Cecily also stood out as a candidate as her brother-in-law Fred Emery, a fellow graduate from the University of WA, was an academic in the department.

One week after my exams, I was offered a job heading up the Hobart lab of the Commonwealth Acoustics Laboratories, a research and hearing service initially set up for children and war veterans. The salary was much higher than the Melbourne Uni job, and I had to attend training in Sydney.

I felt guilty that I was leaving Rona and Alec to the chaos of our mother's decision-making. With Rona having started university the previous year, the rash behaviour had reached epic proportions. She had mortgaged the family home and used the money to trip around the eastern states, abandoning Alec, then aged about 12, to fend for himself without money or food. He found himself a part-time job carting wood. Being the person he was, Alec eventually upped and followed our mother, finding her in Mildura. I had been oblivious to my mother's absence, and the house sale, until she turned up in North Perth. She had rented a home with four tennis courts, which she leased out. She expected Alec to push the heavy roller across these courts up to three times a week. He developed strong muscles. I helped Alec, as did Rona, but it was still hard work and most inconsiderate of our mother.

I had encouraged Rona to enrol at university, promising to send her money each week from my salary, allowing her to live at the University Hostel. Though she only passed two subjects, she dearly wanted to continue.

Daphne was tearful at our parting, while I tried to make a joke of my going away. I felt mixed up and lonely but excited about Sydney. Around the same time my old flame Joan Ryan had returned to Perth from two years in Melbourne studying physical education. She was about 14 stone and, although very keen on me, it was finished between us. Between a man and a woman there comes a critical point in the relationship at which, if either one retreats, the relationship is doomed. That time at the farmhouse was that critical point. We parted as friends.

I borrowed £30 from friends for my train fare to Sydney – £15 from Bert Anderson and £15 from Vivian Voss. Both were paid back, but as Voss became a multimillionaire he may not have noticed a loss. Voss ended up leaving university. He built up a mini wheat trucking empire, before moving to England to earn his fortune in commercial printing, eventually returning to Perth.

Travelling to Sydney, I dropped into Adelaide to see my brother Jack who was studying medicine. Western Australia offered only pre-medicine before 1957. Talking to him and seeing what he was studying, I realised the big gap in my knowledge. I studied the psychology of people and the conditions under which they change. I knew nothing about their physical being. This planted the seed of studying medicine in my mind.

Going to my new job, I felt more than the usual nerves. Even though I was leaving my political colleagues behind at university, I felt I would need to keep my political leanings secret if I was to remain in the public service.

On December 10, 1949, the Chifley government was defeated and Robert Menzies came to power. I felt certain that if the public service checked my Perth record I would be out on my ear. Like thousands of others, for years I felt I needed to fight to be considered part of my country of birth.

After arriving in Sydney and meeting the laboratories' director, I got a room at the YMCA. Never have I felt so lonely in all my life. I knew no one, and felt under threat from the security police. My precarious job and its income were all I had. Poor Rona was relying on me, too.

The work was hardly compensation for the loneliness and stress. The testing technique for hearing loss and various types of deafness were easy to learn. The psychological impact of deafness, especially paranoia, was all too apparent. When a person cannot hear what is being said, they are always wondering whether every outburst of laughter is at their expense.

Every day in the papers, someone claimed they were going to rid the public service of communists. It was a sign of things to come when, in 1952,

Richard Casey – then minister responsible for the Australian Security Intelligence Organisation – told parliament that a senior government official had passed secret information onto the communist newspaper *The Tribune*. There was a "nest of traitors" in the public service, Casey said.

Day after day, I worried that my political leanings would be discovered. I moved into a small boarding house in Glebe, though this only seemed to magnify my isolation. My fellow boarders were all connected to the Education Department. Not once did I hear them talk about politics. They would recite their salary scales, their classifications and their promotion trajectory while I ate my breakfast, wondering whether the secret police would pounce on me by tea time. With the money I was sending to Rona each week, along with tram fares, board and buying paper to finish off my thesis, there was little room for joy.

When my boss's friendly attitude suddenly changed, I knew I was finished. After a week of stewing, he called me into his office. Handing me a letter, he simply said: "Read that." I was given one week's notice – no reason provided, just a blank. All the director would say was: "You know why." I replied that I had guessed. He told me he had been on the phone for a week to Canberra arguing my case but that they were adamant no communist could work for the public service. Despite expecting the news, my knees were shaking. I had to sit down. The director got his secretary to make me a cup of tea, and asked me what I would like to do.

I explained my position: no money; supporting my sister; I knew no one in Sydney and only a few people in Melbourne. I resolved to go to Melbourne. He told me to take the week off and claim a return fare to Perth, which would buy a bit of time and get me to Melbourne.

When I told my fellow boarders, one just went on slurping his soup. The other said, "Bad luck," and nothing more.

Desperate for a friendly ear and hope, I went to the Communist Party headquarters and spoke to journalist Len Fox. He invited me in for a cup of tea but gave me the impression the party was resigned to this sort of discrimination. They had no idea on how to fight it.

After a few days, I packed my bag and caught the plane to Melbourne. The Sydney job had lasted three months. It was now late March.

On the plane I sat next to Jeanette, a beautiful young woman who turned out to be a squatter's daughter. By the end of the flight she had asked me to dinner at The Savoy Hotel in Little Collins Street. Not knowing where else to eat, I decided this would be a bloody good feed. But with my Savoy dinner date a week away, I turned my attention to job hunting.

Again, I stayed at the YMCA, this one located where Hamer Hall is now. (The only time I have ever had any trouble at a YMCA was once in Perth when I was in the shower and someone stole my trousers. I got them back but had a bit of trouble getting to the police station without them.)

After unpacking, I set off for Melbourne University. The first person I saw at the uni café was Fred Emery, a fellow WA psychology graduate from Narrogin and communist, now tutoring at Melbourne.

"What? Have they thrown you out of the job already?" Fred joked.

His face fell when I assured him this was exactly what had happened. Fred suggested I see the chair of psychology, Professor Oscar Oeser.

Good fortune at last: A Perth recruit to the department was on the brink of returning home and a teachers' conference had produced a lot of material that needed collating. I was taken on as a junior tutor. Oeser was delighted when I told him I had done statistical maths, and we started on a friendly basis.

To his credit, he took me on even though he was worried about employing someone who had already been victimised out of the public service.

Oeser told me he was in Germany when the Nazis came to power. I later learnt that his professor, a Jewish man, had thrown himself under a tram to avoid the hell of Nazi persecution. Later still, I learnt that Professor Oeser was part of a British code-breaking team that cracked the Nazis' "unbreakable" Enigma and Lorenz encryption machines.

My feelings about this larger-than-life character are mixed. He played a strong part in the anti-fascist movements that developed at the university over the next few years, but I resented his version of psychology as manipulative and exploitative. Like many academics, he had left active research and creative thinking behind and rode the coattails of others' research later in life.

Professor Oeser was urbane and intimidating, a small man who believed in the superiority of European culture, especially over Australia's. His steely silences were famous. Yet, I am grateful that he gave me work when I was desperate for it.

On my first day, I began analysing teachers' responses to an educational conference held by the department. I broke the responses down into four parts. Firstly, how teachers viewed themselves and how they viewed their pupils. Then how teachers reported pupils viewed their teachers. Lastly, how pupils viewed other pupils. Impressed, Oeser said: "I liked your quadripartite analysis." I'd never heard the word before but grunted the equivalent of "Aw, shucks."

After organising the responses, Oeser wanted a book written by teachers who participated in the conference. I was set to work editing the chapters. All this happened in the first two to three days of my arrival. I was given a room in the department, a kerosene heater and a telephone. The work was well within my capabilities, but it was an anxiety-provoking situation with my financial responsibilities to Rona, my low pay and rumours swirling that the Menzies government was planning to round up communists into camps.

At night I went back to the YMCA, had tea, then walked the streets for an hour or two before going to bed.

Then, on my first Friday night in Melbourne, I was off to my big feed at The Savoy with Jeanette, the squatter's daughter. I dressed in my best suit, with 12 shillings in my pocket. More than enough, I thought, in case I had to pay for myself.

At the hotel, Jeanette greeted me with her cousin and her cousin's husband. The husband and I did not get on. He seemed to think I was a real con man, out to seduce Jeanette and rob her blind. He was out to stop me by keeping her morals intact.

At dinner, a huge trolley arrived with hundreds of little trays of oysters, prawns, olives, cheese, meatballs and pâté. Never had I seen this before. I had a helping of everything. Eyeing my plate, this convinced the husband I was a sponger. He peppered me with questions, and I answered them with mouthfuls of prawns and pate.

At the YMCA I was used to rissoles with gravy, a dab of potato and a light green lump of cabbage for 1 shilling and sixpence. A cup of tea was threepence extra. The Savoy's menu was staggering. There was duck, lobster, ham and beef, at 12 shillings and sixpence just for one plate. I thought of my 12 shillings and decided I couldn't even offer to pay, so ordered ham steaks and vegetables. With a great flourish of white napkins and a "Mind the plate is hot, sir," my two ham steaks arrived. It seemed pretty lousy to me, no veggies at that price, but I followed the others and waited with my glistening ham steaks looking up at me. I must have looked decidedly twitchy for the keeper of the morals shot me a stare at the slightest movement towards my knife and fork. Eventually, another waiter sailed up under full canvas and placed little silver bowls of vegetables in front of everyone. Like a flag fall in a race, it was the signal that movement was allowed. I began scooping everything onto my plate, then I noticed the others take a little piece at a time, leaving a bit in each bowl.

The conversation centred on Jeanette, or "Babs", as they called her. During dinner her cousin and husband would ask her questions, she would ask me something, and I would speak to her, but the other two and I never spoke.

At one point Jeanette asked me to escort her to a wedding the next day. The silence hit the deck with a bang. The bloke said not to worry, he could take her in his car. But Jeanette wasn't going to have that.

The meal ended and Jeanette paid the bill. She then suggested we all return to her room for a drink. The bloke and his wife got into the lift in a most determined way, pushing through the door of her room and planting themselves on her bed, leaving me a small chair.

Our hostess ordered a jug of beer, which cost 5 shillings. The husband ordered the next, and then I had to part with five of my 12 shillings. By about midnight it was clear to me that Jeanette wanted the couple gone, but they weren't budging. I too wanted them to leave, though I was giggling inwardly at the whole scene. We had another round and I was reduced to 2 shillings. After Jeanette had bought another jug, the bloke looked at me expectantly. I dodged his gaze. He was now convinced I was out to seduce Jeanette and, gallingly for him, she didn't seem to mind. I could almost see him explaining to Jeanette's parents how she had run off with an adventurous psychologist to South America. Unable to afford another round, I eventually bid farewell. As I left, Jeanette reminded me of the wedding. It was 3am when I crawled into bed at the YMCA.

I slept in the next morning and didn't hear the maid come in. Instead of turning to leave upon seeing the room occupied, she closed the door and pretended to sweep the room. We had spoken over the past four days, but now she came over and stood by my bed, breathing hard. I put a hand on her leg. She moved closer, so I ran my hand up her leg. She leaned the broom against the table and half turned towards me. My hand was well up now. She was flushed and excited, and so was I. Then I started to think about venereal disease. The more exciting it got, the more I convinced myself she would have it. In the end, *it* won. I told her I'd heard someone coming so she grabbed her broom, opened the door and started sweeping the corridor.

Given I was intent on academic honours, this was an unnecessary and perhaps dangerous situation. So, after a week, I moved to a boarding house in Parkville, opposite University High School, at 28 Story Street. This was run by Bert Pickett and his wife. For 22 shillings and sixpence, you got a good breakfast and dinner.

"Let Mrs Pickett know if you will not be in for dinner," Bert told me.

There were two bathrooms for 30 boarders – men only; women were too much trouble. The shower was gas-heated – 1 shilling for about seven minutes – and if you were lucky you could duck in on the tail end of the last bloke's shilling.

With so many boarders, there was usually something to do.

One boarder, Frank "Salty" O'Rourke, was a second-year medical student. He would go on to be the Austin Hospital's director of medical services from 1957 to 1988. Although *Salty O'Rourke* was the title of a 1945 film, it was said he got the name when someone kidded him into answering an advertisement for a crew to sail a yacht around the world. In the grip of one of those fantasies that students sometimes have, he agreed to go. But the whole thing was a hoax, and Frank landed the nickname Salty. I always thought he hated it, so I made it a practice to call him Frank.

Then one morning in May, over porridge, Bert Pickett told us that Mrs Pickett had had a breakdown, and we would all have to leave. I'd been there for about two months.

Round the corner on Royal Parade, I found a small room in a large terrace for 25 shillings a week. It was a basic room at the top of the stairs, with a small bed, a dressing table and a wardrobe. I had a bottle of milk delivered each morning as there were no facilities for cooking breakfast.

By now two things were apparent. Firstly, the psychology department was ruthlessly competitive. And secondly, life wasn't going to get any easier for me or my comrades. By October of 1949, Menzies had wedged Labor in the Senate, ushering in the Dissolution of the Communist Party bill of 1950, aimed at outlawing my old party. The East Sydney MP Eddie Ward alone has my admiration for standing firm against the bill.

So vicious was this period that anyone vaguely left-wing was frightened of discussing any politics. After Sydney, I knew I was a marked man with the secret police. I had no one to turn to if I was arrested.

From my desolate little room, the situation looked bleak. A malaise hit me that I have never understood. I could not get up in the mornings. I felt so weak I could barely stand. My limbs were heavy. I aimed to arrive at the psychology department by morning tea time, but I rarely made it. Had the political situation brought on neurasthenia, or nervous exhaustion? To this day, I still don't know whether I was ill, paralysed by fear, or if I had a virus.

Mooltan Street

Securing a room in a house on Mooltan Street, Flemington, changed all that. It was a typical suburban house. The elderly owner was a Mrs Nichols. Thin and rigid, she was the deserted wife of a minister – he had apparently gone off with the church's organist. But Mrs Nichols kept a stiff upper lip, and a well-ordered garden, in which she served tea at precisely 4.30 every afternoon.

It seemed that Mrs Nichols hated having boarders but loved the rent. Her children, Shirley and Geoff, also lived in the house. The other boarder was an Indonesian-Chinese plastics engineering student known only as "Bob".

Shirley soon married Australian historian Don Baker. Geoff, a taxi driver, married Gloria, the taxi company's switchboard operator. Miffed at her son's choice of daughter-in-law, Mrs Nichols nearly refused to go to the wedding. Geoff was an uncomplicated person and Gloria a good match.

It was Geoff who, in his own particular way, introduced me to the neighbourhood, including the rather uncouth bloke next door.

"Most of the chaps in the street wear decent bags [loose trousers] of a Sunday," he told me. "But he [the neighbour] whistles around in old overalls."

My living conditions were so much better here. I could study at night without having to go to the psychology department. It was now June, and Melbourne's winter was a shock to my system. But with my obligations to Rona, I had no money to buy singlets or an overcoat. I accepted the bitter cold as a challenge.

With my home life settled, I was regrouping and getting back to basic living. In about August, Fred Emery asked me whether I would re-join the Communist Party.

"Give it a bit more time," I replied.

Soon after, an historic industrial dispute reinforced my commitment to upholding workers' rights. From October 16 to December 8, members of the Australian Railways Union and the Australian Federated Union of Locomotive Enginemen went on the longest strike in Victorian railway history. J.J. "Jack" Brown was leading the charge as the ARU's state secretary, and the issue was wage parity. In sympathy for their cause, I took up a collection within the department early in the dispute. Nearly everyone contributed. The plight of the striking men affected me a lot. As it would in 1951, when New Zealand's wharfies went on strike and I took up another collection, the proceeds of which I sent over the Tasman Sea. Each time I got a polite thank you note from the unions.

Throughout all this, I couldn't get over how friendly everyone was in the psychology department. At the time, I put this down to them succumbing to my friendly Western Australian charm, for which the west is famous. I was about to discover that there was a little more to it.

Before the year was out, Fred Emery again asked me to rejoin the Communist Party. I gave him my application as he was the only communist I knew in Melbourne. At my first branch meeting that November, I could not believe my eyes. At first glance, everyone from the psychology department was there. Among the few exceptions were: Professor Oeser; Donald McElwain (who would found the University of Queensland's department of psychology); and Paul Lafitte (later to gain international attention as author of the theoretical work *The Person in Psychology*).

After I was welcomed, the discussion centred on my strike collecting efforts and a few other activities. Fascinatingly, everything was discussed in a political context. I was used to this kind of political filtering in my head, but I had never shared my thoughts with anyone. It was a curious atmosphere but one I experienced frequently in the Communist Party, particularly at the university. The political climate was discussed as if it was not happening right under our noses; the political threats as if we were not the target of those threats.

Being in the party meant sacrifice and, in Cold War politics, the truth was sometimes a casualty. I convinced myself of the value of the cause. Where opposition and uncomfortable truths were held up to me, I would find some way to justify what was happening. Commitment to Marxist ideas, and the party, was paramount. As guardians of Marxist theory, the branch leaders also claimed to be our spiritual leaders. This had a cruel effect on personal relationships. Staying true to the theory trumped any sense of love, loyalty or responsibility in a relationship. Our prime responsibility was to the political ideal. Many broken marriages, including my own, would become a testimony to this fallacy.

Intense, fleeting associations were inevitable. For instance, in 1953, on the night that Julius and Ethel Rosenberg were executed for espionage in New York's Sing Sing prison, I was demonstrating outside the then American embassy in Collins Street. During our all-night vigil we were heckled as we walked up and down the street, holding our placards. A woman I was protesting with developed an intense relationship with me that lasted only a few weeks. I broke it off because our party involvement was in different Melbourne locations. Our party work meant we just didn't have time to cultivate the friendship.

Such commitment to the cause also prevented us from forming deep relations outside the party. It became accepted that many women were introduced to the party only after establishing a relationship, sexual or otherwise, with an existing party member. In many cases, they eventually became members.

Despite this, our causes were noble. We fought attempts by the Menzies government to impose a dictatorial rule over freedom of speech and thought. We opposed the Korean War, nuclear weapons in general and the re-arming of Japan and Germany. Yet our silence over Stalin, the Russian atomic bomb and the Communist Party of Australia's corruption came at a cost to us as individuals.

My re-entry into the party was a time of intense development for me. In three years, I had gone from an uninformed country lad to a person capable of political thought, discourse and political leadership.

I remained silent during the early meetings, impressed and intimidated by the likes of Fred Emery, who led the party members from the psychology department. A big drinking, big talking, dominating character with a reputation for extra-marital dalliances, Fred's intelligence was matched by unbelievable self-opinion. He once boasted that students wrote their masters' theses based on glances at his jottings on his blotter paper.

When Emery didn't know, he bluffed. This, I came to realise, was part of a defensive strategy forced upon us by the Cold War. I soon found that if I was unable to produce the facts to counter an accusation, I too fell into the habit of fudging. This often left me on shaky ground.

Back then, I must have been pretty intense. Realising my ignorance in so many areas, I tried to learn the lot at once, which meant I picked up a little about a lot. But the fudging habit was hard to break, and I only truly stopped when I realised the hollowness of Stalin's declaration that communists were of "a special mould".

The ever-intense Fred Emery brooked no opposition. His manner in replying to an opposing argument made the opposer feel a bit ridiculous.

Everyone else was just glad it wasn't them and tended to laugh with relief as much as agreement.

Psychology department colleague and prominent branch member Geoff Sharp was accepted as second-in-command. On reflection, he was by far the department's most consistent and profound party thinker. Only when Emery went on sabbatical did Geoff's star emerge.

The year passed quickly enough. I was given the job of looking after practical classes and a tutorial once a week. The rest of the time I read or helped the party. There were always meetings, rallies, classes and cottage lectures. I never did resolve the conflict between what I felt was my political responsibility in opposing attacks on Australian democracy and the need to sit quietly in my room and study in order to keep my job.

At lunch, we would go to the university sandwich bar to get two rounds of banana and peanut butter sandwiches, plus an apple. I had noticed a very attractive woman who made a point of serving me. All the sandwich girls had favourites. I found favour with Peggy Berman. Exchanging a few words each day in her Irish lilt, she found out where I worked and almost every other detail of my life. Likewise, as we gradually became friendlier, she told me she had a son and was separated.

She wished me well when I told her I was heading back west for the holidays. I bought a pocketknife, borrowed a backpack from psychology colleague Freddie Katz, and set off hitchhiking just before Christmas, 1950.

As I travelled I reflected on the months gone by, feeling that I had had a year to last a lifetime: losing my job; feeling the strain of political persecution; fighting Menzies on the Communist Party ban; coping with the demands of tutoring; and enduring a lonely private life. And yet, it would end up being one of my easiest years.

Chapter 4
Go west, and left, young man

My Melbourne colleagues thought I was mad to hitchhike across the country, and would have been mortified to have seen me sleeping under a truck to avoid the rain. But I took it in my stride, making it to Adelaide within 24 hours. I was met at 11am by my brother Jack and his wife, Dorothy. They were also on the move – returning to the west as Jack had secured a job at the Royal Perth Hospital.

With Jack and Dorothy having booked to travel to Perth by train, I paid for a ticket to Port Pirie to join them for part of the journey, but that was all I wanted to spend.

As we boarded, I tried to explain to Jack what had happened to me politically, but he blew up at the mention of Communism and Russia. We then had a terrible argument about Yugoslavia for over an hour. Jack had worked at the Taxation Department, and this experience coloured his thinking on politics and the public service. He never failed to mention this. Back then, the department was "packed" with Irishmen – that is, Catholics – which, given our father's bias against his own Catholic family, was the first black mark. Jack was also told to work much slower than he liked to and ended up playing cards for much of the time. In his mind, this experience justified Jack's prejudices against both Catholics and public service "bludgers" – hence, socialism would not work in Australia. His bitterness was reinforced by having to work while others in his medicine class went on holiday trips.

At Port Pirie, I said goodbye to Jack and Dorothy and walked out onto the Wilkins Highway towards Gladstone. From there I would take Main North Road, as it gave the best hitchhiking options to Port Augusta. Arriving in Gladstone as night fell, I stopped at a house to ask for a glass of water. The surprised English family invited me to stay the night. The newly arrived family were lonely and longed to talk about how different Australia was to England. I didn't get much sleep but had a good breakfast and set off the next morning for Port Augusta.

I walked for miles through the tail end of the beautiful Flinders Ranges, promising myself I would return. A truck picked me up on the coastal plains, dropping me on the outskirts of Port Augusta. The only person I saw after sleeping under the desert sky was an Aboriginal woman who had camped about half a mile from me. With no lifts coming by, I soon finished what little food I had with me – one pound of tomatoes and two oranges.

Eventually I was picked up by a truck, which dumped me at the Iron Knob turn-off. After waiting a while, I got out my sleeping bag and rested. About 11pm, the driver of an old van pulled up and asked me if this was the road west. I confirmed that it was, hopped in beside him, and we shared the driving over two days all the way to Hay Street, Perth.

For better or worse, my "home" was still in North Perth, where Alec and Rona were still pushing heavy rollers across tennis courts. Despite my financial help, Rona had failed her university subjects. She blued with my mother, who bemoaned the ingratitude of children towards their ever-loving parents. Rona was made to feel guilty every time she felt joy in her studies or in the company of others. It was so intense that even when Mum was not haranguing her, Rona worried about what she might say. The tongue always returns to the sore tooth.

I got in touch socially with the University of Western Australia's psychology department, where the interest in my return piqued and then quickly waned. No one was concerned about anti-communist repression. Some were embarrassed to discuss my public-service dismissal.

At the same time, the papers in the west were frothing anti-communist bile. Undeterred by a High Court challenge to throw out his unconstitutional act against the Communist Party, Menzies' new plan of attack was to hold a referendum to change the constitution. As if the general population wasn't frightened enough, authorities were talking of cracking down on the communist threat – meaning me.

Distracting myself from the political tumult, I rang Daphne. She invited me over, but the atmosphere was like ice. Having been teaching in the country for a year, she had met a stock agent who asked her to marry him. Her mother, quietly triumphant, was all smiles when we went for a walk. Mrs Bennett felt my dismissal from the public service had confirmed her opinion of me. She interrogated me. She could not believe I had done nothing to justify my dismissal. She was firmly supporting the stock and station agent alliance. Out of loneliness rather than love, I asked Daphne to come to teach out east. From there, we could see what happened. I didn't offer marriage. How could I when I could well have been in an Australian-style concentration camp by 1951?

Daphne told me she was going to marry the other chap. He offered security and a chance of happiness, while I was too unsettled and didn't know what I wanted to do. At this, I got a bit angry. I was not the cause of my victimisation. Most psychology students strived for a job tutoring at Melbourne Uni's psychology department. I wasn't arguing for her to join me. I was simply defending myself against the injustice of it.

Our walk around North Perth swamp with its croaking frogs did little to improve my view of my desolate future.

As I said goodbye to Daphne, I heard her mother from the porch: "Did you tell him?"

A weary Daphne replied: "Yes Mum. I told him."

Just before her wedding, she sought a last hurrah with me in Melbourne, but I had gone to Buxton for the weekend and missed her by half an hour. Years later, I met Daphne in a Perth street. She was self-confident and had produced an extremely clever daughter.

Back home in North Perth, my mother was as empty and erratic as ever. We relied on her for meals, but these consisted only of lettuce, cold meat and tomatoes. The only meat we had was mince on toast.

My mother's bitter recriminations came every day: "If I didn't have you, kids I could be ..." and "Why can't you be like other kids who ...." Then there was the mournful self-pity: "I have nothing to live for," and "What pleasure is there for me? I get no fun out of life." We kids had no answers to these questions. Our mother robbed us of the right to enjoy our own lives by alleging our enjoyment was at her expense.

After a few of days of this, Alec and I got a job cleaning windows for a flour mill in Fremantle. Though a welcome relief from home life, it was a heartbreaking job. The flour dust was caked on the glass. Every time I wiped the window a white smear seemed to make it worse.

While Alec enjoyed working with me and we became closer, I still felt there was a barrier between us, which I filled by making jokes about almost everything.

At our tea break on the first morning, I sat next to a thin old man who turned out to be Fred Emery's father, no less. This gentle, kind flour mill worker was so proud of his son. He would not have known of Fred's drinking, or philosophy on marital infidelity.

Alec and I endured the window-cleaning job for about three weeks. Our fares to Fremantle ate up most of our wages. Still, I saved enough to pay for a train back east.

When I eventually left, I again felt I was abandoning my younger siblings to a terrible fate. If I had thought too hard about leaving Alec and Rona, I may not have left at all. I knew it was a betrayal to leave them to a mother who waxed between emotional blackmail and indifference. But what was I to do? I had a job in Melbourne and none in Perth.

My family problems dissipated into the horizon as my train pulled out of Perth.

Newfound Melbourne

On my return to Mooltan Street, Flemington, the new year was already giving promise of change.

A chap I knew out west, Malcolm McMillan, had arrived at Melbourne University. Though he was from the upper-middle classes in Perth and had attended a selective private school, he had become attracted to the ideas of socialism. Frustrated that his family could not accept his socialist sympathies, he had abruptly abandoned his University of WA course to take a job in the Collie coalmines, south of Perth. Hearing this at the time, I had thought him stupid – I had worked my heart out to leave that sort of work behind.

After the coalmines, McMillan returned to study in Perth, graduating in 1950. He too got a psychology tutoring job at Melbourne. When he then joined the Communist Party and approached me about living at Mooltan Street, I welcomed him aboard.

In my first year in Melbourne I had discovered the joy of film and theatre. I had begun attending screenings at the New Theatre in Flinders Street. Inspired by the workers' theatres of England and the United States, as well as the Soviet agitprop movement, the New Theatre produced plays and screened films. It would later merge with another company to become the famed Pram Factory in Carlton.

For me, this theatre was a nice take on Lenin's thoughts regarding Russian film makers of the 1920s: "For us, the film is the greatest of all the arts." Lenin was referring to film as an educational medium, but as I saw it, the New Theatre was a place to enter as a loner, watch the film, and leave as a loner.

I had developed an interest in the early films of David Wark Griffith and Sergei Eisenstein and could see their films *Intolerance, The Birth of a Nation* and *Battleship Potemkin* any number of times. Another favourite was *Nanook of the North* by Robert Flaherty. One of the most exciting films was a short documentary by Joris Ivens, titled *Indonesia Calling*. It was made with the support of the Waterfront Unions of Australia. Set in Sydney, it told the story of Australian and Indonesian wharfies who refused to load Dutch arms onto ships during the Indonesian-Dutch independence struggle of the late 1940s. Though hundreds of ships were caught up in the black ban, only a handful were depicted in the film. This campaign played a big part in the Indonesian victory and never failed to inspire me.

Returning to the theatre in 1951, after my time in the west, I was welcomed as an old friend and asked to stay. I sat around drinking coffee, discussing film. To my surprise, when I got up to leave a young woman said she would leave with me. I explained that I didn't live nearby but at Flemington. She just walked along with me. Our hands brushed and the next thing we were holding hands. She was a fairly intense, good-looking girl who worked somewhere in the city. I gathered she was unimpressed by the usual blokey chatter and that she had liked what I had to say.

It was a tricky situation. I couldn't take her to Flemington and she didn't offer her place. I suggested we walk to the university. She was giving off the vibe in a dozen ways and, since 1950 had been a dry year, I was keen to find a place for us.

Unlocking the door to my university room, I took my coat off then helped her out of her coat and jumper. I had drunk a fair bit of coffee so I went to take a pee against the fence outside. Suddenly, she was beside me with the same intention. I lunged for the swinging door, but it was too late. The Yale lock had clicked and shut us out.

Our top clothes, my keys and my money were inside the building. We were stranded outside, freezing, with no hope of getting home.

Back then, the psychology department was only in its fifth year and was housed in an old army hut. I wandered down the back and found a small clinical room unlocked. We huddled and cuddled for hours. The juices be-gan to flow and she was on the floor telling me it was her first time. I was very slow, and she claimed it didn't hurt. It certainly didn't seem to hurt her the second time. At dawn, I wandered out to find the night porter. He rec-ognised me but gave me a very old-fashioned look as he opened the door. I

71

went back and got my companion. I escorted her to her home in Glenhuntly and returned by tram and train to Flemington.

Once a sexual drought breaks, I've noticed a deluge sets in.

During the whole of 1950, the closest I got to sex was one Saturday with an Egyptian woman. I was catching up with a WA friend, John Mulgrew, at a coffee shop. He was down from Canberra, and the pair of us had got talking to the woman over coffee.

I had one word of Egyptian to establish a cultural link, and I used it to ask the woman to the pub for a drink. From there, the three of us went to her flat and it became obvious one of us would try to seduce her.

Mulgrew fancied himself as a wrestler and issued the challenge right there and then, in front of the woman – the winner to stay. I hadn't wrestled much before but was fairly strong and agreed. After two minutes Mulgrew became fair dinkum, lost his block and started holds and grips in earnest. I responded, eventually pinning him with a half nelson. I warned him to settle down or I would break his bloody leg. God knows what our hostess thought of all this. Mulgrew eased up and got to his feet. When the woman went out to make coffee, he offered to toss me for her. By this stage I didn't care, but I agreed, and won the toss. He left before the woman came back. When she returned, she said: "You won the toss."

I sensed the night was not meant for romance. We kissed, and she said she would like to see me again, but I needed to leave as she had work in the morning. I haven't seen Mulgrew since then. If I ever do, I will have to tell him we both lost – or perhaps she did?

The referendum campaign

Film, sex and work all came a far second to my main concern of 1951: Robert Menzies' campaign against freedom of speech. In March, the High Court found that the Menzies' Dissolution of the Communist Party Act was unconstitutional. Menzies then used the Senate's refusal to pass the Commonwealth Bank Bill (aimed at reversing Chifley's proposed nationalisation of banks) to force a double dissolution election on April 28. The Menzies government was returned with a majority in both houses.

In his victory speech, Menzies claimed that Australia needed to arm itself for another "great war" within the next three years and declared "war on communism". I would rail against Menzies on the Korean War and did not rest in the fight for freedom of expression.

The battle lines were redrawn when Menzies declared a nationwide referendum, to be held on September 22, to ram through the changes the High Court had refused him. He sought an explicit ban of communism and communists. The referendum asked Australians to vote Yes or No to the question: "Do you approve of the proposed law for the alteration of the Constitution entitled 'Constitution Alteration (Powers to Deal with Communists and Communism) 1951?'"

All year I threw myself into the "No" campaign. We felt the referendum was there to stifle opposition to Menzies' Korean War plans with the United States. It spurred us on.

Never have I spent so much time at meetings, let alone raising money, painting up "VOTE NO" slogans, handing out leaflets at factories and letterboxing all over Melbourne. I soon found out that I lived two doors away from the barrister Ted Hill, who was state secretary of the Communist Party of Australia (becoming chairman of the CPA from 1964 to 1986). Between us, we covered every inch of Flemington with leaflets, posters and doorknocking.

Money poured into the party. People gave £5 and £10 gladly. Each time I went out collecting, I would return with more than £100 to pour into the campaign coffers.

Suddenly, on June 13, Ben Chifley died. H.V. "Doc" Evatt took over the campaign reins as Opposition Leader. He campaigned magnificently and stormed the country. Evatt was heavily invested in the outcome. At the High Court hearing, Evatt, while still an MP, represented the waterside workers and ironworkers' unions.

Evatt did not enjoy his party's full support. Many ALP members remained silent but, again, East Sydney MP Eddie Ward campaigned loudly against the referendum. Ward despised Menzies as much as I did. He famously described Menzies as "a posturing individual with the scowl of Mussolini, the bombast of Hitler, and the physical proportions of Goering". The name Menzies was hated by so many. There were reviews, plays, short stories, anything to highlight the danger of this referendum getting through.

In Victoria, the campaign was scuttled by the Catholic-backed groups. Industrial Groups were formed within the ALP to stop the influence of communism on the trade union movement. From this, the "Groupers" faction within the ALP was born. Catholic Action – a laity group started by anti-communist activists Bob Santamaria and Frank Maher – fought for a "Yes" vote, despite a manifesto stating that members should not discuss politics. Meanwhile, the Catholic Social Studies Movement, known as "The Movement", also started by Santamaria, modelled its organisation on the Communist Party, yet it was an anti-communist force. We fought on.

Somehow, I kept up my university work. I was even promoted to the senior tutor position at a much higher salary. I was also enrolled in biology and should have been doing my master's degree, but I was too busy posting stickers on lamp posts and speaking at street meetings to a drunk and two dogs.

At the university café one day, my sandwich-girl friend Peggy Berman asked if she could talk to me after work in my room. By 4.30pm, her intentions were clear, and she followed up with an invitation to dinner. "Just chops and peas," she said, in her Irish accent. "We can talk."

I went out to her home at Boyne Street, North Coburg, where she lived with her little boy, Peter, who went to bed soon after I arrived.

Peggy was a witty, well-informed and highly intelligent woman. As the evening progressed in the loungeroom, we became more and more friendly.

Having had an affair with senior law professor Norval Morris, Peggy knew every detail of law school gossip. She knew who was sleeping with whom and the political feelings of all staff. Through her sandwich shop observations, she was even able to tell me who was in the Communist Party – so much for our much-vaunted party security. She could also name the campus police spies. But then again, so could we.

She was lying on the couch with her knees raised, her dress falling more and more down her thighs. I went over, sat on the lounge and touched her leg. Without changing her conversational style, she told me she did not intend on having an affair with me. When I eased her dress over her belly and her pants down, she did not shy away. She had her first-ever climax that night. After that night, she tried to include herself in everything I did.

From then on, I got my sandwiches free. And I needed an ironclad reason for not having tea with her or not seeing her in town.

I told Peggy from the outset that I was a revolutionary and that I could not become involved with a woman. Like every communist, I expected to be visited by the security police at any time to face legal proceedings, either instituted or trumped up.

Back then, only a woman with Peggy's resolve and toughness, or another Communist Party member, would chance becoming intimate with communists. Financially, communists risked losing jobs and were denied promotions. Personally, associations were broken and families alienated over the commitment to the party beliefs. The Cold War forced party members to stick together long after they would have happily dispersed.

Peggy was undeterred by risks. In her teens, she was involved with Geelong gangsters and once hid in the bushes while shots were fired in a police raid. She was unafraid of police or much else, and that steel came in handy when dating a communist.

Frequently, I would finish a meeting or finish letterboxing, then go out to Coburg. I'd then leave Peggy at about 2.30am and catch the all-nighter tram to Flemington.

The all-nighters, combined with an irregular diet, led me to develop boils – one of the most painful lesions in the non-serious category. These persisted one after the other for two years.

During this period, Peggy snuck into Mooltan Street to bring me some fruit. She was on her way to Geelong with her mother, while I was in bed with a plaster on my leg from a boil. With her mum waiting in the car, engine running, Peggy slipped into my bed. It was difficult, but not impossible, for her to ensure I "had a good night's sleep".

Boils or not, the fight against Menzies' campaign and the referendum was a seven-days-a-week effort. Thousands of people who had never uttered a political word in their lives were drawn into the fight. They were always careful to state "I am not a communist, but …."

Our catchcry of "Vote No" was painted on bridges and walls in the dead of the night. We all laughed when police caught a chap in the act of painting up a slogan. At court, our clever solicitor and fellow communist Rex Mortimer established that no paint had been splashed on the wall and congratulated the police for preventing a crime. As no crime had been committed, Mortimer submitted there was no case to answer. The case was dismissed.

There were other lighter moments amid the campaign's seriousness. My departmental colleague and fellow branch member Geoff Sharp came from a monied family. His father had a huge house in Kew, overlooking the Yarra River, and Geoff himself had a flat that became a hub for accommodating members as he carted them to and from meetings. During one conference, Geoff asked me to stay at his father's house, as the place was empty for the weekend. We went to bed at 10pm. Some time in the night, I heard a woman calling out to "Geoff, darling." She was outside, wanting to be let in. Geoff allowed her inside but not into his bed. Unbeknownst to me, an entourage of friends was emerging from the bushes, giggling. Unsuccessful with Geoff, the late-night visitor entered my bedroom. In a husky voice, she said: "Percy, are you awake?" Sensing shenanigans in the air, I leaned over and pulled her onto the bed. Startled, she screamed, the light went on, and about half-a-dozen men poured into the room. The event, and subsequent party, became the stuff of myth and we finally got to bed at 3am.

The vote

On Saturday, September 22, 1951, the referendum was put to the Australian people. On the day of the vote, I was allocated the Melbourne Town Hall polling booth. The Communist Party had won few seats in elections, but we knew how to organise polling booths, putting other parties and candidates to shame. Every two hours volunteers were relieved of their post. If your shift ended at 10am, you were relieved at precisely 10am, when a car arrived to pick you up. Coffee and food were always available at a nearby house.

At the polling booth, you often knew the other communists. If not, you got to know them quick smart. Back then, the Labor Party people could be friendly with us. Catholic Action members were decidedly unfriendly. The Liberals, on principle, were the enemy. Usually, they were elderly ladies, young Liberals or paid workers. The board game, club-type executives never distributed how-to-vote cards.

At the Melbourne Town Hall, the feelings were high. We watched the Liberals handing out Yes how-to-vote cards, making sure none of them got close to the entrance.

By law, no propaganda could be distributed on polling day, yet the Liberal Party ladies were distributing cards which read: "Smash Communism, Vote Yes." It occurred to me that the slogan "Smash Communism" was propaganda. I informed the Liberal ladies that they were infringing the law, and told them to desist. I then went to the nearby police station to report an infringement of the electoral act. The sergeant I spoke to was flummoxed. He wasn't sympathetic to me, but he did frighten the Liberal ladies enough that they stopped distributing their cards. For two whole polling hours, no one was handed a "Vote Yes" card at the town hall, until the Liberal Party heavies arrived and reversed the situation.

The day dragged on. With our Dandenong forces needing relief, I spent the afternoon and evening at a windswept booth almost in the countryside.

That night a party was held at the home of Fred Emery and his wife,

Frances. Their rented house in Ross Street, South Yarra, was a regular venue for psychology department parties that raged until 2am or 3am. The highlight of the evening was the singing and dancing of *Git Up Off'n the Floor, Hannah*, a folksy satirical song by Red Ingle about "them hogs who is gotta be fed." Unfamiliar with folk dancing, I was the caller for most of the dances. God knows what the neighbours thought, but the house did shake. On reflection, these were hectic, nothing parties that acted as a pressure release valve for the constant half fear, half aggression and frantic activity that characterised our lives.

Amid the partying that night, we crowded round the wireless as the "No" votes increased. The cheers went up and the drinks went down. Late into the night, it became clear that Menzies had failed – the "No" vote had edged out the "Yes", and the referendum was not carried. Amid the excitement I distinctly remember hugging and kissing a woman by the name of Noni Mainland and thinking she was a bit bony.

It was a narrow victory but a victory nonetheless. Of the 2.37 million votes cast nationwide, 50.56 per cent were against using constitutional change to "smash communism". In spite of general expectations, and Gallup polling suggesting that more than 73 per cent of Australians favoured banning the Communist Party, we had succeeded. The Menzies government would make no further attempt to openly ban us. Instead, it would use ASIO – formed two years earlier under the Chifley Labor government – to spy on party members.

Commentators called it Menzies' greatest defeat and even suggested he could be challenged for the party leadership.

For my part, my neighbour and Communist Party leader Ted Hill thanked me in a letter for my efforts on the campaign. I kept the letter for years but destroyed it when my respect for Ted Hill as a communist fell to zero.

Chapter 5
Reverse psychology

I found it very difficult to settle down and study after all the excitement of the referendum. The campaign win robbed me of the time and interest in pursuing my academic work. The chaos of the year forced me to drop out of studying biology. Journals were left unread, I did no research and was lucky to be able to prepare my lectures and tutorials.

While we had stopped Menzies' direct assault on our freedom of thought, there was still the threat of university students acting as security agents. We knew who they were and, one day, a mysterious bundle of leaflets appeared in the café naming the agents. One of these agents had been spying on Asian students. But it turned out that his weakness for Asian women – particularly Chinese women – helped reveal his identity. He would boast of how much he knew of their movements – gleaned from his spying. The Asian women, in turn, informed us of every move he made, particularly his military intelligence conferences. His hand was forever clicking on his camera.

Another agent infiltrated the Labor Club. He managed to become a campaign organiser for Sam Goldbloom, a peace activist. In 1951, Goldbloom stood as an Independent Labor candidate in the federal seat of Isaacs, in Melbourne's south-east, on a single issue: opposition to Nazi immigration. The agent's double-crossing was uncovered, and he later ended his life in a mental asylum in Melbourne.

Two other agents faded out of university. I later heard there were many more in the university's administration. Sometimes our friends turned informers.

Through these years, we assumed our phone lines were tapped and did not use them to communicate. Before I would go to a public meeting, a rally, a demonstration or lamppost pasting, I would empty my pockets of all papers, identification and money. Although I was never roughed up by authorities, it was known that such an encounter would leave you with only your keys.

Organisational details were never discussed in a restaurant, on public transport or in the presence of a third person. Details of our branch or section were the only topics we bothered to discuss. I always believed the less I knew of the wider party, the fewer details could be bashed out of me.

Even though I was a tutor, I enjoyed good relations with the students. I tried to take an interest in more than just their work. And though I was older than most of them, I didn't feel it.

My main problem was my growing conviction that psychology was a gigantic fraud. Attitudes, feelings and instincts were nothing I could hold in my hand, but these were considered "facts" in psychology. I was interested in what actually occurred inside the brain when these "facts" were playing out. I was beginning to think sociology or physiology was the main game.

My answer to these nagging doubts about psychology came in the form of newly arrived senior lecturer Kurt Danziger. Born in Germany, Danziger grew up in South Africa, where he studied chemistry and psychology before gaining a PhD in psychology at Oxford University, using rat studies. A progressive, he was said to have chosen Melbourne University because it was the only Leftist psychology department in the British Empire.

Up until Danziger arrived in the latter half of 1951, we studied German and American psychologists who, at best, ignored the brain and, at worst, explained stimulus and behaviour as a mathematical equation. He was soon putting forward experiments and areas of study that had the potential to disprove these American and German psychologists.

Danziger was interested in the way in which human social relations were reflected in their consciousness. He wanted to investigate how the cerebral cortex – that part of the brain that produces conscious thought – processed information.

At the end of 1951, we mapped out a research project to investigate the relationship between the processes of excitation and inhibition in the cerebral cortex of rats. I knew the general theory of the conditioned reflex (a dog salivating at the sound of an opening door signalling the possible arrival of food), but when I read studies by Russian psychologist Ivan Pavlov, they burst through to me like a thunderclap. There were questions to be asked, but Pavlov had something.

Also, around this time, a cloud was lifted. Fred Emery left Melbourne for London, where he was attached to the Tavistock Institute of Human Relations for several months. Brilliant as he was, Emery discouraged

79

individual development, seeing it as a personal threat. He treated any challenge to his thinking with withering contempt. He was a staunch believer in the "social psychology" of Kurt Lewin and Sigmund Freud, both of whom paid little heed to the brain's physiology. With Emery gone, I felt I could instead pursue Pavlov's theories regarding the physiology of the brain.

Fellow tutor and housemate Malcolm McMillan pushed Pavlov's theories dogmatically and without understanding. At first, I countered them with the arguments that Pavlov did not consider, like the subjectivity of concepts. We needed to resolve these various views and decided to hold weekend conferences to achieve some clarity on the subject.

A breath of fresh air, these weekend gatherings were among the best psychology discussions that I ever attended. Pavlov, Freud, Lewin, Clark Hull and various other schools in psychology were dissected.

To rise to PhD status in psychology, it was necessary to have a fixed idea. You then had to get known for that idea, by pushing it through journals and conferences. However tenuous in its link to reality, any idea was given a fair hearing. It produced some crazy theories, but the principle was too good to abandon. Ageing European academics would try to defend Freud's theory of society, explicable in terms of the generalised psychoanalytic concept of the Oedipus complex. We listened patiently while they talked for too long. Everyone thought they were cracked.

With Fred Emery gone, the mentor dynamic shifted to Kurt Danziger. A modest intellectual who did not regard others as a threat, Danziger encouraged us to grow and develop our ideas under his mentorship.

Kurt proudly introduced us to his wife, Mavis Waters. Mavis had an Oxford Bachelor of Arts degree with a history major. She became the history expert at our in-house conferences. Unfortunately, she had neglected to read the Marxist classics and suffered badly at the hands of some conference members.

Ratted out

Heading into 1952 with renewed enthusiasm, I stayed in Melbourne over the summer break and began studying and summarising journals with Danziger. So began my many months of studying rodent behaviour.

We set up a circular, divided field to note every aspect of rat behaviour: from how far they ran to whether they defecated, urinated, washed their faces, licked their bodies, clung to the wall or ventured into the centre.

The results showed that when there was a degree of excitation, there was evidence of inhibited behaviours among the rats. If we sounded a loud bell next to the rats, they would go into a state of extreme agitation, then collapse. Their limbs would be plastic and would remain in place if you bent them. It was an extraordinary phenomenon. I tried to assess what the cerebral function was during this time. We further noted a marked difference between various types of rats, which seemed to support Pavlov's theories of various types of nervous systems.

It took about five months to finish the detailed experiments, and this included weekend work. Around the time I finished, China's Communist Party had begun to highlight the importance of self-criticism and personal re-examination. We all felt it was a good idea to evaluate ourselves. One day, Danziger suggested we evaluate my work with the rats.

"I think we must conclude that your work suffers from the defect of functionalism," he said.

I politely asked what in the hell he was talking about.

"Well, we have fallen for the American trap of finding variables without examining real processes," he replied. "Write it up, but we will have to be critical."

After all my effort, I didn't feel like explaining to anyone that I had wasted my time. I felt my studies of the rats were worthwhile. But I got no more support from Danziger. He was only interested in critiquing my work, rather than supporting it.

Still, he holds my respect. Danziger later left Melbourne for a professorship in psychology in Johannesburg and a two-year stint as a psychology professor in Indonesia. Some hard-bitten lefties regarded Danziger as an agent, planted to spy on the psychology department, but I refused to accept this. He has my highest regard.

Undaunted, I intended to continue with my work. But towards the end of the year, a blow fell from an unexpected quarter.

With spies and turncoats about, it was customary when someone left and rejoined the Communist Party that an investigation was carried out. I fully supported the process.

Despite all my work in the referendum the previous year, I was suddenly regarded as a security risk. My old Western Australian branch had told the party's Central Control Commission that I showed right-wing deviations and I had been sectarian. They questioned why I had rejoined.

I laughed at the irony: barred from any government or private employment in Australia for my communist affiliations yet suspended from the Communist Party for suspected right-wing tendencies.

By the second half of 1952, I was very much alone. I did not go to meetings or attend classes. Previously friendly people now hurried by. Kurt Danziger and Mavis Waters became very curt and cool. Psychology department colleague and prominent party member Geoff Sharp remained loyal, if very correct.

Various fellow Western Australians filed critical reports about me for the party's Central Control Commission. Back from England, Fred Emery filed a report, likewise Malcolm McMillan, with whom I had had an ideological falling out over politics. McMillian's report held sway as we had been in the Perth branch at the same time. Wracking my mind for the impetus of these accusations, I could only think of the time when I dared question the renaming of the Labour Club as "the Marxist-Leninist Club". Damn Ian Turner (the Melbourne University activist who bristled at my impertinence after he spoke in Perth). The situation looked dire. Back then, to lose the respect of your comrades was equivalent to social death.

I requested an interview with the party's Central Control Commission. Victorian state executive member Ernie O'Sullivan was looking after my "case". Back then he was a powerbroker, but years later when I saw him again he had withered.

Ernie had a good deal of sympathy for me as I had been a worker, and these attacks were coming from the middle-class ranks. It was hardly a defining reason, but to Ernie it was significant.

An old foe revealed

It was around September that I had word from the Communist Party's Central Control Commission: I would have an interview in Sydney. I was given the name of a comrade who would meet me at the China Club and put me up for the night. As arranged, the chap gave me his address and apologised that he needed to attend a meeting. I took the train and found the street, looking for the number on the houses. When the numbers suddenly finished, I was forced to count along until I found what I hoped was the house. With no one home, I went round the back and found a door open. I waited half an hour. Still no one came home. Finding a little room with a bed, I fell asleep. When I woke there was still not a soul about. I washed the dishes that had been left in the sink. Still, no one appeared. I collected my gear and walked out. To this day I don't know if that was the right house or whether someone is still trying to work out who washed the dishes for them.

When I got to the control commission rooms, I found my accuser was my old friend Brian Carey, the former University of WA branch president. There were two older comrades present to hear the evidence.

Brian opened by repeating his accusations about my right-wing leanings. He produced a file eight inches thick on what was alleged. It was pretty impressive.

I started by outlining my history, my family history and how I viewed the politics at the Perth university. I told them the claims against me were absurd and made me laugh. Carey, a lawyer, had carefully documented how I had helped in some campaign against him in February and March of 1949. I asked him to repeat the date. Was he sure? Yes, absolutely. I pointed out that during those months I was 1000 miles away in Port Hedland. He had confused me with Bob Rogers (no relation) who, with his brother were Catholic Action group leaders. After that, Carey seemed more than a bit confused about whether the other data he had squirrelled away was about me or Bob Rogers.

The two commission members were quite irritated. They didn't castigate Carey but told him he should check his facts a bit better. Generally, the control commission exonerated me of all charges.

A couple of weeks later, I attended my first branch meeting again. Geoff Sharp spoke about my exemplary manner and conduct during the investigation. Fred Emery tried to make some fatuous distinction between revolutionary courage and revolutionary conviction, which didn't apply. Malcolm McMillan was a bit shamefaced as he had said several things which he felt were in line with party feeling against me. Thankfully, he had already moved out of Mooltan Street with his then-girlfriend. In all, it was another reminder that friendships and even marriages were damaged as we stuck to our beliefs in these times. Years later Malcolm and my friendship was patched.

If I was in Russia I would have been shot for what was levelled at me – principally, that I was anti-party and anti-working class.

Chapter 6
A taste of pre-medicine, a school of hard knocks

With the academic year finally ended, I had decided to study medicine at Melbourne University. I had put this decision off because I wanted to be certain. The cost was high. I had just £120 saved, which was not a lot to start a six-year medical degree. Before that, I had to do a year of pre-medicine. I needed to live and buy books and clothes. But I worried that if I waited and saved, I would never make it. I had to bite the bullet.

The trick was working out a way to pay my way through medicine. An opportunity presented itself, but it wasn't going to be easy. At the end of 1952 I had applied for a position as a half-time teacher. With the Department of Education desperately short of teachers, I was offered a job at Richmond Technical School, teaching maths and science to Forms 1 and 2.

Meantime, as a Bachelor of Science graduate, I was given right of entry into pre-medicine. My science degree meant I was granted an exemption from studying physics. I bought the textbooks and began studying biology and chemistry for my pre-medicine year.

Another piece of the puzzle fell into place when I took up new room and board. A psychology colleague, Don Anderson, asked me if I would like to board at his place in Mont Albert. The board was to be 25 shillings per week, much less than I was paying in Mooltan Street.

Don and his wife Joan were a Christian couple with no children. Like many Christians, they felt strongly about opposing wars and oppression, but they were not campaigners. To give voice to those feelings was to invite victimisation. For people like Don and Joan, it was safer to campaign for Indonesian independence and support Asian students by inviting them to Australian cultural events than to march in the streets. By seeking out these safe causes, they could display their essential humanitarianism without committing themselves politically. Taking an overt stand was to invite the accusation of being a "commo". To my mind, the only way to deal with this label was to wear the badge with honour.

Don, Joan and I got along very well, although I tried to be out of the house as often as possible. Don and Joan were not a very social couple then, but would occasionally entertain the neighbours. I often felt embarrassed at these evenings.

During these days I got to know an Eva Wolf. She was the daughter of rich Jewish parents who had fled Vienna. I think she held sympathy for this poor struggling academic for she was too rich to have known what it was to have no money or leisure. I took her home a few times and had tea with her family, but I always felt the poor boy. She spent as much on her wardrobe and a chest of drawers as I had earned in a whole year. Feeling a gulf between us, I soon broke it up.

In February of 1953 I began the juggling act of being a part-time teacher at Richmond Tech and a pre-med student at Melbourne University.

On my first day of teaching, I was impressed to find a long driveway with vast playing fields. I went into the headmaster's study and introduced myself.

"God," he said, "I wish the bloody department would let me know who they are sending."

I was a little taken aback. "Oh well, here I am," I said. "Although, it's a big school for a tech."

The headmaster pointed out that this was not a tech. It was Melbourne High School. I had overshot Church Street and ended up in Chapel Street, South Yarra. I returned up the street to a squalid red brick school next to a tram track in Richmond.

The headmaster welcomed me in, introducing himself as "Stormy" Waters. He took me to the staffroom, flung open the door and said: "Here's Mr Rogers, a university man." I could almost hear the anti-academia hisses from the tech teachers.

My fellow teachers weren't my problem. The logistics of my work and study was the main problem. Sometimes I had just 15 minutes to get from the university lectures to Richmond Tech classes in Church Street.

My landlady Joan Anderson solved that problem when she sold me her James motorbike. This bike was the greatest curse and blessing of my life at the time. When it went, I could scoot around Melbourne. But mostly I remember having to push the damn thing because it had oiled-up spark plugs or a flat tyre. I left the bike all over Melbourne, yet it was never stolen. I could always get the bike going again, so I persisted with the pushing and put-putting.

The impression created by my leather jacket and high leather gloves was dented a bit by the bike's pitiful engine.

One time I was visiting my old flame Peggy Berman when we heard a motorbike roar down the street. I leaped up, thinking my not-so-trusty two-wheeler was being stolen.

"No, Perc, no," said Peggy. We both burst out laughing. To think I mistook a passing, proper motorcycle for my put-putting struggler. Still, I liked to imagine my little bike roared.

When I rode from Richmond to the medical school, I would leave my bike outside the chemistry department and rush in, usually as the doors were closing. Biology was so absorbing that had I not been doing medicine, I would have done a biology major.

Soon even my weekends were taken up with hard slog as well. I started working every Saturday and Sunday as a gardener, as well as doing fruit picking. I earned £2 and 15 shillings a day. This paid my rent and allowed me to save for my fees and education expenses.

This was all well and good, though with the gardening job I'd been hired as a professional. I was good at weeding and watering, but that was all. I had to use a process of elimination, common sense and guesswork to try to work out what a delphinium was and which bulbs were tulips and which were anemones.

Perks of the job included cups of tea. One woman brought morning tea out on a silver tray in fine china cups, with a silver sugar bowl and spoon. I had to terminate our gardening arrangement when she asked me to babysit and then didn't return home until 3am.

In Doncaster, I worked for a man called Tully, an orchardist with a cool store. I was more confident with picking than gardening. It was difficult to make mistakes with fruit, and I was a fast picker of apples. I would end up working almost every weekend of that year out at Tully's orchard.

Meanwhile, at Richmond Tech, I was given two classes of Form 1 science and one of Form 2 maths. It was a rough and ready school. After just two days, two secondary training college students abandoned their posts. I braced myself.

In the staffroom, a well-meaning teacher told me there were two accepted discipline methods at the school: "lumbering" and "ironing out". Lumbering involved hitting the boys with a 15-inch lathe belt that was about two inches wide and one quarter-inch thick. This was usually administered twice on the hands. When the situation was desperate, you hit the boy on the chin, intending to knock him out – ironing him out. The staff related with enthusiasm how one teacher, Danny Costigan, had not had a scrap of trouble since he ironed out a student last year. I had got "the cuts" at school – a strap across the hands – but this was a new league.

My first class was a double period of maths in the late morning. I entered the room to an unbelievable row. I shouted in my best wheat-lumping-style voice and had quietness after a fashion. When I introduced myself as Mr Rogers, one kid shouted: "Buck Rogers!"

"Come out that boy," I said. I reached for the strap, but it made me shake. I vowed not to use it again.

The strapped boy was Peter Walker. He was a big lad who lived away from home in tough circumstances. I can't say the strap taught him or anyone else anything.

Rather than use the strap, I invoked a method where the boys voted on punishments. The infringements were pretty liberal, but if they occurred I would stop the class and say something like: "Look lads, I've told you not to talk … or throw ink wells out the window … or shout … or try to throttle the boy next to you." I would then identify the boy and the infringement, and ask the class: "What do you vote?"

It was always one of four things: let him off, give him lines, keep him in, or give him the strap. Letting him off was the favourite for a while, with me addressing the boy in question by his Christian name, to try to improve his behaviour.

"Now look, Fred, the boys have shown a lot of confidence in you," I would say. "They reckon you're not the sort of bloke who usually punches Bill or Louis in the face, and they have voted to let you off. Now don't let them down."

I don't quite know what it achieved, but the atmosphere in the classroom was pretty good after a let-off.

Occasionally, if punches were thrown, the boys might vote for the strap. I would always get the instigator up and say: "Well, Bill, the boys have voted for the strap, do you agree with this?"

Bill: "What do you mean?"

Me: "Do you agree I should give you the strap? I won't give it to you unless you agree."

They used to look bewildered until they realised that if they agreed to the strap, they were not humiliated and could even be proud of the way they took their medicine.

After a mumbled agreement, I would ask them to put out their hand for a whack. Afterwards, I struggled to think of what to say, but it was usually: "Good lad, Bill." It seemed to take the sting out of their hand.

While some private schools boasted a microscope for each boy from the third form, at Richmond Tech we had one microscope, usually booked weeks in advance, for the whole school. Maintaining the fragile balance between myself and the boys was always a battle, especially with trams trundling by so close that they shook the windows.

In my science class, discussion time was one of the best ways to hold the boys' attention. On one occasion, the toughest thug brought his butterfly collection in, and jealously guarded it. He told me to watch the collection "in case Louis got to it". Louis was a gentle soul. The son of a tailor, he went home every night to help his father sew. For some reason, the bully thought Louis was the most likely to lay his paws on those precious butterflies.

As it was for me in my time at Perth Tech, one boy always fell asleep in class because of his work – this boy was exhausted by his early-morning paper round. The same boy once brought in a hand grenade from Puckapunyal army base. When he handed it to me, I dropped it, and every boy ducked beneath his seat before the grenade hit the floor with a harmless thud. The boys would bring in old swords, scraps of metal and flowers. I would conjure up some scientific principle to match every item they brought in.

One day, the class came in sullen and silent. I had planned to show slides and films but could not get a word out of them.

"OK, what's wrong?" I asked.

"Oh sir, Mr [name deleted] hit Robbie's head through the window and we're jacking up."

The teacher had apparently ironed out a kid, through a classroom window.

I asked what Robbie had been doing – as if that made any difference. He'd been talking in class. I said I would investigate it. I soon found that the teacher behind the outrage was Davey Burns, a Scotsman who along with myself and one other constituted the staff's left-wing faction. Though a generally kind and sincere man, Davey had a quick temper, which had been strained to breaking point by a morning double period. By an unfortunate stroke of luck, young Robbie had lost balance and gone through the window. On the smell of the story, the other boys had whipped themselves up into a crisis, but the incident passed without comment in the staffroom. Just another day.

There was no doubting it was a rough school. In one staff meeting a trade teacher asked, quite seriously, to what extent he was permitted to defend himself as he crossed the playground to the main school building. He was never answered as everyone laughed.

I started taking the first formers to the museum, the observatory and the beach. The boys behaved like responsible adults on the streets. This was their environment, and they held no fears about public transport or traffic.

At the same time, my pre-medicine lectures in chemistry and biology were watered down to be given to my form classes. At year's end they gave me a tie, which increased my range by 100 per cent, and a pen with a printed appreciation, "Thank you, Mr Rogers".

Medicine, and membership limited

As an aspiring medical student at Melbourne University, my timing was not great. In the years leading up to my run at a medical degree, the number of places available to pre-medicine students had been steadily shrinking.

The Dean of Medicine, Professor Sydney Sunderland, had told the medicine student magazine *Speculum* that numbers had to drop to maintain standards and avoid overcrowding. He also said there were too few cadavers for students to study. Sunderland cited a letter from the US State Medical Board saying it would refuse to recognise the qualifications of ex-servicemen who had studied at Melbourne because the university accepted too many students. It seemed a bit too convenient. I knew some US ex-servicemen with PhDs who were enrolled to study pre-medicine. None of them passed, and they returned home.

In 1949, about 220 pre-medicine students had been admitted to Melbourne University. By 1951, the number was whittled down to about 200. The Faculty of Medicine Professorial Board then introduced a quota system for first-year medical students. This meant that even if a pre-medicine student qualified for first-year medicine, they could still be denied entry based on the quota system.

By 1952, the quota meant that only 180 students could enter first-year medicine. Many of the rejected students ended up swapping out to dentistry. In 1953, the number dropped to 160, and in July, it was decided the number would stay at 160 for 1954. Some of us would be culled.

These quotas were imposed despite an extreme shortage of doctors in Victoria and throughout Australia. The migration policy had swelled the population of Melbourne and some country towns, but the number of doctors had remained the same or reduced. In 1952, the ratio of doctors to population was 1:1100, and the population would only grow. The restrictive quotas seemed like madness.

During my pre-medicine year of 1953, I spoke out against the medicine faculty quotas at a Student Representative Council meeting in the public lecture theatre. I pointed to population growth and other factors suggesting that more, not fewer, doctors were needed. After the meeting, a fellow pre-med student, John Fennell, told me he was pretty worried and was happy to help with campaigning. Another medical student, Barry Forbes, also expressed doubts about the quotas.

We all spoke at other SRC meetings and soon the council was campaigning with us against the quotas. Everyone hit the books to ensure they made the quota cut-off, including John, Barry and I, but we also worked hard on the campaign. We were known as the leading opponents.

During the day I was busy with both teaching at tech and being taught at university. When I arrived home after school I would go straight to bed for an hour or so. When I woke I would have tea and study for five hours, then go back to bed. On Sunday nights, I would listen to *Take It from Here* – a Frank Muir and Denis Norden radio comedy show – and that was my week's entertainment. Occasionally, Peggy Berman would call to say she was lonely and could I take a night off?

After I spoke at a couple of SRC meetings, a fellow pre-med student called Liz (surname omitted) approached me in a café and we talked about the quota. She had the posh tones of a very exclusive schooling, and affected a languid pose. Whenever I went into the café, she would sidle up to me with some news item. She soon suggested that we should study together at my place.

While Liz was in my room, we did study. Though elsewhere it was a different story. As I took her home on the motorbike, she would nearly undress me along the way. We would go on to the front lawn and she would help me take her pants off. I was careful to ensure she did not become pregnant because this would have hampered both our careers. She contrived every way to see me at weekends, but I had to work and only studied with her about twice a week.

Liz was very clever. She knew a lot about chemistry and biology, as she had covered the course completely in her matriculation year. She was a great help. She was also, it seemed, in love with me.

Dalliances aside, I remained focused. I did not see a film or go to a party that year. I worked, I studied, I campaigned.

On the spot

When my teaching duties were done for the year, I looked around for other ways to keep working and saving. With Christmas and a long hot summer on the way, I took a position as a fire spotter with the Country Fire Authority.

A Malayan-Chinese student friend called Fong joined me at the Mount Lawson fire tower, outside Tallangatta, near Wodonga. All day, seven days a week, we looked for bushfires. I have rarely seen more beautiful scenery. Every day, something passed the camp – kangaroos, emus, wombats, thousands of different birds – and the mountain looked different every day. We were connected by a wireless transmitter and would report smoke, taking note of the smoke's bearing. We used an overhanging rock as shelter.

Someone from the CFA told me the next year that I was considered a nice bloke, even though I never reported one fire. Not surprising, as I am so short-sighted. I had difficulty seeing the mountain, let alone a smoke column.

We used to sit on top of the mountain and read. I ordered boxes of books from a left-wing bookshop, the International Bookshop in Exhibition Street. When Menzies began claiming property owned by the Communist Party of Australia, the bookshop escaped seizure because it was not technically owned by the party.

We tried to meet up with Fong's friend Ong Eng Guan, a Singaporean-Chinese student who was coming our way by train on his way back to Singapore to see his wife. We missed the train, but Ong ended up becoming the mayor of Singapore famously refusing to don mayoral robes and throwing out the mace in the council chamber as a relic of British imperialism.

Three weeks in, Fong couldn't stand the loneliness and went back to Malaya. I was told soon after that he "died of a heart attack". An excellent soccer player, he had given no hint of having a weak heart. We suspected that he was in fact killed during the Malayan Emergency, the guerrilla war between the British colonialists and communist independence fighters that lasted until 1960.

After Fong left I stayed on the mountain, living under the overhanging rock which acted like a one-sided cave. I could hear scratching and thumping that seemed so loud in the still night air. I was a bit scared until I found out that the sound was made by mice foraging for food on the rocks. As the weeks dragged on, it got much colder at night. When it rained and the fire spotting was over for the day, the wind was very cold through the mountains. I would light a huge fire and try to stay warm by huddling half under the overhanging rock and half near the fire. It never worked out and I was usually chilled.

Gutted but prepared to fight

Five weeks in and the fire danger period was nearly over. I got a letter from the University of Melbourne registrar saying I had been excluded from the medical faculty quota. Stunned, I could not move for two hours. The sick feeling in my stomach was the same as when I was shunted out of the Commonwealth Acoustics Laboratories in Sydney by the secret police.

The next day a letter from Geoff Sharp got me back on my feet. Geoff had left the psychology department for social sciences and was heavily involved in the Labour Club. The Labour Club was incensed at the quota. Geoff said it was essential that I run the anti-quota campaign. About 23 pre-medicine students had been excluded.

Coincidentally, within a day or two I was pulled off the mountain to Tallangatta. I was ready to return for the fight. Sporting a dark brown beard, I set off for Melbourne in a car with a CFA chap around lunchtime. He was a mild-mannered, vague bloke who looked clerical with his rimless glasses.

We left Tallangatta and had gone about 20 miles when I saw an encampment of itinerants on the side of the road. The kids were holding up an old tube and when we stopped they rushed up asking for a tyre patch. Within minutes their hands were in everything.

"What you got here, mister?" they asked as they pulled my fire-spotting cheque from my shirt pocket.

"No, leave that alone," said the CFA chap, rushing round to the boot where other kids were opening cases and handling the contents.

A woman came up and offered: "Cross my palm with silver and you'll have all the luck."

I got bloody annoyed. I slammed my door and wound up the window. My CFA mate got the idea. He apologised to the itinerants, saying we had to get to Melbourne. He lost 10 shillings and god knows what else from his boot. The car then broke down in Kilmore and I had to get part of the way home on the train. At 5am, I staggered into the Andersons' place in Mont Albert.

The next day I caught up with the news. While not all of the 23 pre-med students who were excluded were part of the anti-quota campaign, every vocal campaigner was on the list of students who didn't make the cut. There was John Fennell, Barry Forbes and Brian Essex, plus three others who had only spoken out once or twice. We had all passed but would be arbitrarily excluded. My friend Tim Loh was excluded the year before and was now studying medicine in Hong Kong, but he was desperate to come back. We would campaign for him too.

While others, including the less vocal opponents, accepted their fate, five of us – including one other who did not continue with his studies and whose name is now lost – vowed to fight the quota.

We sought an interview with the university's vice-chancellor, George Paton. Though very sympathetic, he said it was a university decision. My fellow campaigners were pessimistic about our chances, but I was more confident we would break it.

Unsure how to proceed, we mapped out an initial battle plan. We enlisted the help of the SRC, then we made a statement to the press. A reporter for *The Age* who was based at the university was a great help. Soon the State of Victoria knew there were five medical students who were fighting to become much-needed doctors. Victorians also knew that the medical faculty quota was somehow immoral given the critical shortage of doctors in a booming population.

The University Council members were all canvassed and their views published. The five campaigners then split up and went to every union in the Trades Hall Council. We went to the Country Women's Association, the Ex-Prisoners of War Association and the Brotherhood of St Laurence. We asked all these organisations to write to the council and the press. Soon the correspondence began arriving. The Trades Hall Council passed a resolution condemning the university.

Then it was time to hit them legally. I set in motion a possible lawsuit. University regulations stated that pre-medical year students had to be assessed in order of merit. In my case, I had already completed a bachelor of science, with a dispensation for the subject of physics, which I had completed in Perth. Daryl Dawson – later to be Sir Daryl, the High Court judge who ran the 1998 royal commission on the Longford gas plant explosion – got me some time with Maurice Ashkanasy, QC. The barrister's legal opinion supported my contention. This was submitted to the University Council, and the council agreed to alter their ranking procedure in line with its own regulations.

After re-ranking, it was possible that some of us would be readmitted.

Five of us then attended a meeting with the university's registrar, Frank Johnston, and faculty secretary, Frank Elford, in the University Council room. Johnston read out each name: "Rogers – you're out; Fennell – you're out; Forbes – you're out. Essex – you're out. [Lost name] – you're out." Others, including Tim Loh, who did not attend, were also named and ruled out. All that campaigning and the re-ranking was of no benefit to us.

But the registrar had made a critical error. After reading out the names, he added: "We only took into account a person's academic record. We did not consider his politics, his religion, his race."

If this was the case, why mention it? Especially as our number included quite the mix of potentially divisive subsets: a Catholic; a communist; an Orthodox Jew; a homosexual; and a Chinese chap. Others were readmitted, although the final figures are not known to me.

We took up the campaign with renewed enthusiasm. In three days we gathered 2500 signatures on a petition.

In April, a prominent law student by the name of Barry Jones made a mistake that threatened to derail the campaign. At the time, he was president of the university's Australian Labor Party Club – on his way to becoming, among other things, ALP national president and federal minister for science.

In his flamboyant way, Jones opened a speech at an SRC meeting by saying: "I was talking to the premier this morning …." This drew hisses from the crowd. But no one could stop him. "He told me," Jones went on, "that he would be glad to receive a deputation from the SRC".

Yes, Barry Jones had got us a meeting with the Premier, John Cain Snr, but he also got the backs of the staff and the University Council up – this looked like political interference on campus.

At the meeting with John Cain were the excluded students, along with Jones, SRC members, and, in a strange kind of date, Labor Party Club member Keith Hancock and his girlfriend. Hancock went on to be a Flinders University vice-chancellor.

Cain was a typical politician. While we were there, he rang vice-chancellor Paton.

"Now look, George, what about these students?" Cain asked. "We've given you an extra million this year and you start knocking students back. See what you can do George, OK?"

My heart sank. For some years, the Communist Party had been campaigning strongly against government interference in universities. Yet here was a Labor Premier directly interfering in internal decision-making at the university.

By the time we got back to campus, the staff were angry. Government meddling was now the issue, not the quotas. The excluded students tried to mend the fences, but it was hard work as the staff were so riled about being told how to run their affairs. It would not have mattered what the issue was – interference was interference. The University Council voted again to uphold the medical faculty quota.

It was a very disheartening night. The story was broadcast on the ABC national news. We told *The Age* reporter we would go on fighting. Barry Forbes didn't much like our chances, but John Fennell was an iron rod in support. He thought we could still win. He convinced me to persevere.

The key was the University Council. Months of campaigning had softened them up. We pushed our case again. We went to every member once more and asked how they intended to vote at the next council meeting. The council had taken its stand over political interference. Now it seemed they were quite happy to vote on the quota question.

Relief – we had a majority.

I was going back to school, but it was July 1954 and I could not begin classes until the following year. With the campaign having decimated my finances, I would need to work hard to restore my bank balance and join the first years in 1955.

The Richardson Street commune

In January of 1954, around the time I returned from fire spotting, Theo Hammond and I crossed paths in the university café. Theo was a tall, languid bloke who was doing his final year of architecture.

His parents had lived in a tent on the Mullewa line, near Geraldton, for years. His father was a fettler, a long-lost job title for someone who maintains railway lines. I recalled Theo's brother Sam was a Geraldton State School monitor when I first went there around 1935.

Theo and I had met in Melbourne through the Communist Party. He once visited me at Mooltan Street. We talked well into the night, and he missed the last tram. My landlady Mrs Nichols was away for the weekend, and I suggested he borrow her bed. If he was careful, she would never know. He was not careful. Theo got up in the morning and the lazy bugger just pulled the blankets up over the sheets, leaving the impression of his body still on the sheets and mattress. No doubt the smell of his cigarettes hung in the air.

Mrs Nichols hit the roof. I said nothing but she carried on for days. She slammed saucepans, banged doors, did everything but chuck me out. In a way, I suppose, Theo owed me a place to live.

When we met up at the university café, Theo asked me to join him and two others in sharing a house at 323 Richardson Street, North Carlton. Its immediate past use was as a brothel. But the rent was cheap and it was close to the university, so I moved in.

It was a rundown brick house. It smelled like a slum because it was a slum. The place was filthy. I suggested we divide into teams of two, with each responsible for duties in cleaning, cooking and shopping. Filthy conditions always irked me. Even my camp in the bush was clean and tidy, bordering on the anal retentive, I would suggest.

Theo was a team with Shin, who was Malayan-Chinese and a terrific cook. I was in the team with Sammy, the most untidy Chinese student I've ever met.

After two days on the tidy-up campaign, Sammy locked his room and refused to tidy it. There were piles of dirty clothes on the floor for weeks. The drawers of his bureau were scattered around the room. They contained everything from old papers to car parts. We picked the lock to his room and cleaned it anyway – much to his annoyance.

It took a week but we had swept through the place, scrubbed the kitchen table, washed clothes in a copper boiler and had fresh food in the kitchen from the Queen Victoria Market.

It felt like home. We developed a method of keeping the place clean as people began to drop in. Saturday gatherings became very popular and, after the market, we had plenty to feed a regular crowd of up to a dozen for lunch.

Throughout the months of the quota campaign, many of these Saturday meetings involved arguments and beer, and would go on for all hours of the day and night.

Sammy had a job at a Richmond ice-cream factory, and when he offered me a night shift I readily agreed. With campaigning taking up so much time, I hadn't earnt a penny since my fire-spotting gig.

My job was to wrap banana ice-cream blocks in pieces of paper, then stack them in cardboard boxes. Sammy was a wizard. His hand never stopped. He could pack about three boxes to everyone else's two. Gradually I found a rhythm.

At some point the conversation turned to a recent management decision to allow women on the night shifts. As everyone on night shift took a two-hour sleep break between 1am and 3am, I couldn't help but ponder the possibilities. These thoughts kept me awake for quite a while.

Unfortunately, this wasn't all that kept me from sleeping during my crib break. We were allowed to eat as many ice-creams as we liked, and I had eaten quite a few. I had also eaten the tomato and onion sandwiches I had prepared. Onions and banana ice-cream do not mix. At 4am, I started vomiting. The taste was terrible: Half-digested onion with banana ice-cream and vomitus. Once the retching started, I couldn't move without heaving. No further work was had from me. At 7am, we knocked off. I went home to bed for a 10-hour sleep. To this day I cannot eat banana ice-cream.

Sammy never asked me to assist on a night shift again. Once he bought a car, he moved out of 323 Richardson Street.

Another Chinese student, Siew, from the Royal Institute of Technology (RMIT), moved in. Also an excellent cook, he more than helped in keeping the house running smoothly. Every Saturday morning, while two of us shopped – writing down everything we bought in a book – the other two did everyone's washing, scrubbed the kitchen, swept and cleaned up the backyard.

The market shoppers cooked lunch, but from then on meals over the weekend were community affairs with anyone lending a hand, visitors included. During the week we each took our turn in preparing the evening meal. My meals were nothing special, either rissoles or curry, but when the two Chinese students cooked, that usually attracted a crowd. Rice was the main staple of every meal, so we all knew to put on the rice if we were the first home. The Chinese students' meals were a far cry from Dad's bachelor meals of rice when I was a kid. Shin could do anything with rice – with one exception. The only known way of making him sick was to suggest he eat rice with milk and sugar.

Chapter 7
Tramming it

Still flat broke after my ice-cream dreams melted away, I headed in a new direction for work. In April 1954, I took a job as a tram conductor, or a "connie", as they were known. I joined the Melbourne and Metropolitan Tramways Board, as conductor number 626, with Essendon Depot as my base. Not that I was the 626th connie employed, as the tramways reused the numbers when a connie retired.

I felt a bit of a gig dressed up in a jacket – like I was in fancy dress – wearing a tie, a trammies shirt and a trammies overcoat. But I became so attached to that overcoat that I bought it after I left the tramways. I kept it till it fell apart.

Before being let loose on the public, I had to attend conductors' school to learn how to collect tickets and get to know the sections. The school consisted of two long tram seats facing each other. We were given a book of tickets and a punch, and we went on a pretend trip, in which we had to punch the appropriate sections. I soon realised the system's beautiful simplicity. The tramways board and we trammies could tell in an instant the date and time the ticket was issued, who issued it, and the tram it was issued from. You could also identify the street that passengers got on from. In disputes, this was invaluable.

We all punched tickets and called out: "Fares, please … Move down the car … Keep the doors clear."

When we could say this, and punch tickets, we were given our first tour of operations.

Mostly I worked broken shifts from 7am to 11.30am, then I got a break before the afternoon shift from 3.30 to 6.30pm or 7pm. A lot of the trammies spent the break in the pub, a few went home, but it was useless time off. For mine, it was a quick lunch, a rest and then time to return.

The job could stretch into a 13-hour working day, from the start to closing the doors.

My first shift was with one of the old connies, Jack Griffiths. A socialist from way back, he was beside himself when I told him I agreed with his politics.

Jack filled me in on the history of the Australian Tramway Employees' Union (later the Australian Tramway and Motor Omnibus Employees' Association), which he said started under the Princes Bridge, near Flinders Street Station, when two trammies met in 1910. One became president and the other secretary, then they recruited members.

Jack told me how he'd worked with the renowned and feared Clarrie O'Shea, the union's state secretary.

"A real white man," he said. I winced inside. Jack was a decent, well-read, articulate man, but he was part of a working-class set who were benevolent racists. They could not conceive that such a statement might cause offence or harm.

On my first day as a fully-fledged connie, the union held a "work to regulations" strike. The union took the action because its log of claims was delayed in court.

Most folk in the tramways union loved Clarrie O'Shea but had no understanding of politics and did not realise his purpose in instituting the "work to regulations" action.

Court decisions were usually rubber-stamped disputes that had already been won in the depots. Clarrie knew the log of claims was a foregone conclusion in the courts but pushed the action anyway. While work to regulations strikes could bring the whole network down, if workers were at work, they were still paid. The tramways board developed and used the regulations as a shield when there were accidents or collisions – blaming the worker if they failed to follow the regulation. The problem was that when the rules were followed to the letter, the tram network came to a standstill. For instance, if trams stayed the regulatory distance apart, the Elizabeth Street trams could not turn around and would instead bank up the street. Just following the regulations, sir. Work to regulations was a clever tactic.

This meant that on my first day, I found myself working to regulations I knew nothing about. But by lunchtime, I saw how the regulations caused the tram network to collapse.

The anti-communist Catholic Groupers were at the time in a bitter struggle with Clarrie O'Shea, who was a well-known communist. During lunch break, a defiant Irish trammie and grouper tried to break the strike by barging through without waiting the regulated time. The groupers were well organised and undermined O'Shea at every turn.

Within hours, O'Shea had shut down the depot and a meeting was called in the meal room to discuss the Groupers' actions.

"If I ever did a thing like that I'd go away and shoot myself," O'Shea said.

Another trammie, Billy McClean, slapped a hand on the table in agreement: "The man's a scab."

The dissenter didn't turn up for the next shift and was transferred to another depot.

All this on my first day. This was the real guts of the class struggle.

My respect for the militancy of the trammies union ebbed slowly over the next few weeks. One of the depot's most militant members told me he didn't agree with strikes. I had to try and convince him that it was the workers' only weapon. Whether he believed in striking or not, if his union boss said "strike," he should join the members on strike. Those members were loyal to O'Shea, and adored him. He was one of the wisest trade union leaders to have lived. When Sir John Kerr jailed Clarrie in 1969 for contempt of the Industrial Relations Court, it triggered a post-war national strike. That legislation was never again used to jail a union leader.

Incarceration and political fighting seemed the order of the day back then. Around the time I joined the tramways, Menzies announced that spy Vladimir Petrov was defecting from the Soviet Union. The Petrov Affair gave ammunition to Catholic Action. It attacked the ALP left daily.

Plainclothes police got free travel on the trams with their police pass, so I got to know many of them. Quite a few were at the protests over the Petrov frame-up. Perhaps they too were protesting at the lack of democracy in Australia. I never threw them off the trams and they never arrested me. In fact, I had very little to do with the Petrov protests.

In the tramways meal room, I followed the union discussions and always joined in. Fellow connie Jack Mitchell asked me to a meeting of a group called "The Industrial Labour Party." It was an attempt to break the grip Catholic Action had on the ALP Victorian Executive. Catholic Action was also reaching to control the Federal Executive. This Industrial Labour Party was entirely unrelated to the group that opposed NSW Premier Jack Lang in the late 1930s.

Mitchell was an old-time Catholic Irish Labor Party supporter. He voted for Clarrie in union elections and for the ALP in parliamentary elections. After attending the Industrial Labour Party meeting, he asked me to join what he described as a pro-Evatt Industrial Labour Party, backing Menzies' ALP archrival "Doc" Evatt against the Catholic Action crowd. After a few weeks, he asked if I would stand as a pro-Evatt party tram depot delegate. I told him I was a Communist Party member and was just starting a medical course. He tried to talk me out of the medical course. He flagged that Clarrie O'Shea would need to retire one day and that I could be in the box seat. My Communist Party membership was no barrier. He thought highly of communists.

I explained to Jack Mitchell that I was grateful for his good opinion, but I couldn't accept his offer. The depot delegate elections came up a month later. The militants had selected Albie Gay, a quiet but sensible man, to stand.

On election day, I was handing out how-to-vote cards for the militants next to a fellow militant supporter. We were standing outside the depot master's office when a tram driver came up and, without a word, smashed his fist into the other chap's face. I grabbed the attacker and we struggled. The bloke's mates told him to run, so he broke out of my hold and raced up the stairs.

With my militant mate too dazed to go on, I handed out the how-to-vote cards alone for the next three hours. Then I started my shift. Albie Gay won.

Classic characters

I was friendly with just over half of the Essendon Depot. One driver, Stan Cunningham, frequented rubbish tips. He once found the first part of a two-volume work on chemistry. He knew all about beryllium, calcium, cadmium and contraceptives, all the way up to magnesium, but there his knowledge ended. His tip finds included a do-it-yourself condom kit. As we rattled along Alexander Parade, he explained how molten rubber was poured over condom moulds, then allowed to dry. It was essential to test for holes.

Most of the female connies had been at the depot since the war. Male and female trammies were the first trade to get equal pay, so no woman was keen on giving up her job, and who could blame her? Each one had developed into a "character," and nothing was sacred.

One of the roster shifts called for a connie to be stationed at the Abbotsford tram hut. These huts were a rest spot for trammies, and a place to swap shifts.

This particular shift was part of a standby roster in case another conductor was ill. Your duties included cleaning the hut and ensuring there was boiling water for tea. It was an easy roster and left a lot of time for discussion.

One day, at "Abbie," a group of trammies were arguing with two German-accented tram drivers. The Germans argued that the Australians were lazy. Just eight years after arriving in Australia, the Germans and their wives had worked six-day weeks, and now owned their own homes and cars. Running the line that the Australians were caught by the consumer ideal of wanting a house and car while not being overly keen on the continuous overtime, these Germans were winning the laziness argument hands down.

At the moment of victory, in walked Fran, the connie. Small and tough, she listened to the accents, ignored the logic, and said: "Youse can't tell me anything about German girls. I read about how they fraternised during the war." This stunned everyone. The Germans shut up, I suspect because they felt a bit guilty about Germans and the war. The Australians, not sure what the hell Fran was talking about, shut up too. The hut soon cleared out. Fran finished her tea, then turned to me: "What does this 'fraternise' mean anyway?"

When I was on the 5am early shift, I rode the all-nighter tram. This meant getting up at 4am. Most times I could catch the alarm before it woke up the others. I would heat some rice or leftovers for breakfast, get dressed and walk across Princes Park to Royal Parade to catch the all-nighter to Flemington Road.

One night a police car picked me up and drove me to the depot. The whole time the officer talked about flying saucers.

Another night I stepped on the all-nighter and found I had forgotten my cap. It was compulsory to wear your cap, so I raced back to the house to pick it up. When I got back to Royal Parade, the all-nighter tram driver had waited for my return. Trammies stuck together, despite passenger protests.

To get to the Essendon Depot I'd take another all-nighter up Flemington Road. This driver had been on the same run for years. He went from Elizabeth Street to Matthews Avenue, a mile away from Essendon Aerodrome. He seemed to think being a driver was ripe for sexual exploits. He had favourite stories to illustrate his point:

"I picked a woman up in Flemington. She spoke very nice and asked me if I'd take her all the way to the 'drome. Yes, I said if you make it worth my while. 'I'd like to driver,' she says, 'but it's the wrong time of the month.' So, she fucking well walked."

"Another time I hadn't been sleeping too well. The wife was away so I picked up this woman and took her home after the shift. I had the best night's sleep I'd had for weeks."

In my experience, a man of the trams had to be married to enjoy any woman's company. I was just too tired to fraternise. I met no one on the trams or at the house. I envied the home lives of the married men I worked with. They seemed devoted blokes who felt they were working to advance their families. When I met their kids, those kids seemed to love their fathers, and were proud they were trammies. Not for the first time, I started to feel the urge to have a family of my own. Wandering and working since I was 15, I had a strong desire to settle down.

One bitterly cold night, a driver came in without his overcoat.

"Where's your overcoat, Bill?" one of the trammies said. "Don't tell me. You couldn't take it off the kid's bed."

Bill blushed and tried to joke it off, but his overcoat remained on his child's bed.

More than any other time, the loneliness hit me on the trams.

While I was on the trams, I never gave up hope of getting back into medicine.

Even while campaigning, I studied anatomy, preparing myself for my inevitable return to medicine in 1955. I started to learn muscular attachments and descriptions of the clavicle, humerus, radius and ulnar bones.

Coming home at midnight, I would meet my pre-med mate John Fennell, who had a job making hats in Essendon. While we rattled along we would test each other's knowledge of muscular attachments and plan out what bones we would study next. The camaraderie kept our hopes and knowledge up.

While thinking about muscle attachments, I realised I had lost my ability to run. The slightest effort left me out of breath. I felt a slob. In the break between my broken shifts, I threw on sandshoes and tried to run around Princes Park. From Richardson Street, I got over to Royal Parade before both of my legs cramped up. It took me two weeks before I could run the full three-kilometre course round the park. At one stage I could do 10 laps of the park. Except for a few years here and there, I didn't stop the laps until I was 70, when a farm accident ended my running career.

Every week I collected thousands of passengers, mostly on the Number 19, 49, 56 and 59 trams. Like all trammies, I tend to remember only the passengers who caused trouble. The prickly burrs stuck in your mind long after the ordinary decent folk faded with their smiles and well-wishing.

One time I was taking a packed tram out to the Moonee Valley races. Two little kids were having a glorious time half swinging out the door, pretending to be ship captains and first mates. A passenger standing near them said: "I'm an inspector on the trams. Get off the steps and show me your tickets."

The poor kids crumpled. But before they could produce their tickets, I asked the bloke to show me his identification.

"Don't worry about that, conductor," he said.

Then I asked to see his ticket. He refused, so I rang the three bells and told him the tram would not leave until he got off. Trams were piling up behind, ringing their irons. Cars were hooting. The tram driver leaned out of the door and asked what the hell was going on. Eventually, Inspector Fake got off and, from the safety of the footpath, let out a torrent of abuse. Near to the door, another bloke stood straight, almost to attention. When the tram took off, he said: "I nearly hit the bastard when he started on those kids."

Another time I was travelling in from "Crackers," as the Maribyrnong munitions factory was known, when a drunk chap got on with his mother. He refused to pay his fare. I told him he would have to get off. I rang the three bells on the tram cord. The tram would not start until he got off. His mother, very upset, tried to haul her son off. I had swung my bag to my back and closed it as I expected a fight. The drunk threw a punch at me that missed. He then abused me in a loud roar as he went. As the tram started, another passenger offered his name in case I needed a witness.

Another time, near Haymarket (the roundabout at the top of Elizabeth Street), I picked up a drunken man huddled over. He wanted to get to the city, but we were off to Pascoe Vale. I suggested he jump on, saying, "Stay on mate, we'll get you there eventually."

The driver called me up to the cabin, saying: "You know that's the gangster 'Red' Malone. Just watch it. He usually carries a gun."

Red Malone stayed asleep until we got to Pascoe Vale, then stumbled off the tram. I'm sure he thought he was in the city. Half expecting shots at any moment, I had that pole down from the tram wires and the bells clanging quicker than any turnaround before.

Then there was the old Irish militant tram driver Chris Donnelly, who used to take a liquid pub lunch during his shift break. Once he missed the stop near the Royal Park Homes for the Aged and Infirm and landed an elderly woman away from the stop. She declared she would report him to the board. In a drunken mutter he pointed out that she had nothing to complain about as she was now closer to her home.

Working as a conductor gave me time to contemplate the difference between manual and professional work. Manual workers are involved in repetitive tasks that allow for a limited display of creative imagination. Thus they become bored with their labour but vitally concerned with the conditions of their work. Professional workers have a much greater interest in the creative potential of their work, and tend to relegate their conditions to a secondary position. The position alters when professionals enter institutions such as the public service, hospital departments or large medical practices. Here the institutions assume the dominant, significant relation, and passage through the hierarchy takes the place of creative endeavour.

With repetitive work such as collecting tram tickets, industry relationships become important and loyalty builds. It was so apparent to me that I felt an affinity with anyone wearing a trammies uniform.

In October, the union staged a mass meeting of 5000 tramway employees at West Melbourne Stadium, which was soon to burn down and be rebuilt as Festival Hall. The half-day strike was part of a wider industrial campaign. Outside the hall, Clarrie O'Shea greeted more than 50 per cent of the men by name, shaking hands with nearly all of them. Men waited just to shake his hand. Huge, burly, workshop men were as gentle as kittens when in Clarrie's midst.

In the hall, Victorian Trades Hall Council assistant secretary Mick Jordan spoke and sounded very hot. He got a few boos and a good hand clap. When Clarrie O'Shea spoke, not one interjection came; everything he proposed had almost guaranteed approval. We would be back at 4pm to take the workers home.

Later, I walked to the city as there were no trams because of the strike. The first person I spoke to after the meeting was a toilet cleaner in Elizabeth Street, outside the General Post Office. He asked about the decision. When I told him, he nodded and smiled.

"He's a good man, O'Shea," he said.

Peggy and I part ways ... almost

When my need for female companionship overwhelmed me, I would call Peggy Berman. We would sleep together erratically, although at the end of pre-medicine we had broken up. In front of the Old London Inn, at the corner of Flinders Lane and Market Street, she cried.

"You're a fool, you're a fool," Peggy sobbed. I wasn't sure if they were tears of anger or grief.

Late in 1953, at the behest of her other lover, Norval Morris, Peggy had sought the services of an East Melbourne abortionist. He was immediately taken with Peggy and asked if she would work with him in his practice. She agreed. She could earn up to three times more than she did at the sandwich bar. But since abortion was illegal at the time, I was wary of being involved in any way. I knew Melbourne abortionists were paying police protection money, and I felt that by keeping up my association with Peggy, I was jeopardising the Communist Party. It had enough battles without skating up beside police protection rackets.

If Peggy agreed to work for the abortionist, I would have no more to do with her. She took the job, so we were finished – officially, that is. Through 1953 and 1954 I would go out to see her once in a while.

On my way home one night in 1954, I suddenly thought of Peggy. I quickly changed trams at Flinders Street to head towards Burnley, and Peggy's new home in George Street, East Melbourne. Her son may have been with his father at the time. When I knocked there was no answer. The lights were out. Around the back, I found the door unlocked. As I was tired, I found a bed in a spare room and fell asleep. About 1am, I heard noises in the kitchen and a man's voice. Soon the light went on in the spare room. "Hello Peg," I said. She took the situation very calmly.

"Oh Allan, I'd like you to come in and meet Perc," Peggy called.

106

Allan shook my hand and said that it looked like I had the jump on Peggy. I agreed.

"You mind if I have a cup of tea?" the hapless Allan asked.

"Go ahead," I replied.

Peg and Allan had a cup of tea in the kitchen and then he went home. Peg came back in, nearly killing herself laughing. We laughed so much we nearly forgot what I'd come for, but not quite.

Medical school acceptance at last

Every week I would go down to the North Carlton Post Office and bank either £5 or £10, depending on whether I had worked six days or six days and a Sunday.

Infrequently, I would go to the university to check up on the latest news. Going to the uni café in my trammies uniform always caused a stir, as my socialist friends liked to be associated with a genuine worker.

I never lost hope of returning to medicine, but it was becoming harder to instil in the others who had missed out.

About mid-September, we all got a simple letter to say we had been accepted into the medical quota for 1955. It was almost an anticlimax. We had struggled and fought so hard we felt our acceptance was our right.

After we were accepted, Barry Forbes' parents became my friends and took me into their hearts. Mr Forbes, for that is what I always called him, saw me as the person who got his son back into medical school. Mrs Forbes thought I was Barry's mentor.

They were a close Jewish family and I relished watching Barry and his father's honest relationship. His mother provided a warm supporting home. Thinking of our poverty and later emotionally impoverished home, I couldn't believe homes could be like that.

Barry's father was a socks salesman. He had a wisdom about him. We were mutually appreciative of each other, and I liked the way he treated his son. He used to tell us about his whiskey-drinking contests with other salesmen. There was no hint in denying to his son that he drank, nor of moralising and saying, "I may, but you should not." He trusted Barry in all things. I even noticed he used to tell funny jokes – violent or clean, it made no difference.

When I strained my ankle on the way home from their place in nearby Pigdon Street, Mr Forbes was round the next day to massage, bandage and insist on hot and cold compresses. He even brought one of Mrs Forbes' apple strudels.

On one occasion, a girl I had vaguely known for some years was visiting the Forbes' house when I was there. I left for home after a short while. I had just crossed Pigdon Street and was entering the lane when she called out. We walked up the lane together. Previously, after taking her home from a party, we had cuddled a bit. When I touched her more than ample breasts, she had almost melted. She was one of those women who could climax from fondling their nipples.

This time, I turned the light off and waited before I touched her. When I did, she was trembling. I touched her hair and she almost shook. She stayed still like a frightened rabbit when I ran my hand down her neck and onto her breasts. She seemed to be more frightened than excited, so I turned the lights on. I knew she thought me an unselfish lover, so I couldn't understand what had happened. I still don't really know.

We talked for a while and I walked her down to the tram.

New housemates, new beginning

After some months we were required to vote on whether another friend, Ken Turnbull, should join the house. As a psychology tutor, I had taught him, and we kept up a distant acquaintance. After a couple of years working as a country school teacher, he was now working on psychology research. Theo knew him too. The other two agreed to our recommendation.

Ken was a breath of fresh air. The house remained as organised as before, but it became much more light-hearted. Ken's friends came over just for fun. Our meals doubled once again. We could feed as many as 30 people for Saturday or Sunday lunch. Chinese meals are great for expanding and contracting to fit your numbers.

Writing about friendships that continue to this day is difficult, as the present tends to colour feelings from years back. Safe to say, Ken Turnbull and I have been mates for a long time. From the moment he entered that house, we started to laugh. I have a feeling it was one of the best communities he had been in. The life of the place was reflected in the people who swarmed to it.

After a while, it became obvious that I was the butt of a lot of Ken's jokes. I have always been pretty good-natured and tolerant about jokes at my expense. Ken was too solid. Very formally, I one day asked him if making jokes at my expense was designed to change me. Still serious, I agreed there was much room for improvement but felt that his sniping made me resent change. To his credit, he admitted he was aware of what was happening. He told me it was largely because I tolerated the gibes. He vowed to cut it out in future.

This episode made us realise we needed a safety valve to stop petty resentments piling up. We insisted that there should be solid Marxist criticism, and no bourgeoisie carping. Every Saturday lunchtime we had an agenda set, with anyone allowed to add an item to the agenda. We went through each item seriously. Agenda items ranged from someone leaving the toaster dirty to an organisational restructure of our food buying. Our lunchtime guests tended to join in. We felt the neighbours had a right not to hear us swear, so we started a swear box. There was a graded scale of fines. "Bloody" was a penny, "bugger" was threepence, "bastard" a zac (sixpence). "Fuck" and "cunt" were up to 1 shilling a time. Some visitors used to come in and say they would have five bobs' worth as they felt lousy. We made quite a sum out of that tin.

Even having something of a spy across the road only added to our merriment. A man called Williams ran the milkbar opposite our house, and he kept a critical eye on us. Williams and his brother, a local butcher, were prominent names in Catholic Action. The milkbar owner noted who entered our place, and who came out. I don't know whether he had any links with security agencies, but he did a real job on that house of ours.

With people squawked up day and night, we did give Williams plenty to narrow his eyes at. When we weren't feeding all comers, we were preparing banners for the May Day march. We would roar out the socialist anthem *The Red Flag* after dinner, although our favourite was the rousing Robert Burns song *Scots Wha Hae (Wi' Wallace Bled)*.

One night we were dancing in the kitchen to a Scottish tune when our boots went through the kitchen floor. The whole floor was rotten. This added to the complication of living but was no barrier.

After I had my letter of offer to study medicine, I contacted Tim Loh to tell him we had effectively broken the quota. Tim was studying medicine in Hong Kong. He was destined to become an exceptional surgeon who had bridged the gulf between China and Australia – later starting an acupuncture college. He wrote and spoke Mandarin and Cantonese, was a correspondent for a Hong Kong newspaper, and enjoyed the friendship of some of the most right-wing people in Australia.

Tim was accepted to study medicine at Melbourne University in December 1954. He moved into Richardson Street just as our housemate Shin was leaving.

With Theo's final-year thesis on architecture due around this time, we all pitched in. It needed to be handed in by 5pm on a set date, and the clock was ticking. At 4.30pm on deadline day, Tim, Theo, Siew and I were drawing lettering and packing Theo's thesis. A taxi waited outside. At 4.50pm, we bundled Theo and his thesis into the taxi to race to the university. Theo returned hours later, pissed to the eyeballs, but he passed his year.

At the time, Theo was courting a gifted painter, who would later become Mary Hammond, part of the Melbourne Realist Group of artists. Mary was infatuated by Theo. Though they married, it didn't last. Theo became one of Melbourne's leading high-rise building designers.

Tim started courting a woman called Morag Foster. Morag was a vivacious, frantic woman. Rather refined, she was put off by crude Australian males. She and Tim soon became inseparable. Morag even cultivated a slightly clipped way of speaking, similar to Chinese English. She and Tim would marry in 1958, with Morag becoming an author of Australian history and children's books.

Morag and Liz – my pre-med study partner and sometimes lover – became constant visitors to the house. Liz had been accepted into first-year medicine in 1954 but was said to have failed that year so she could be in the same year as me.

Resigning from the tramways in February 1955, I started studying seriously for the first year of the medical course proper. As part of the ritual, Tim and I rose every morning at 7am, made tea, and recited the muscular attachments and descriptive feature of every bone in the body.

Chapter 8
First year med: Far from bone idle

From my studies with Tim Loh and John Fennell, I was way ahead in my knowledge of bones by the time I finally started the first year of medicine in 1955.

On our first day, Tim and I walked to the university, between the Melbourne Cemetery and Princes Park. I doubt the park had every looked greener. Then we headed on through Trinity College to the school of anatomy.

Every morning at nine the doors to our anatomy lecture were locked. We had allocated seats and an attendant made note of the vacant seats. Professor Kenneth "Red" Russell took us for most of the lectures. Some of the students found it difficult to keep awake. Red would take aim and let fly with a piece of chalk at the sleeping student. His shots mostly went astray and he would have to say, "Prod that person, thank you."

We had numerous mnemonic strategies for learning anatomy, but there was no substitute for knuckling down and making sure it was in your head.

Immediately after the morning lecture, it was coffee and coffee scrolls in the café, before we started the day's dissection.

Tim Loh, Brian Essex, John Fennell, Barry Forbes and myself arranged ourselves into a dissection group. There was one other irregular dissector in our ranks, but his name escapes me.

Dissecting generates jokes. It is probably a reaction to the whole notion of death. Our time was spent half in dissecting and half in black humour. A Brian Essex remark could have me almost doubled up laughing. The whole group could be convulsed. Some deadly serious students frowned at us but most did not look askance.

Along with our daily anatomy lectures, we would have two classes a week on biochemistry and physiology. We would usually finish up by 4.30pm and then go home.

A mystique, like a pale shadow, was cast on medical students. Although we were part of the university, we felt and acted like a separate student body. I was surprised how well-dressed most medical students were. Many wore suits or thick ski jumpers. It was only a small band of us who had worn clothes, or who walked to university rather than drove cars or motor scooters.

The competition was intense. Some of the Jewish students stood out as being particularly bright. They jockeyed, competed and bitched about each other in an undignified way that I had never seen before. The private school "old boys" were a large contingent – all different, all pleasant enough, but somehow cut from the same pattern. They were conservative without thought. Society afforded them privilege and they accepted it without question. The school tie bound them socially – old boys' reunions, football matches, and socials – and they mostly met their girlfriends through the old girl networks. They were confident and assured of a straightforward medical course with a further degree if they desired it.

They were buffeted against any economic struggles and were granted any book simply by displaying an interest. Telephone calls home fixed most problems and bought tutorials as needed. After they had eaten the tea their mother placed on the table, they could retire to a regular room and study.

Unlike the Jewish students, the old boys had nothing to prove. They were uncompetitive. Their place was assured and they could afford patronising conviviality. Politically naive, they didn't know or care what my leftist friends discussed beyond the field of medicine. They knew nothing of the process of work. Trade unions were an emotional cliché. We got along fairly well because most of the time they had no idea what I was talking about.

Tim and I continued our 7am study hour, warming ourselves in the kitchen by a one-bar radiator. After breakfast we would leave for uni at precisely 8.43am. On the walk home I picked up pine cones from Princes Park as I couldn't afford wood to burn in my bedroom fireplace. Once home, I got changed and ran as hard as I could around Princes Park. After showering I helped with tea or the washing up. By 6.30pm I began studying, finishing in bed at midnight.

This was my basic day. It paid dividends. Although the workload was hard, the subject matter was easy to comprehend. I won some grudging respect as a good student.

Liz from my pre-med year continued to come over to my room and study. She certainly came over a lot. She made herself available but I respected her and did not take advantage of her feelings. I walked her to her share house across Royal Parade sometimes but nothing more, I let her drift away rather than hurt her feelings directly. It was easy to start a romance, but I did not know how to break them off. Rather than reignite our affair, I never allowed it to begin again. She was silly and fun, but I could not see myself married to her. I suspect she was disappointed, although she never mentioned it.

My desire for a family continued to develop. Living in groups with women friends did not constitute a close family for me. My loneliness generated idealistic visions of family life as I looked on with envy at close families. Yet, I pushed the vision away as I could not afford a girlfriend, let alone a wife.

Tim and Barry were my only close friends. Outside that little circle, I saw friendships as requiring time to give freely. I just couldn't afford that sort of leisure.

The split

With my time already tight, the Communist Party university branch asked me to sell the communist newspaper, *The Guardian*, outside the campus café. This presented an internal struggle. The branch executive members all had comfortable homes, with plenty of leisure time and money. They seemed on easy street while I was struggling to stay afloat. I worked at weekends to avoid taking too much money from the bank. My study time was limited, and I had no one to haul me up if I sank. Medicine and law were the two most reactionary professions, always resisting change, and I was trying to navigate my way into one of them. Yet, here was the branch asking me to take an advanced, exposed position during the Cold War period. It seemed grossly unfair.

In my conflicted state, I countered this internal argument by remembering why I joined the party. This type of action could make "men of a special mould" who could cope with this task and a thousand others. My fellow medical students would react badly, but it would be an honest political statement. This argument won the day, and I started to sell *The Guardian* outside the café.

On the first day, the vice-chancellor, George Paton, stopped by to chat, smiling. We were on speaking terms. He dubbed my quota campaigners and I "Rogers and his four musketeers". He didn't buy a paper though. A few others did. Some of my fellow medical students walked past and just nodded.

I sold *The Guardian* for about 18 months. Years later, fellow medical student Alan Isaacs recalled stopping a Polish emigre from beating me up. The Pole was a right-wing fascist type who thought any communist was fair game. Alan had quietly pointed out that I had a right to sell any paper.

Animosity also came from Catholic ALP supporters in the thrall of the anti-communist activist Bob Santamaria. Things began heating up when Labor leader Doc Evatt blamed the October 1954 election loss on the Industrial Groups (the "Groupers") and ALP members in the Catholic Social Studies Movement, orchestrated by Santamaria. Then in February 1955, the ALP federal executive dissolved the Victorian state executive, replacing it with a new one. The old executive turned up at the 1955 National Conference in Hobart, and was excluded. The party was then split between pro-Evatt members and the anti-communist Catholics. The new Victorian executive reacted by suspending 24 members suspected of being under Santamaria's influence.

Initially, we in the Communist branch were heartened by the move, as the right-wing anti-communists could now be excised from the ALP party. We expected an influx of members into the Communist Party from Labor, but this did not occur.

The expelled members formed the Australian Labor Party (Anti-Communist) group, which allowed the then state opposition leader Henry Bolte to move a no-confidence motion in the Cain government. Our lower house local MP, Bill Barry, with fellow anti-communist and upper house member Les Coleman, led the group across the floor to vote with Bolte. This forced Premier Cain to dissolve the parliament and face a state election on May 28, 1955. Barry had 30 pieces of silver thrown at his feet.

The election in Carlton was bitter. Bill Barry ran as the ALP (Anti-Communist) candidate. He was opposing Denis Lovegrove. "Dinny" had suddenly thrown his lot in with the pro-Evatt faction but for years had been a stooge of the Catholic Action group in Victoria. The Communist Party was running a candidate, but we were basically against Barry.

Barry lived in Wilson Street, Princes Hill, a few hundred metres from our home. He was known as "Old 10 Percenter". It was rumoured that when he was Minister for Transport if a person wanted to buy a taxi licence, they would need to meet with Barry in his office. From behind his desk he would peek under his blotter and then leave the room, expecting a sizable sum to appear. Kate White also alleged other corruption in her 1982 biography of John Cain Snr.

For many nights we hit the streets to put up campaign posters. It was the battle of the lamp posts. We began after midnight, when Geoff Sharp would call around to 323 Richardson Street. Ken Turnbull, Theo Hammond and I would usually join him.

To stop others from mutilating our posters, we stood on Geoff's car and slapped the poster as high as we could.

We occasionally slung dead rats over Bill Barry's election posters and altered his signs, but we never put rats in his letterbox. That was another disgruntled constituent. We did, however, pull his election material from other letterboxes and replaced it with ours.

The Carlton campaign was considered the most violent and bitter of the election. I was reminded of Dinny Lovegrove's description of his rival Bill Barry as a man carrying a "crucifix in one hand and a dagger in the other". With the "Groupers" using knives and hammers on anyone they caught messing with their election material, we armed ourselves with a large spanner and a couple of solid pieces of stick. The cops were active, so we would empty our pockets of all identification and money.

On election day, we Communists and left-leaning volunteers handed out how-to-vote cards at St Jude's Anglican Church hall in Lygon Street. We were standing on the steps when Barry, wearing a homburg hat, drew up in a black car with his wife, Mary Barry. Communist comrade, Dave Davies shouted: "Here's Old 10 Percenter!"

Immediately there was a fight. A little bloke sprung up, hit Dave on the cheek and ran down the road as fast as his little legs would carry him. Bill Barry walked up the steps without pausing, but Mrs Barry started to abuse us.

"Pack of coms, all traitors, should be in Russia," she said. Jeered by our group, she started to attack us individually. She turned to me and said, "You … you brainy looking individual." She had to retreat eventually to our cries of "No brains in the Groupers" etc.

That night we partied at Richard Malone's house. He was an old-lefty who lived nearby at the corner of Garton and Paterson streets. We sat on the floor and waited for the result. By 10pm, John "Jackie" Brown, former Australian Railways Union state secretary, came in.

"I can tell you comrades, Barry has been done like a dinner," Brown said.

While Cain was beaten, the Groupers were positively annihilated in the Victorian Parliament.

On Sunday, I went back to my books. On Monday, we started dissecting cadavers as though no other world existed beyond our medical realm.

Not a word was said about the elections, even between us and the Old Paradians at the next dissecting table. We remained friendly, even though their alma mater was Parade College – a Catholic school that was strongly supporting the Bill Barry-Les Coleman-led party. I remained friends with Kevin Rickards from that school for years, and he later became a renowned haematologist in NSW.

This splitting of fundamental aspects of my life would become a characteristic of my entire career. Medicine is an all-embracing way of life. Those teaching it made it clear that students could admit no rivals. There was only limited questioning of medicine's structure and role in society. This would irk me as a doctor, and my rebellion against it would coincide with a revolution in medicine.

To be a communist within the medical profession was a contradiction that could not be resolved within the head of a single person. I never did resolve this clash between these two institutions. It was only when the institutional commitment was gone that the resolution was achieved.

Chapter 9
An added Factor

In September, at the Mission to Seafarers in Flinders Street, in what is now Docklands, I attended a wharfies' progressive barn dance. I always felt obliged to support socialist unions.

It was here that I noticed June Factor. This dark-haired young woman had caught my eye at the party. She had been the only unattached communist female at the post-election party. Nothing was said between us that night, but I pondered her.

At the wharfies' event we danced a few times and agreed to meet at the university, where she was studying arts. Another woman took my fancy that night too, and I tossed up whether to go for her or June. The other girl later married an Indian man

At uni, June and I drank coffee and talked. She was obviously pushing for a relationship. She later told someone she met me that I was an "inspired student". This was an idealistic conception, even then. I was simply poor and hardworking. I didn't have the money to fail.

With so few women in the Communist Party, June was a welcome sight. I was now keen to find a wife and had always felt I needed a woman who thought along the same political lines as me. Back in Perth, the poet Dorothy Hewett was among the university branch's party members, along with a woman called Jo Williams, but that was the sum of it.

About a week after our dance, June invited me to her parents' house in Brunswick for tea. She was the only child at home. Her parents had adopted a French orphan after the war, Jacqueline, who was now married and living out of home.

Compared to Richardson Street and all the homes of my current friends, the Factors' Edward Street home was opulent. There were mirrors over the loungeroom fireplace. The open fire had been swapped out for a new gas heater. There were matching carpets in the lounge, dining room and bedrooms.

The real eye-opener, though, was the toilet. It was indoors, and barely recognisable compared to the chain-flush, cement-floor outhouses of my childhood. Our toilet at Richardson Street was a lean-to tacked on to the back of the house. The Factor toilet had ceramic floor tiles and the bowl was pink, with a half-concealed flush button.

June's father, Saul Factor, I half knew from rallies. Her mother, Mary, was a friendly woman, although she made some incredibly naive or ill-thought-through statements that made me look into my plate. They owned and ran a dress shop in Swan Street, Richmond, and were among the Polish Jews that came to Australia just before World War II. It was an average suburban dress shop with frocks, blouses and skirts for working-class migrant workers. The Factors made reasonable, if not spectacular, living from it.

It was more than seven years since I had eaten a meal in a family home, and it felt good. Mary had built a lovely, homely home and spared no effort to make it comfortable. In my lonely search for a wife and family home of my own, this was alluring indeed.

June spoke at length about how much Jews valued family life. The ducks seemed to line up for me – a politically aligned woman who wanted to be married too. I did not resist.

I thought June shared my abilities and interests. I was quite wrong on that account.

Rather than gaining a family, I began to feel the Factors were etching away my independence.

One Sunday I was late arriving for dinner. June met me at the door, her face like a hard rock.

"My father doesn't like waiting for his dinner, and he wouldn't start without you," she fumed. "Why weren't you early?"

My impulse was to turn and walk away. On many occasions, I regretted not doing so. Time has taught me to trust my gut feelings in intimate relations. Instead of feeling welcomed and included by Saul's insistence on waiting, I felt pressure to arrive on time thereafter.

But as a committed communist, my personal feelings were secondary to my drive to find a mate of pure communist thought. Though I could not afford to keep a wife yet, I hoped, in time, for a small home as comfortable as the one Mary Factor had made.

Looking back, it was like standing in the smoke of a bushfire. It can be all around you, enveloping you; it might be mildly worrying, but without a direct threat, how do you know when to flee? Events were happening to me, but I felt like an observer. My opinion was rarely given or sought. It was as if my presence was incidental to the relationship.

When June and I announced our intention to marry, the Factors announced they were inviting a few people to their house to meet me. Expecting a small gathering, I had gone out for some beers with friends beforehand. Shuffling in the door in my old faithful double-breasted suit, I was greeted by more than 50 family members. The women were loud and suntanned, the men sharply dressed and almost effeminate. They came with cash and lavish gifts like lamps and toasters, luxuries I had never imagined owning. I felt they were all trying to impress something upon me.

Mary served up an elaborate supper of cold dishes, hot dishes, tea, cakes and toasts. We all drank *l'chaim* ("to life"), and everyone wished me "all the happiness I would wish myself." I got sick of saying thank you and wished I was well out of the house. I felt removed from the whole scene. I wondered what the wheat-lumping gangs or the trammies, or even my fellow students, would have made of it all.

At evening's end, I went home and studied for hours. Later I lay in bed, pondering the gifts I had never wanted and the large family gathering arranged without my consent.

All the same, an engagement party was planned. My trammies money did not extend to a ring. I refused to waste the money I had saved for books, clothes or food.

As my driving passion was studying, I took only a passing interest in the engagement party preparation.

Saul and Mary insisted on buying me a new suit.

"Why spoil their pleasure? What does it cost you?" June needled.

Saul took me to a tailor he knew. The tailor asked me to take my trousers off. I couldn't afford underpants so I was left standing there in the raw. Saul did his best to look away. The tailor tried too, but this was tricky for someone taking an inside leg measurement. It was an embarrassing half-hour all round.

For Saul, the engagement party was also a strategic social event. As well as family members, he invited political allies and anyone else he felt he needed to impress. The numbers blew out to 400, three of whom were my friends, Lloyd Churchward, John Fennell and Brian Essex. I had invited my WA family, but they had declined – finances and distance a barrier. The event was held at one of Melbourne's most exclusive reception centres at the time: Stanmark, in Inkerman Street, St Kilda East. It was a sit-down dinner with grog laid on. The catering was excellent.

All these events and family gatherings took time that I could ill afford. Yes, dinners at the Factors each Sunday saved me money, but I was expected to dine out at expensive restaurants with them too, and I couldn't pay my equal share. Embarrassed, I expressed my dismay at this.

Whenever they introduced me, at some point, they mentioned "doing medicine". While having a doctor in the family might provide cache, it did not provide me or other university-educated individuals with respect. Mary and Saul had an inflated sense of their own medical knowledge and never missed an opportunity to attempt to pitch this knowledge against university-educated men and women.

Saul and I clashed. But Saul, backed by June and Mary, enjoyed the fight. Were he alive, he would say the same but give his version of events. He always did. I found his ego difficult. He could not conceive of relationships or discussions in which he was not directly involved. He could turn any discussion into a story of his own experience, his feelings, his opinions or his character assassination of another.

Emotionally, these events meant so little that I just didn't care about the arrangements – including those for our impending wedding. I was interested in studying and this caravan was rolling along quite nicely without me. Everyone seemed to be having a good time. Now and then I woke up with a start to realise I was jostling behind the caravan on a rope.

Hits and misses in medicine

The dissecting room was a large, high-vaulted space with 40 to 50 slabs. Around each body, five or six of us would huddle in our dirty white coats. Near the door were about 25 clean, starched white coats, worn by the mostly female physiotherapy students. All eyes turned when a med student sidled up to one of them. Several marriages began in that room, but most did not last.

Gradually, faces and personalities emerged from the fat-stained white coats of the dissection room. You grew to know a colleague's mettle, although some grew larger than life.

One of our number at the dissecting table was quick to make himself known – and just as quick to vanish. Sid Kosky was a great pianist around the traps but not an exceptional medical student. He had sat around the first day fidgeting over his part of the cadaver's upper arm. He then said, "Look fellas, I've gotta go for a haircut."

Some three months later, in Jimmy Watson's in Lygon Street, we caught up with Sid and asked how the haircut went. The whole time he was absent, Sid had been telling his parents he was "studying with Perc", or that the dissecting group was making a special review of the upper arm. Sid failed, but convinced his parents that the exams were unfair and that he had done so much work for them.

The end of year exams came in a rush. Week after week we had been terrifying ourselves with what "they" (the examiners) could give us in the "vivas" (oral exams, from the Latin *viva voce*, meaning "with the living voice"). The vivas were held at the anatomy museum at the medical faculty, where specimens were kept to help students learn about the body. We were sure the specimens used in the vivas would be rarely seen items from the collection, specially chosen to trick us. Of this we were certain.

We wound each other up with tales of crafty examiners who would try to catch us out. Traps might include covering up everything but a fine white line. Or we would need to pick a sciatic nerve from a single blood vessel running down its flat surface. Or the examiners might hide vital structures just so they could laugh as the student missed, fumbled and retired, panic-stricken. Every examiner was crafty, we decided.

By comparison, the written papers were straightforward descriptions of nerves, arteries, muscles. Biochemistry and physiology were not difficult, but "you wait for the orals," was a line we heard constantly.

On the day of the viva, one Chinese student, in an effort to put the examiners off guard, dressed up as a Chinese opera singer, with thick makeup, eyebrows darkened and plucked, and a dress split either side up to her waist. We forgot the viva exams just looking at her. We knew she would pass. We all had our best suits and ties on – no scruff for a viva. One urban myth told of a student who turned up in his golfing clothes and was instructed to take his clubs and get out. We were too wise (and scared) for that.

We were called in alphabetically. All my student days, I was scared by "Robertson!" In turn, "Rogers!" no doubt scared "Rose!"

Six tables were lined up in the museum, and the examiners were very polite: "Would you mind naming the structure in this specimen?"

"Mr Rogers, I would like you to …" make a fool of yourself (ha ha).

The first table was dead easy. The examiners did not wear masks, and

I recognised one. When I named half the structures – tendons, arteries, bones – someone handed me a difficult dissection of the leg. I happened to know this, so was then moved on to a postage-stamp-size opening of the flexor tendons crossing the wrist. All the viva horror stories had ensured that and I was expecting, and knew, this one. Five minutes were already up and I moved on. At the next table was Professor Leslie John Ray, or "Creeping Jesus", as he was known. He was quite dark and swarthy, with a kindly smile that served to disarm an unsuspecting student. That was before he threw the trickiest of questions. We had been warned to watch the bastard.

Creeping Jesus picked up a piece of gumph – it looked like ragged thread – and asked me to identify it. It was a small branch of the glossopharyngeal nerve, which I quickly named. His eyebrows went up in surprise at how fast I had nailed it. We moved on to the brain at the next table. For five harrowing minutes, I tried to work out the nuclei. I did my best to humour him and answer his questions. He seemed quite pleased.

The tables came and went so quickly, and it was all over. I was free. Back at 323, I had a few beers in relief that it was over.

During the summer break, I learnt that Barry, Tim, John, Brian and I had all passed our subjects. When we all met up, we couldn't stop laughing about the vivas. Everything seemed to be a witty remark.

"How did you like the bloody median nerve at the elbow?"

"I was just lucky I saw the artery."

"How about the glossopharyngeal nerve?"

"They're all bastards."

"But how do you like it? No supps (supplementary exams)."

"Have another (beer)."

Despite my misgivings, Professor "Creeping Jesus" Ray and I became great friends as time went on. Students do work themselves up into a state over exams.

June had tea with us that night at 323, and I walked her home afterwards. Her parents were in bed, but she told them I had passed all my subjects. Mary said, "You didn't get honours? We are only used to honours in this house."

June was a top arts student and did get honours, but I couldn't bring myself to answer this slight. If I had, the words would have poured out. With vehemence, I would have described leaving home at 15, having grown up in a house with just five books. I would have let loose about my bloody hard struggle to educate myself with no daddy with a cheque book to help me out. I would have told of being victimised for my politics in my career, barred from the public service, and thrown out of medicine; of how I had led a campaign to get back into medicine while working 13-hour days on the trams. To think June's mother had the nerve to dismiss my pass and speak of "honours". I was so wild with fury. I fumed all night.

Beyond my initial rage, the implicit snobbery of Mary's remark disturbed me. Intellectual snobbery is strong in the Jewish community, leaving satire as one of the few defences. I suspect that is why Jewish comedians rightly do so well.

A country boy at heart, I believed anyone associated with the left would also reject these haughty attitudes, rise above them and be actively opposed to them.

Chairman Rogers

In early 1956, I was made chair of the Communist Party's university branch. I felt duty-bound to lead what had diminished to about a dozen members. The university communists had a reputation out of all proportion to their numbers. It always surprised me how a small movement at the university could evoke such a wide response.

I could ill afford the time, but I was obliged to attend weekly meetings plus take on other duties. During my time as chairman, the university branch sparked the party's campaign to block Australian troops from joining the fight against the Malayan freedom uprising.

Even so, 1956 for me was mostly taken up with study, more study, and the Factor family's social calendar. Politics did take up some time but not in the same way it had. I didn't need to work because I had been frugal with my tramways money, drawing just £4 a week and paying 30 bob (shillings) for rent and board.

But by the end of the year, it was clear my money would not last through 1957. The day after I finished my exams, I started work in the biochemistry department as a bottle washer, working with senior lecturer Jack Legge.

Jack was an old communist who had joined the party before the war. In 1954 he had been called as a witness to the Royal Commission on Espionage, triggered by the "Petrov Affair" Soviet spy scandal. Jack was a brilliant man, but his politics had blocked any chance for academic advancement. Everyone liked him, even the students who could never understand a word he said about the Krebs cycle, also known as the citric acid cycle (the series of chemical reactions used by aerobic organisms to release stored energy).

Jack had brought his son, John Michael Legge, in to help in the laboratory. Together, father and son spoke a strange kind of Legge family lingo. Michael, as he was known then, was a self-assured boy who assumed his father's intelligence naturally fell to him, though he lacked his father's work ethic. He later became an economics lecturer.

My newfound work clashed that summer with the National Union of Australian University Students conference, held in January of 1957 at Victor Harbour, South Australia. The party wanted me to attend but to do so would cost me two weeks' worth of lost wages – £10 a week – plus I would need to draw another £5 a week from my savings. I told the party I could not afford £15 a week, so it agreed to pay me £5 a week for the two weeks.

Travelling to Victor Harbour with June, we were joined by the political activist and academic Lloyd Churchward and Max Marginson, later a founder of University House and supporter of *Overland* magazine.

At any meeting, conference or campaign, the Communist Party always appointed a fraction – an aligned group of members – to lead it. The Marxist thinking was that, unlike a *faction*, a fraction did not aim to divide members. It was a very effective method of achieving unity and responding to the shifts within a gathering. Mostly, these comrades were experienced in making decisions, even if those decisions were occasionally stupid.

The NUAUS was entertaining three People's Republic of China students. They were on exchange with Australian students. It was a great breakthrough, and we all felt a responsibility for ensuring no scandal enveloped them. Security police were following them everywhere and were easy to identify.

Poet Max Harris, founder of the literary journal *Angry Penguins*, gave a talk on communications that was as empty as it was long. Davey Burns, my Scottish teacher friend from Richmond Tech, spent a lot of time attacking Harris's ideas. Davey was an arts student at Melbourne Uni and part of the university branch of the party.

Breaking up is hard to do

During the conference, I spent a lot of time with the fraction discussing tactics and working out resolutions to put to the conference. June would sit in the conference room biting her nails. She was never jovial, but I felt her presence increasingly dragging on me.

One night we went for a walk and I told her I was sick of her critical, superior attitude. We were never in a mood for cuddling or making love. Her interests were biting her nails, eating and being critical. I called for an end to our relationship.

We parted – me for the men's dormitory and she for the women's. Someone woke me to say she was sobbing in her bunk. Guilt-ridden, I went to her immediately. She sobbed louder when I told her that separating was for the best, so I pacified her by saying we would try again.

The conference broke up and we made our way back to Melbourne around the south coast.

Around this time, Tim had been offered a job minding the phones for a Clifton Hill medical clinic, in exchange for a free room and £3 a week. He wasn't interested but was I? I went and saw the clinic, the room, discussed the conditions, and promptly agreed. I minded the phones every second night and every second weekend, sharing the work with a Mrs Rigby.

It was a sad parting at 323 Richardson Street, but the boys understood the allure of income and a free room.

When I told June's mother Mary of my plan, she said: "I will tell Saul when he comes in and he will decide what you should do."

Incredulous, I asked her to repeat herself, which she did. I pointed out that I made my own decisions. She dug her heels in, insisting it was a family decision. When Saul heard the news, he told me in a pompous voice, as though I had consulted him, "Yes, it is worth taking. You don't pay out anything, so what have you got to lose."

Though tempted, I could not afford to reject the job and room just to spite Saul. Under the guise of concern, the Factors had once again undermined my self-rule. The option of rejecting Saul's "approval" was no option. These kinds of issues came up time and again, and every time I made a stand I lost. Behind my back, manipulations were at play.

I shifted my books and clothes over to Queens Parade, Clifton Hill, and set up in a small room next to the bathroom. It was an ideal studying environment. I was forced to stay in the house every second weekend from noon Saturday to Monday morning. If anyone rang for the doctor, I was to give them his number at home or wherever he was. From the moment I entered this phone-minding monastery, I started studying.

The clinic had five doctors, but one was on leave for a year, so four were working. Previously, practice partners Sam Benwell and Cyrus Jones had operated a clinic in Queens Parade, next door to brothers John and Gordon Trinca, who ran their father's old practice. They joined forces to create a four-room clinic inside the large Edwardian house in which I now lived. Others employed at the clinic included a Latvian receptionist, an accountant and a trained nurse.

Mrs Rigby, with whom I shared the house and the receptionist work, was a hypertensive harridan housekeeper. She was a talkative bore. She would keep nattering as I backed out of the kitchen, following me up the hall even as I closed the door in her face.

One time she talked solidly for one hour while I cooked, ate a meal, washed up and backed away. My only words to her were, "Yes," "No" and, unfortunately, "Go on?" She was unkind about most people.

The Factors invited me over for many meals and, as a result, I never quite made the Clifton Hill place my home. When I was working, the weekend was too long to go without food in the house, so I lived on scrambled eggs and grilled sausages.

Sometimes June would come over to my room. We would cuddle on the bed, but she didn't want to make love – I thought it was an opportunity too glorious to miss, but she did not agree.

Stretched

Occasionally, to fit branch meetings in, they would be held in my room. As the chair of the branch, I was also expected to attend section meetings, and metropolitan and state conferences. This became extremely difficult with my uni workload and my job at the clinic. Somehow I coped with the meetings, university campaigns and selling *The Guardian*. The worst was close at hand.

The Factors continued their constant demands for meals together and visiting relations' houses. Each meal was served with a course of politics. These discussions were as difficult to describe as they were to digest. Saul would make a declaration. Mary would find some point of difference. He would almost always shout her down. June sided with her father. Although I have always enjoyed a political argument and we were of the same persuasion, I did not want to add fuel to the already explosive dining table. I kept my own counsel and ate my meal.

I was concerned that June lacked humour and only perked up in the presence of her father. It also worried me that intimacy was not developing between June and me. I could not understand it. We were both Communist Party members and I assumed our compatibility was inevitable as we were both "men and women of a special mould".

June was conscious of her weight, and to be fair so was I. She said she wanted to lose some pounds but baulked at my suggestion that she go easier on the bread, sweets and heavy Jewish cooking. Scorning me, she laughed at the thought of giving up her mother's meals. I wondered whether as a married couple we would eat every night at her parents' house, as she had never learnt to make those dishes she loved so much.

Our upbringings were so different in this regard. I had grown up in a house where food was never plentiful. Being overweight was rare. I was nicknamed "Mutts" for being the exception to the rule – my "mutton chop" cheeks were unusually chubby. I had long felt a moral imprimatur that weight should be kept in check, a philosophy that health research agrees with.

When June bought marshmallow snowballs from the café and crammed them into her mouth, someone in our group commented that these treats would make her fat. She just laughed, her mouth brimming. Her full moon face, teeth coated with white goo and coconut, hovered before me. My face must have registered disgust because she told me to keep my mouth shut. It was an awkward, embarrassing moment for the whole table. As I left, June followed, asking me what the matter was. That was my chance. I really should have stopped everything there and then. I told her I was ashamed of her. She claimed this was my puritan upbringing and that if she enjoyed her food, she would eat as much as she liked.

This turned into a row, which continued outside the university. Riding home on my bike, I vowed again to break off the engagement. Then I considered the repercussions. I felt responsible for all the lamps, bowls, coffee sets, toasters, electric coffee percolators, cash and other gifts we received. People would think me irresponsible to break it after all they had spent. On top of this, we were both party members – what were the implications for the party if a chairman was seen to be acting recklessly?

I had no idea what marriage entailed. I just wanted to study, and it seemed possible to do this married.

The rest of the extended family had shown me hospitality and kindness – especially Mary's sister and brother, and Saul's three brothers. When I so wanted a family, their warm familial embrace was hard to reject.

Now and then one of the extended family would include me in an invitation to dinner. Often an old Polish or Jewish dish was served and, although originally meant for a cold climate, I could fully understand why they maintained the traditions.

Meals usually started with thick or thin borscht, with fish, sweet or sharp. There would usually be a traditional dish of cholent – a slow-cooked bean and meat stew. The poultry, a must, would be brought out on huge dishes, followed by other meats and vegetables. The table would then be cleared for sweets. Cakes, fruit and coffee would be eaten at the table. Not once did I ever see anyone at these dinners or at any party who was drunk. There was always a wide choice of alcohol, but little of it was touched.

The meals were huge but so well cooked it was a pleasure to feel bloated. I would have a dinner like this at a relation's house once every six weeks.

Some relatives would attend four, five or six of these meals a week, complaining all the time about the amount of food they were eating. Then they would pop into the doctor's to ask for pills to stop eating.

The conversations at these dinners were lively, usually funny, but always egocentric. Everyone had an opinion; facts were unnecessary, and it helped if you had a loud voice. One of Saul's brothers told me that Australian medicine was years behind Austrian medicine, with American medicine leading the world. He could read the directions on an aspirin bottle, but that was about the sum of his medical knowledge. I told him he didn't know what he was talking about. This precipitated a real row as I had done worse than oppose an opinion – I had dented an ego. This was a real hurt.

Still, the family was kind. In deference to my lack of Yiddish, they would always tell jokes in English, except for the punch line. When the punch line was then translated into English it fell flat as a wet fish. I learnt a little Yiddish just for the jokes.

If conversation waned, there was always the culture wars to fall back on. European and Yiddish culture was held up above Australian. It seemed to be a given that culture began and ended with music, a few books, European galleries and the Yiddish writers. It was a point of honour to attend concerts and plays, and to see any visiting celebrity artist. The level of analysis varied, but mostly it was on the level of, "Well, I like it (or her, him or them)." This was usually accompanied by a thrust of the head, a lift of the jaw and an arrest of the soup spoon, the spoon signalling: "Defy me if you will but I stand alone against the world to say so." Murmurs and slurps indicated responses: everything from a tacit agreement to disagreement; unable to attend; refuse to go; or the children have measles.

It would have been hard to leave this newly acquired family behind, and so, I stayed. My abiding hope was that things between June and I would change when we were married and rid of outside influences.

Chapter 10
Dangerous games

While I had been knuckling down to study in 1956 and maintaining my fractious relationship with the Factors, a time bomb had been ticking in Russia. In February, Nikita Khrushchev, the First Secretary of the Communist Party, had delivered his "Secret Speech", officially titled *On the Cult of Personality and Its Consequences.* Denouncing Joseph Stalin, Khrushchev had said the late Soviet leader used weapons of mass terror in the Great Purge of the 1930s. Khrushchev confirmed what anti-communists had alleged for years – that innocent communists had false accusations of espionage and sabotage pinned on them and, in the name of political expediency, they were tortured and executed.

By June, the speech had been leaked to *The New York Times, Le Monde* and *The Observer,* via the Israeli intelligence agency Shin Bet. At first, we had dismissed it as Cold War scuttlebutt from the United States.

The exams had come and gone with a slight air of unreality. I had been on duty at the clinic and bunkered down to study in my room. The place had become something of a real bunker as it offered a cushion against the political and emotional maelstrom that had been building in the party outside.

It had been against this backdrop that the 1956 Melbourne Olympics were held, from November 22 to December 8. Australians had been confused and edgy in the lead-up. Years of conditioning meant many Australians hated anything to do with the Soviets. Mother Russia had done herself no favours by not only leaking Khrushchev's secret report but also twice invading Hungary, in October and then again in November of that year.

With my third year of medicine providing a month-long break at what had previously been the end of the third term, I was part of an organising committee to welcome the Soviet Olympic team to Melbourne.

Although newspapers of the day had tried to project the Soviet reputation onto the athletes, this had failed. The crowds at the Games loved the good performers, and Russia had some outstanding athletes. Vladimir Kuts won the 10,000-metre and 5000-metre runs. As something of the darling of the Russian team, he had countered the anti-Soviet propaganda more than anyone else.

The police had been given instructions to let nothing upset the Games. When I joined 300 students to march down Swanston Street in a protest, we were met by a line of 100 police with batons drawn. We turned away without further protest. Some of us had been marching against the British-French-Israeli attack on the Suez Canal on October 29, and some against the Soviet invasion of Hungary on November 4. I had carried a banner calling for a hydrogen bomb ban, as I thought the situation both in Suez and Hungary could lead to the third world war. I wanted the hydrogen bomb banned no matter which nations were fighting. I was grateful that US President Dwight Eisenhower had cooled things down using economic sanctions, and he led the move to place UN peacekeeping forces in the area.

The welcoming committee had worked for a month selling tickets and organising a hall to host a party for the Soviet delegation. But on the night, they didn't show up. After about an hour of waiting, a chap from the Australian Soviet Friendship Society got up and told us the reception would now be on the wharf: the delegation was not disembarking from their ship. Everyone left the hall and went to the wharf, but I went home in disgust.

The stench of Stalin

As 1956 crossed over into 1957, a miasma, like that of a mustard gas bomb, began to pervade the Communist Party. It had become apparent that the allegations against Stalin were true. He had used his power to crush dissention from good communists.

There were huge divisions within the party over what to do with the fallout from this bombshell. Some used it to crank up their rhetoric; others left the party, lost their minds or took their own lives. Decent people within the party were crushed and disillusioned. After placing so much faith in the Russian version of communism, they were disgusted by its implementation. It was heartbreaking. This implosion had a far greater impact than anything ASIO or Menzies could have done to us.

We wanted the local leadership to start the painful process of self-criticism. The leadership said we were rocking the boat and it would blow over. We initially stuck by them because Menzies and the Cold War had created a climate in which we needed to band together. We didn't want to give the security police, the press, the Menzies government or the right-wing maniacs any ammunition.

For my part, I accepted all that had been said about Stalin. But I wanted to change the party to make it truly socialist and more in tune with Australian political realities. At the time, the ALP seemed to me to be more a grassroots party than the CPA, especially after the split of 1955.

It soon became apparent that Australia's Communist Party leadership had little intention to change its work style or the democracy within the party. Worst of all, the leadership had no plan to state or assess the role of Stalinism in Australia.

Intellectuals within the party held a public meeting at which both Stalinism and the local party leadership were denounced. The intellectuals were immediately expelled.

I was chairman of the university branch and on the executive during most of this period but drifted away towards the end of 1957 rather than resigning. One meeting after another was taken up with infighting. My view was we should stay in the party and campaign for change from within. Still, friends were resigning from the party: Davey Burns, Michael Masser, Neville Green, Jimmy Grew and dozens of others.

A chap I had known for years, Jack Preston, turned up one day at the university and started shouting about Stalin. He attracted quite a crowd of students who baited him. I went up and led him to the café. He had cracked up under the strain. Another fellow Communist, a poet, had put his head in a gas oven.

At one meeting, Fred Emery, back from the UK, went on a tangent that made me think he too had gone mad. He had become the leader of a group in North Melbourne who plotted a socialist uprising for Australia based on Lenin's teachings rather than Stalin's. The more beer they drank, the more they became convinced that they were little Lenins in the making.

Fred Emery still harboured a grudge over his toppling as branch leader of the psychology department. This, combined with the split between those calling for action and those staying the course, unsettled him. He was also troubled that the party did not bow to his genius. Now, ordinary branch members were attacking him in branch meetings. His bitterness grew. Max Marginson would later allege that Emery gave ASIO a secret dossier on every communist in the psychology department. Max said Emery spent six weeks on the ship back to England – post the Secret Speech – trying to convince him not to send it. Max sometimes embellished with booze, but if he was telling the truth, Fred Emery was the only comrade who ratted to the enemy.

Meanwhile, in the argumentative Factor household, the battlelines continued.

Saul Factor was a Stalinist hardliner. He believed that Stalin had acted in the best interests of Russia's defence and that we, the workers of the world, needed to support the Soviet Union as the first socialist country. Mary Factor knew all the time Stalin was no good. June bit her nails rather than oppose her father.

One curious thing I noted at that time was that June never addressed me or spoke to me directly in front of her father. She always made it clear that I took second place. She seemed to be spelling out the message to me that while she might have been marrying me, her relationship with her father was paramount.

I hoped that this would change when we set up an independent home. I felt June never related to me as a person. She related to me as a communist medical student – someone studying, working, even someone who was going to marry her – but not as a living, breathing man.

The humanity of medicine

My fourth year started in September 1957. In this term, we took intermittent bacteriology classes and had pathology classes. We also attended hospitals two afternoons a week to observe clinics in action. The following year we would be based at hospitals most of the time, working as student doctors and attending clinics and lectures mostly in the hospitals.

I found the studies fascinating and absorbing. I felt I was biting and chewing on solid medical knowledge. The pathology course was so good that since that year I have followed the dictum of the renowned Canadian physician and philosopher William Osler: "As is your pathology so is your practice."

My first session as a trainee was at The Alfred Hospital. At the ward, we met Dr Menzies, who wore an impeccable suit, cufflinks, white shirt and dark college tie. With his surname and appearance, I assumed he was a Liberal supporter and feared it would not take him long to work out my political sympathies. And this man was to be my examiner!

While he was talking over a patient, my mind was back at the wheat-lumping gang. The heat of the bagging tables and the weight of a bag on my shoulders came back to me. I wondered which world was real. I wasn't really a part of the wheat-lumping gang – they made that clear when I told them I had got into uni. Yet, I felt alien in the company of Dr Menzies and the other well-dressed medical students. Their progress to this point was uninterrupted, I thought. They came from comfortable middle-class homes, private colleges. They had parents who talked to them. They had been conditioned for years to be standing exactly where they were now, listening to the well-modulated voice of Dr Menzies discussing the pathology of a cerebrovascular accident.

At odds with my initial perception of Dr Menzies was the man's obvious knowledge, his sympathy for the patient and his friendliness towards the students. He was delightful. I admired him so much I never wanted to know if he was related to my most hated prime minister. His politics never emerged and I did not venture mine.

On this particular Tuesday afternoon at The Alfred, I had to make a conscious effort to relate to this man who represented everything I could not resolve. It was perplexing. How could doctors generally be good and knowledgeable yet be political reactionaries? The only true humanists were socialists, weren't they? At present, the soothing tones of Dr Menzies could do more to help the patient in front of us than I could with all the humanism in the world.

It took some convincing, but eventually, I started to listen to him. I decided that although the middle classes had the monopoly on medical knowledge, I was going to imbibe a reasonable share. In my awe, I never asked his first name.

During our years of anatomy, physiology and biochemistry, we rarely came into contact with our lecturers personally. They were so remote that their opinions and politics hardly mattered. They were at a university and, to an extent, shared in the liberating effect of an academic environment.

Consultants like Dr Menzies were from the ranks of practising doctors and were conservatives of a different kind. I had not realised at first that these "conservatives" were conserving medicine and preserving it in its purest form. They would not run with half-baked, unproven theories – show them the evidence. Only then would they consider introducing new theories on treatment.

Dr Menzies spoke to us for about an hour that day. Having solved my philosophical difficulty of relating to him, I listened so intently that I can remember now most of that clinic.

It was my first taste of the brotherhood of medicine. Only later would I full appreciate the way in which being a doctor gives you a ready-made community. Doctors could be prickly in training mode, but once you were in the club, you were in. This restricted male-dominated brotherhood, which is international, provides very clear obligations or ethics for its members. Gradually the rules were revealed by anecdote and example rather than by precept. Personal convenience is set aside if a doctor or any of his family is in trouble. Dr Menzies, with his personable attitude towards us, gave us a taste of that brotherhood.

The other vivid impression I got was the difference between the generality of a disease and the person who has a disease.

The old chap in the bed had had a cerebrovascular accident (CVA), also known as a stroke. It altered his life profoundly. It changed relations with his wife, his children and his work. But the pathology of the disease – its diagnosis – was curiously immaterial to the pathology questions before us. I watched as Dr Menzies displayed a deep knowledge of pathology. While the doctor's pathology was independent of the patient, he had compassion.

I wondered how the old chap felt as we discussed the factors which produced atheroma in his arteries and the three types of common CVA's. He listened as keenly as most of the students around his bed.

On my way home, I decided that clinical medicine did allow for the fullest expression of humanism. I felt no contradictions between my strong beliefs and the practice of medicine. Back then, I had no inkling of the role money played, and still plays, in the practice of medicine.

We were introduced to histopathology. This is the alteration in tissues seen at a microscopic level after these tissues have been subject to a pathological process. It is like viewing art and science at the same time. One could see the beautiful arrangement of the normal cellular pattern and the obvious interruption caused by the disease agent. The process of sorting out cause and effect read like a detective novel. By knowing simple facts, it was surprising what could be deduced.

Deducting reasons and causes from accurate observations is, in essence, pathology.

In fourth term, we were also introduced to bacteriology. Like most doctors, I got into a habit of excessive handwashing, as I viewed most objects as possible carriers of bacteria.

The term passed. We had to study one book on general pathology, which some students claimed they had read nine times. One student failed the exam because, while he knew the book word perfectly, he seemed to lack the imagination to put those words into effect.

The term finished and still, I did not contemplate my approaching marriage much. Looking back, I had no experience on which to base the two biggest decisions of my life – my job and my marriage. Both were a shot in the dark. It has been pointed out to me that the third vital decision – becoming a parent for the first time – must be made without experience as well.

The wedding

With the end of 1957 in sight, my marriage date of December 10 was looming. I felt that my part in the wedding was only to say, "That's nice," and "Thank you very much."

I would have liked a stag night – a few beers and a song, a few jokes and everyone shouting. But by then I had no close friends. The Factor family had consumed my free time to such an extent that I never saw friends apart from Tim Loh and those who attended party meetings.

The wedding was held at the Registry of Births, Deaths and Marriages in Queen Street, Melbourne.

The reception was again at Stanmark and, again, many people were invited. But less than a handful of my friends were there – Lloyd Churchward, Tim Loh and Barry Forbes were there for me. At the door, I received and thanked the guests for the expensive presents and wondered how in the hell I had allowed myself to be in this situation again. The food was standard, well served, with plenty of wine. Then came the speeches. The first was by humanist and 1952 candidate for Isaacs Sam Goldblum. He gave a good speech on happiness, on how he had to struggle for it with his wife and how you couldn't take it for granted. It was a plea for unity, and there was not a sectarian note in the whole 30 minutes.

My historian and activist friend Lloyd Churchward spoke next. He said when he first heard of me he was told I was a boxer from Western Australia. He went on to say I had a remarkable facility for relating to people in quick time. June, he felt, stood above people. She tended to look down on them, and this, he felt, was a matter of maturity.

The family table stiffened. Saul got up to debate in reply.

He started by recounting how he had fostered June through school, how he had watched her do well as a student – brilliantly, in fact. He was proud

– yes, proud – of his daughter. He wanted everyone to know just how proud he was. His wife was proud. They were both proud of their daughter.

Next, June rose in the debate. She declared that as soon as her father had joined the army during the war she knew the war would be won. She was proud of her father – yes, proud – and in honour of him, she would always sign herself June Factor.

If I hadn't felt so removed from the whole proceedings, I would have moved a motion calling for a show of hands from all those at the high table on her "name". Although she never spoke to me about this beforehand, I was not surprised at her decision.

I was a spectator here. Not one of my family turned up. I felt like I was being pitched into something that was beyond my control. Besides, I was worried about whether I would have enough money to support myself over the next three years as I qualified as a doctor.

Sand and study don't mix

That night June and I went to our flat in Elwood, in a street parallel to the beach, organised by relatives. It was £4 a week, more than I had ever paid. It was eight miles to university and took me two trams and an hour to get there. I had wanted a room in Carlton, but that was considered not good enough. After a two-week honeymoon in Marlo, at the mouth of the Snowy River, I hoped to settle into a life with fewer social obligations.

I thought when we married the time with Saul and Mary would diminish and I would be left to study in peace, but this was not to be. They came at least three times during the week, with lunch somewhere on Sunday. It was all done in the name of love, so I could not fight it.

When Saul and Mary came to tea, the best tablecloth and silver would be laid out. June had developed a repertoire of meals and when her parents came over she would go out of her way to make it special. June was quite the blushing bride when her father praised the meal, as he always did. Saul picked up his political pronouncements where he had left off. With his presence lingering in the air long after he had gone, June often took to being critical of the "limitations" of her mother. In the aftermath of these visits, I felt that any soft intimacy between us was utterly destroyed.

Over the 1957-'58 summer holiday, I did no paid work. When I lived in Clifton Hill I had spent next to nothing and saved money. I still also had money left over from the tramways. During the year, I had taken on some gardening work and a well-paid position polling people on their opinions. But now I could see the money running away and could not seem to stop it.

By chance, I met up with student counsellor Bob Priestly at the university. (I had known him for years and had always felt guilty about taking a bottle of whisky from his house to another party. He never held it against me.) After chatting, he invited me to apply for a university bursary, which I did. I think it was due to Bob's influence that I got a double bursary, worth £100 a year.

At the start of that summer break, I had a third-year therapeutics exam but I found it impossible to study in our one-bedroom Elwood flat because of the constant stream of noisy family members in bathers, bearing food, who wanted to go to the beach. I waited until they had gone to the beach and would study then rather than waste two hours on trams commuting to the university library.

Outside of her family relations, June was an isolate. She had very few friends, although for a time was close with Joan Kirner, who would one day be Premier of Victoria. When her few friends came over, June came to life. She was vivacious and would talk with them about "the good old days." She was then 20 years old.

It was a mucky year and I was forced to repeat my therapeutics exam. I passed the supplementary exam but was bloody angry that June allowed those crowds to descend on us, repeating their endless inanities, when I needed to study. I was so wild I think they got the story. They could be as stupid as they liked as long as it didn't shatter my concentration. My study came first and would remain first.

After tea, June would not bother about the cleaning up. Her mother had done that for her for so long that June didn't see why she should have to do it. I would hurry to clean the table so I could get my books out.

I would set up my reading stand and try to focus, but out of the comer of my eye, I could see June biting her nails. She did this with a pathological intensity that transferred itself to me. I would start to watch her and tense up myself. I told her to stop a thousand times. I tried turning around but I could hear the click-click of the teeth wrenching at the nails.

The Factors operated within two belief systems – both Jewish and Marxist. To me, Marxism was truly without borders, race or religious ethos. How could a communist have a religion too? They were communists but never resiled from their innate Jewishness nor addressed the paradox.

Yet, I had chosen to marry a communist, and here was my paradox. I needed intimate relations. When I did finally work out the full implications of choosing a mate based on political alignment rather than physical attraction, the contradiction was shattering.

Although there was politics to talk about, June would pick a time when I was studying to ask my thoughts. I always tried to reply and then found it hard to get back into the feeling for my chapters. It was during this year I realised my studies were the most important thing in my life.

Throughout 1958, I studied, attended lectures, and had practical classes and ward rounds. I also attended party meetings and executive meetings. I should have been joyously enthusiastic with just one year of my medical degree to go, but my home life was ruinous. To my mind, June was selfish. She could not care less about my studies but expected me to be concerned with hers. Sexually, she rejected me so much I had almost given up trying. I thought this marriage was not worth the trouble. I began to not desire her and began to appreciate her parents' visits as a welcome distraction from my relationship with her.

Halfway through the year, I developed symptoms of a duodenal ulcer. A barium meal diagnostic test showed nothing, but the discomfort and belching was relieved by antacids. I believe the strain of my home life, the implosion of the party and my studies were all contributors.

As I hadn't seen my family for some time, I went across to the west alone at the end of the year. June was pregnant before I left. I was pleased at the thought of having our own family, although this was secondary in my mind to my preoccupation with medicine. June still had exams and so remained in Melbourne.

Tin lids and tears

My visit back home to the west was pretty flat. Visiting Jack, I had a one-sided conversation about his medical practice partners and the difficulties of practising in a group. My big brother was out to impress me with his wealth, as he had started making money on the stock market.

After Perth, I travelled to Albany by train to see Mum. She had fallen on hard times, some of which she had brought upon herself after selling the Narrogin house to go tripping around the eastern states. In a story that became family legend, she was retrieved by Alec, aged about 12, who travelled solo across the country to bring her back. With Rona, they moved into the house in North Perth with the tennis courts, but Rona moved to the University Hostel.

Eventually rejecting the punishing routine of rolling the lawn courts, Alec made his way to Albany, travelling alone again, aged about 14, to attend high school. Albany was a cheaper place to live than Perth, but with no money and no friends, it was a most unlikely venture for one so young. Alec not only survived but thrived. The high school principal arranged for him to board at the home of the primary school principal.

Meanwhile, penniless, with her children gone, Mum had apparently answered a newspaper advertisement for a partner-housekeeper on a 600-acre property outside of Albany. The wife of the owner had died, and he had effectively advertised for a new one. My mother had married this stranger out of the blue. I felt uneasy about the whole situation.

From Perth, I called Alec to find out where Mum was, and I made my way out there by train. Arriving at a lonely siding, I jumped down from the train. There was only bush for as far as the eye could see. I followed the directions I'd been given to a small bush track. At the end of the track was a clearing with a two-room shanty. One room was the bedroom, the other was a large kitchen, containing a long, cheap deal table, a dresser and a large wood stove.

My mother couldn't see who it was when I came to the back door. When I called out, "It's Percy," she burst out crying and hugged me. Her dress and body stank. There was no bath and she did all her washing in a tin dish on the kitchen table. The shack had electricity but next to no conveniences.

She offered me a cup of tea. It was then that I noticed her hands shook in jerky movements. She had some kind of neuromuscular condition. The movements were asymmetrical. She had become so uncoordinated that she had to tie the lids to the kettles so they wouldn't drop to the floor when she removed them. Her hands tremored so badly when she picked up a plate that she couldn't place it on the table without a clatter. Alec later told me that the old man beat her with a stick whenever she broke a plate.

Over tea and biscuits, I told her what I had been doing for the past few years. She tried to tell me about her recent past but kept saying how good it all used to be in Geraldton and Narrogin: "Do you remember when ...".

The present meant nothing to Mum as she suppressed her current intolerable situation. She was kept alive by looking to the past. Up until that point, I had never realised how little insight she had into her relationship with her children. The reminiscences were episodic, usually humorous, and ending sadly.

"Do you remember the time you brought that dog home? I called it 'that dammed mung'. You called it 'Steamboat Bill' or 'Mr William' and Alec called it 'Skip'. The poor dog didn't know who to respond to. They were happy days."

I recollected that time in Narrogin entirely differently. Rona was sullen and resentful of my mother's insensitivity. Alec was so lonely he was almost inarticulate. I felt like a stranger in my home. Happy days? They were terrible days.

Yet, in this bush shack, I agreed and laughed with her about this and many other stories that helped keep her going.

The old man who owned the property, Tom Atwell, came in, met me, and went out again. He was a pinched, miserable stooped little man with a mean mouth.

As the afternoon passed I got brighter and brighter in my conversation with my mother but inside I felt more and more depressed. We drank our last cup of tea. I had to leave as there was nowhere for me to stay and old man Atwell didn't like visitors.

Mum struggled down the track with me, clutching my arm. I tried to be cheerful with her until I said goodbye. Only as I left and she walked inside did the tears start to fall. I sobbed as though my chest would break. I couldn't see the road. Everything flooded my mind – the sheer rotten loneliness of it all. Nothing replaces the intimacy of a happy family relationship in the home and once that disintegrates, there is an aching longing for it.

I stumbled rather than walked. It was now about 6pm and the shadows were lengthening across the road. This is a beautiful time in the bush, but – stuck miles from a bed and a meal – my one thought was to get out of it.

Survival in the Australian bush requires preparation and organisation, and I had done neither. All I could do was wait and hope for a lift. I was eager to see my little brother Alec now that he was all grown up with a young family. He was living in Manjimup, about 20km away, on the road back to Perth.

When teenage Alec had boarded with the Albany primary school principal it was only meant to be a short-term arrangement. But he became ingrained in the family. He was taken on picnics. He and Wendy, the eldest of the family's three girls, fell in love. Wendy looked at Alec and never looked away from him for 25 years, when after a lifetime of toil their love burnt out.

Still, they had romantic beginnings. Wendy and Alec eloped to Perth as teenagers. When they returned, Wendy was pregnant, and they married. They were both now schoolteachers, with three daughters of their own. After the desolation of visiting Mum, I was anxious to see them all.

A fruit truck dropped me off at a post office in a town about 35 miles from Manjimup. It was dark when I arrived, which meant I had little chance of getting another lift.

The local teenagers were shouting and skidding their bikes around the post office, acting as they felt – bored. Like the youngsters I encountered in Pinjarra all those years ago, these teenagers lived for petty distractions. On the look out for a victim, they eyed me off but allowed me to pass when I dumped my bag.

I had lost Alec's phone number on the journey and called the Manjimup Police Station. The police gave me a number for one of Alec's friends. I called and started to explain the long story, but the friend cut me off as Alec was standing beside him.

Alec and a teacher colleague collected me by car an hour later, and we shook hands. Even with this stranger behind the wheel, it occurred to me how different I felt in the presence of my family. When I was without them, my experiences felt personal – my joys or hurts were private – but in their presence, they become common property to us. It became easy to slip into a conversation that appeared not to have started or ever to have finished. With the teacher friend listening in, I told Alec only that I had seen Mum. I wanted to leave it at that for now. Family tragedies are family affairs.

We arrived at Alec's timber cottage to find Wendy had prepared a large roast meal. But everyone wanted to talk rather than eat. The teacher friend was almost living with Alec and Wendy. It was clear that my brother and his wife made instant and enduring friendships and that Alec's mates went to no end of trouble for him.

Wendy and Alec were happy. Shy and at times inarticulate, Alec tended to venture few words. But he seemed proud to be able to show his brother his household. I told them about my medical course and what had happened to me in the preceding years. I could never sort out exactly how Alec had survived year by year, but I knew Wendy played a big part in keeping him from disintegrating.

Wendy's sisters were staying with them at the time, and I found they were rude and insolent to Alec. They ordered him around, almost as if he were a servant. I suspected they resented my arrival. By dint of showing Alec the utmost respect myself, and refusing to countenance one word against him, they slowly got the message.

I returned to Perth the next day to stay with Jack and Dorothy in their newly built home in in Floreat Park, a fashionable part of Perth. The house had a four-car garage and a swimming pool, which suited their tastes and Jack's pocket. Jack's sharemarket punting had paid off and would continue to do so. In years to come, Jack would make a killing in Poseidon Nickel, buying in at just a few cents a share. At its peak, Poseidon shares boomed to around $280 a share.

Like old man Atwell, they did not like guests. I was the first person to stay overnight at the new house and, apart from one other person, the only overnight house guest.

Though my relatives in the west regarded my visit as a homecoming, I knew I could never live there again. Jack, in particular, struck me as insular and parochial, with no interest in the events which had shaped me. Jack felt compelled to oppose and correct any philosophy I had that did not lead to the making of money or the pursuit of pleasure – as if this was the only thing in life.

Western Australia seemed the ideal place to put your feet up on a holiday, or at the end of a working life. To me, it was not the place to attempt serious work. The pleasures were too obvious: the ideal weather, the beaches, the bush. The people were friendly and unassuming but so remote that most of the outside world seemed a bit hostile to them. They had two categories: "them" and "us." By the 1970s, WA's long-running secessionist movement was led by Australia's richest man, then Lang Hancock, who bankrolled the state's failed push to become a republic.

Soon after my WA visit, my mother's keeper, Atwell, died. As his widow, she inherited the acreage. Around this time, Dr Jacobs, who had cared for me like a son over the years, discovered Mum had a neurological disorder that caused her spasms. He arranged for her to stay in Perth's Mount Henry Hospital, which was opened in 1951 to care for mentally ill and disabled elderly patients. Although glad to know my mother was finally being well cared for, I found it hard to recapture any real affection for her. As I have said before, once the family home disintegrates it is hard to rekindle that closeness. Instead, I would revert to my default in a dark situation, playing the fool for her and reminiscing.

Chapter 11
Obstetrics brought home

Returning "home" to Victoria by train, I was met by June at the station. She told me she had lost the pregnancy while I was away and that her father had arranged and paid for her medical care.

I asked her whether she was alright. She said she felt "a bit sad" and I replied that I understood. I knew that 25 per cent of pregnancies were lost and this was not uncommon. I was concerned for June but not, I admit, terribly upset.

While I had been away June wrote that I had passed all my third-year subjects but had not got honours in pathology. I was a bit disappointed at this as I had worked fairly hard.

This was my fifth calendar year studying medicine, including pre-med, and it felt like the course had breezed past me before it had even started. Unlike previous years, 1958 brought with it the promise of some respite from exams in fourth-year medicine, but the following year we could be examined on anything we had studied over the previous six years.

From late January, the school year was divided into four 10-week terms. Each term was spent at a hospital, or a clinic specialising in areas such as dermatology, gynaecology, urology, or ear, nose and throats. I would spend my first two hospital stints at the Royal Women's Hospital and Royal Children's Hospital. The rest of the time would be divided among clinics at the Royal Melbourne Hospital. Attendance was compulsory.

My first 10 weeks at the Royal Women's profoundly altered my attitude to hospitals and the institutional care of people.

About 20 medical students stayed here in live-in accommodation. We had our own rooms but shared facilities on the fourth floor of an old building, which is now demolished. Our student rooms were served by a slow cruising lift that was supposed to "rush" you to the labour ward for deliveries.

Every student had to do 20 deliveries, including any episiotomies, plus assist at one or more breech births. We were expected to attend every caesarean section performed in the hospital – you could be dragged from bed at 2am for this. We were also expected to stay at the hospital at all times. We were on call day and night, to be summoned to the theatre or labour ward. At every call-out, we had to wear a short, white jacket which we called the "bum-freezer". Failure to don this ridiculous uniform was noted.

Obstetric students were disliked by nearly everyone in the hospital. The ward sisters regarded us as dammed nuisances. The trainee sisters saw us as the opposition, pinching their deliveries and doing very little of the slushy work around the labour wards. Only the hospital obstetricians liked us because they taught us, and nearly every one of them responded in kind to our interest. We would be colleagues soon enough, and some of us might even send them cases. On day one, we excitedly trooped into the lecture room with sharpened pencils. Australia's first professor of obstetrics and gynaecology, Lance Townsend (later to be Sir Lance), came in and sat down.

He immediately started on the first student: "What is the origin of the female reproductive system?"

To my utter astonishment, no one knew. He asked each student until he came to me.

"In the development of the Mullerian ducts, there is a fusion at the distal ..." I began. I didn't get any further.

"What is your name, son?" Townsend asked.

"Rogers."

"Well, Rogers, you and I are going to get along together," he said. And we did, until his death in 1983.

Townsend was a hard, ruthless teacher – Australian to his bootlaces, both in his manner and in his national pride. When he discovered my communist sympathies, he felt he had an ally against the Catholics. As a Freemason, he felt the Pope was the natural enemy.

With a sympathetic professor who expected me to be a good student, I rose to the occasion. I knew the angles, the diameters, the curves and the anatomy of the pelvis backwards. I thought obstetrics was a bit like anatomy and pathology but, if anything, more exciting.

Wards both callous and brutal

There were two wards we could be assigned to at the Royal Women's: 19 and 31. I was assigned to Ward 31. When we arrived, panting after forgoing the lift for the stairs, the sisters in charge directed us to our deliveries. Then the sister would tell us to "scrub up" and be quick about it, "as she (the mother) is nearly there." We would then try and ease the baby over the perineum, if necessary cut an episiotomy, deliver the baby and the placenta, and clean up before going back to bed.

In general, there was indifference and disregard for the patients. These sentiments were often masked by platitudes and threats to the expectant women. In response, I felt compelled to talk to the women.

I couldn't believe the atmosphere of the place. It was a charnel house, and those who were in a position to do something about it, the honoraries, stayed silent. (As senior medical staff, they were powerful in the hospital hierarchy, and the relationship between resident and honorary was like that of slaves to masters. Honoraries were revered as if they were one step down from god.)

It seemed to me that obstetricians were almost scared to appear humane. They went about their work while the women were treated like cattle in the labour wards. The obstetricians knew the conditions were brutal, but the expectation was to always appear efficient on the public purse. This began to change when a courageous man, Dr Kevin McCaul, became the director of anaesthetics at the Royal Women's Hospital in 1951. He championed the rights of mothers to remain awake during labour, making the hospital the first in the world to abandon general anaesthesia in labour in favour of nitrous oxide or oxygen analgesia, as well as pioneering epidural anaesthesia.

While Ward 31 was callous, I was sometimes sent to Ward 19, and that was brutal.

The Ward 19 head sister sat behind a desk watching over 10 to 12 beds that lined the room. She often left the desk to make raids on one of the beds and to shout instructions to some other nurse or sister. One Greek girl was so terrified by the unknown pains and surroundings that she tried to climb out of a ward window. No one spoke her language to explain what was happening, but she understood the sister's slap across the face and sobbed her way back to bed. The head sister's treatment for a woman's screams would be to call for sedation: "Sister, a hundred milligrams of pethidine for number 8." And her underlings, like soldiers assigned to crowd control in the Nazi camps, would obey. Little wonder they obeyed. At that time, many nurses had served in the war, and barking orders was the only way to get things done in that hospital situation.

It was in Ward 19 that I witnessed one of the most heartbreaking medical episodes of my life. It was so powerfully awful that it moulded every interaction I had with patients from that date. I was one of five students called in to hear a senior obstetrician speak. We were joined by a senior nursing sister, two junior nurses, an assistant obstetrician and a junior doctor. All eleven of us surrounded a bed where a woman sobbed uncontrollably. Her baby was premature and had died in utero. The consultant stood over the woman, describing what had happened to her and the measures he had taken in the complicated birth. With no regard for her trauma, he spoke as if in a lecture theatre, with the impassivity of a mechanic discussing a car. Hers had been a breech birth and her baby had died. This sometimes occurred in breech deliveries back then. He described how if the cervix could be dilated slowly, with some luck the baby's neck would not be clamped by the cervix. He had draped weights over the edge of the bed and tied them to the baby's feet to draw the baby out. It was cruel beyond words to make this poor woman relive it. None of us said a kind word or offered her a hand in comfort.

Sickened, I vowed this had to change. Even if I knew nothing of obstetrics, I was determined to treat these women with kindness. They were isolated, going through a dramatic and sometimes traumatic experience, without kith or kin. I decided I would talk to them and encourage them. When they took my hand I would get embarrassed and wonder if others thought me soft. Even now, when I am caught being sympathetic and understanding I have to resist the urge to square off and talk it down.

It wasn't just one senior obstetrician being callous. Staff were defensive in the face of a labouring woman. Nurses, rather than being co-operative and encouraging, efficiently fluffed pillows or made doctors a cup of tea. This attitude changed demonstrably over the years, but it was a long struggle to effect the change.

Common room politics

Among the students living in the hospital were several anti-communists and anti-fascists. Some of their families had lived through fascism and communism and they brought those experiences to the argument.

One student's father had been in charge of a munitions factory under Hitler. The student, named George Pohl, claimed ignorance of the concentration camps and denied his father used war prisoners as slaves.

(Incidentally, he and his father were no relation to war criminal Oswald Pohl, to my knowledge.)

A Czechoslovakian student, Frank Kopecek, had fled when the Russians swept through his home country. Some of his relations suffered, and continued to suffer, under Stalinist terror.

Royal Australian Navy students got their biases from accepting the Queen's golden handout, which funded their medical study in exchange for time spent working the naval fleets. Other students were simply conservative.

My only allies were my old friend Tim Loh and Dorothy Rubinstein. She told me of how during the war she and her sister lay in a Polish forest ditch, each holding their mother's hand while the Germans fired overhead. The sisters kept asking their mother if she was still alive. Dorothy could not bring herself to talk to George Pohl and hated anything from Germany.

Our pitched battles were in the student common room, where I was forced to defend every political historical event, every disappearance and every utterance of a Soviet leader. Due to the Cold War, those on the attack felt morally confident and on the side of humanity. Having defended communism for so long during the Cold War, I felt I had to challenge George and Frank's family's personal experiences rather than accept them on face value. This I regret, but at the time I did not want to concede the point.

It was a hopeless situation. I was an isolated absolutist, truthful to the character of my theoretical conclusions. As in my early days in the party in Melbourne, I felt conceding any point weakened my argument. I was doing what was expected of a card-carrying member of the Communist Party. Our commitment had to be strong. Under attack, there was no room for revision and discussion of basic tenets.

The nightly battles continued, yet we remained friends for decades because we respected each other's right to be utterly convinced of our own views. No cynic played the superior person. All of us were fair and helped each other in the clinics. We let each other know where interesting cases could be found and also covered up for absences.

I found the pathology of obstetrics and gynaecology so fascinating that I became an embarrassment in lectures – so enthusiastic was I to ask, and answer, questions. Our lecturer was Hans Bettinger, a German recognised as a victim of Nazism. He would later be given the moniker of Australia's father of obstetric and gynaecological pathology. At the time, his English could not be easily understood, so he used Latin names for most parts and conditions. His teaching method was to flash up on a screen various conditions which we were to name. His method resonated with me. I don't think I missed being the first to spot a condition until Tim told me to hang back and give someone else a go.

Bettinger was overjoyed that someone was interested in his course. He was doubly overjoyed when I met him years later – having continued in obstetrics – at an international congress on obstetrics and gynaecology in Sydney.

As thrilling a time as this was for me, the treatment of women in the labour wards continued to haunt me. I ended up having nightmares about their screaming and suffering. What appalled me most was the women's ignorance about what was happening to their bodies, and how this was fostered. Myths circulated about labour wards. Chiefly, that nurses knew too much to be good obstetrical patients – ridiculous as they often went on to have babies of their own. The other myth I found galling was the dismissal of natural birth as "this relaxation business". They argued if a mother tried to have a baby without intervention she would find it did not work; they would lose heart, become shattered by the birth experience, and never be able to face childbirth again. Nonsense.

Back then it was rare for women to have a vaginal birth without analgesics, even though British obstetrician Grantley Dick-Reid had begun publishing books about relaxing during childbirth in 1933. He claimed that by focusing on the pain it was amplified, and women needed to relax. Unfortunately, he did not consider what else a woman could focus on during childbirth. His ideas were largely ridiculed, but some of his books remain in print to this day.

The women, and we students, were told that nurses and doctors knew how to have babies and that the women should be no more than mute vessels or tools for gestating and delivering babies.

I recall a nurse who was guiding a head through a perineum. When the baby was delivered, I told the new mother she had worked very hard. The sister looked at me, still sweating from the lights, and said: "*She* had to work? What about me?" It was as if the nurse had had the baby.

The nurses used to say they became callous to the suffering of others. They worked and played hard, and their parties were so wild that everyone passed out by midnight. Or so I was told – I never attended.

At the end of our stint at the Royal Women's we had our own, less raucous, party. With barely enough time to catch our breath; we were due to start at the Royal Children's Hospital the following Monday.

Family friction and fatherhood

After her miscarriage when I was in Perth, June fell pregnant again on my return. Early in the pregnancy, around February 1958, she had had a bleed while I was working at the Royal Women's Hospital. I had been given leave to be with her at the Jessie McPherson Private Hospital in Lonsdale Street, Melbourne.

I knew just enough about abnormalities of pregnancy and labour to fear the worst, but did not have enough knowledge to placate those fears. At the Women's, we were well versed in the risks during labour – sudden bleeding, fetal asthenia, cord prolapse – and it felt like uncomplicated labours were unusual and somehow dull. It was no wonder we believed baby making was a dangerous business; at the Women's we saw nearly every rare and abnormal case from all over the state.

The private hospital was the scene of a confrontation with Saul. June's genial, white-haired obstetrician, George "Bonney's Blue" Bearham, had admitted her to the hospital. He was known as Bonney's Blue because of his love of the violet-coloured antiseptic dye used in operations.

Saul, Mary and I were standing at the top of some stairs waiting to be allowed in to see June. Characteristically, Saul started telling Mary what she had to do. Then he turned to me.

"What I want you to do is ring Alwyn Long (another obstetrician) for another appointment," Saul demanded.

From my limited experience, I knew Bearham was giving June the commonly accepted "best opinion possible" and I was a bit tired of Saul's habit of constantly seeking a second opinion. Saul had assumed leadership of my family, but I would not surrender it to anyone, let alone him.

"Listen, I will make those sorts of decisions, and I don't think you can tell me what to do," I told Saul.

Not brilliant repartee, but the effect was instantaneous. Saul walked off in a huff. Mary stayed to placate me.

"Saul is only interested in doing what is best," she said. "He does it out of love for June. He wants the very best for her."

Again and again, they had used this tactic to coerce me in the name of their love for June. Mary now suggested that I was not acting in June's best interests by opposing Saul.

The bleeding stopped and I never did call Alwyn Long, although somehow he ended up delivering our baby.

With a baby well on the way, June and I moved from Elwood to the Factor family home at 138A Edward Street, Brunswick. Thankfully, Saul and Mary moved to West Brunswick.

They charged us £5 a week. I could have got a room with a kitchen in Carlton for under £3. Edward Street was too big, and I knew we could not afford it, but Saul and Mary demanded June be accommodated just so. I felt like we were headed for a financial fall.

On the day we shifted, I carefully budgeted for the removalist. He had no regard for the time and took a circuitous route to Brunswick, dawdling as he moved our things inside. I hit the roof when he demanded £2 more than my budget. We had a loud row on the footpath.

I was angry at Saul for dragging me into debt. When he tried to lend a hand with my things, I was angry that he dragged my good white canvas bag across the ground. Naturally, as June was pregnant she was not expected to lug furniture and she sat on the lounge and bit her nails. Mary sat in the dining room and smoked.

In a grim mood, I wrote to Jack, asking him to lend me money. My brother never hesitated, lending me £5 a week until the day I graduated. I paid him back, but I could never express my true gratitude at his immediate response of a loan with no conditions or haggling.

After the distractions of beachside Elwood, I demanded the quietest part of the house to study. The baby could have the room near the kitchen, I suggested, at the opposite end of the house. The Factors thought this was selfish, but I was driven to finish medicine.

On October 5, 1958, our baby Naomi was born safe and sound with no complications at the Queen Victoria Hospital. All my fears of disaster were unfounded. Fathers were barred from the births, and I worked while June laboured. I recall Naomi's screwed up face and the sense of relief and excitement that June and my relationship now felt very much like a family. Naomi grew to be a pert, lovely and musical toddler. She loved Beethoven and from an early stage could communicate that she loved Beethoven's Fifth more than his Third.

The final dash

The Royal Children's Hospital was then in an old building with wide draughty corridors and large clean-scrubbed wards. It was on land once owned by Sir Redmond Barry, the first chancellor of Melbourne University and the judge who sentenced Ned Kelly to death. The original house was demolished in 1912 and its replacement, on the corner of Rathdowne and Pelham streets, Carlton, was outdated. Work was under way to build a new hospital at Parkville, which would officially open in 1963. That has since been demolished for another new Royal Children's Hospital further down Flemington Road.

In treating children, a pressing question was posed: "What is a sick child?" At the Royal Children's, we had neither the experience nor the understanding to judge this. Children are prey to diseases which make them very ill, very quickly, and young patients must be assessed as early as possible. We had hardly any contact with children in our 10 weeks, and I could not have acquired the skills needed to be an expert. It would take the examination of hundreds of children, as a resident doctor in 1961, for me to feel I had any skill in paediatrics.

Back then, a student doctor's time was largely spent in a series of lectures at the hospital and on ward rounds. With little responsibility and no exams, this was an easy and carefree time. We could study as we liked. To my mind, paediatric textbooks were singularly bad, and my knowledge was general and pretty useless at the end of my term.

The last two terms were mostly at the Royal Melbourne Hospital, in urology, ophthalmology, dermatology and gynaecology clinics. All the while I summarised my learning onto swot cards so I might revisit it later when I was studying for exams the following year. The year raced away.

When I started my final year in February 1959, I had a tightness in my gut that lasted all year. We would rush to a ward, wait for the honorary, stand around the bed and dwell on every word. All of us felt it necessary to read the fine print of exotic diseases, but we were told again and again to know the common diseases, like acute appendicitis, perforated duodenal ulcer, pneumonia etc. In our group we had Tim Loh, Dorothy Rubenstein, Margaret Pickles and myself. Tim tried not to work; Dorothy tried to do nothing but work; Margaret tried everything in between, including yoga, cricket and music – she even tried politics. (Years later I would learn that Margaret, like me, was quite poor and skipped lunch to help pay her way through medicine.) For a bunch of odd bods, we worked well together.

We were mostly cheerful and got along pretty well with the other students. I do recall one occasion at the Royal Melbourne Hospital café. I was upholding some political point of view with fellow medical student Clive Bennetts. I heard another student, Arthur Boardman, say, "What are you talking to him for? He's a communist." Clive, to his eternal credit, said, "I don't give a stuff what he is. He's a bloody good bloke." Friendly banter was the antidote to full-throated McCarthyism.

The final fifth-year exams came and went. Passing fairly well, I was admitted to the international brotherhood of doctors. It is a curious fraternity – at once terribly strong and yet critical. Doctors recognise the eternal conflict. They realised the necessity for brotherhood (very few sisters back then), yet remained critical to the last of each other.

Our registration was held at the Australasian College of Surgeons building in Spring Street, East Melbourne, diagonally opposite St Vincent's Hospital. At 11am we had drinks laid on. One of the Royal Melbourne Hospital ogres, an honorary called Dr King, gave a speech welcoming us into the fraternity. He was most comradely and friendly. Welcome to the club.

Chapter 12
At last, it's Dr Percy Rogers

At 2pm, just hours after my doctor registration, I was off to work at my first job. I worked as a locum for Gerry Westmore, who was in Blyth Street, Brunswick, for £90 a week – an unheard of sum. It was a fill-in job for three weeks until I took my 12-month appointment at the Royal Hobart Hospital.

Whenever the phone rang, I jumped a mile and assiduously attended all patients and calls.

I remember one woman who said her family had complained that she was tired all the time. She described her typical day to me. She woke at 6am, got food for the family, worked in a factory all day, then came home to more rounds of cooking and cleaning. I reassured her that she was fine, if exhausted. I wrote a letter to her family prescribing rest.

At 2am one morning the phone rang. I was told that a Greek lady was in labour at Vaucluse Hospital (now called Brunswick Private Hospital). I rushed over, desperately trying to remember all the complications of a normal labour. Sweating, I was met at the labour ward by the sister, who said: "You know Mrs K is having triplets?"

I turned pale remembering vividly the photos of interlocking twins, of impacted triplets, of the necessity for an anaesthetist etc. I breathed easier when the sister said the consultant had been rung. It was a short breath because the first baby was on its way "now". I could not believe my luck – triplets as my first delivery! The head appeared and I delivered the baby without difficulty, then the second and third, all without a hitch. The placenta came out upon demand. After which, the consultant turned up.

Afterwards, we sat in the surgeons' lounge and drank tea, waiting for the press to arrive for the photo opportunity. What a way to be blooded in obstetrics.

Aside from triplets – and a fresh dint in Dr Westmore's beloved old Dodge car – it was an uneventful and happy three weeks.

Headed for Hobart

Around the turn of 1959 to 1960, we bundled up our meagre belongings and flew to Hobart for my 12-month Royal Hobart Hospital residency. June was about three months pregnant with Ian, and Naomi was about 15 months old. Barry Forbes and his wife Flora arrived to complete Barry's residency at the same time.

A friendly place, the Royal Hobart Hospital was originally called the Hobart General Hospital. From a series of huts in 1804, it became a permanent building, sited at Liverpool Street, in 1820. It's the second oldest hospital in Australia, after Sydney Hospital.

We were quartered in Gore Street, South Hobart, a bus ride away, in converted stables at Vaucluse Hospital, the old infectious diseases hospital. Vaucluse was then mostly used as a repatriation hospital. The stables-turned-flats had small, cosy rooms with long windows that sat inside the two-foot-thick walls. Rising behind the flats was Mount Wellington, which was capped with snow soon after we arrived. The flat setting was romantic and beautiful.

Hospital superintendent Dr Phil Nolan introduced me to the staff and the hospital layout. He was a small, mean, miserable man who got the job when the previous superintendent was sacked. Nolan's nickname was "Old Flip Flop," because he seemed unable to make a diagnostic decision. When confronted with a patient, he would either admit them for a "long investigation" or a "long observation" of pain. Either way, the diagnosis was left to the resident doctors.

The residents and registrars were outstandingly loyal. If I was a bit worried, I need only ring the surgical or medical registrar and he would be in casualty in minutes. The casualty department ran like a general practice, so everything funnelled through casualty. Day and night, we saw everything – incomplete abortions, suicides, car accidents, abdominal pains, lacerations and more. Unsurprisingly, you got very little sleep when working in casualty at night.

To my surprise, my newfound routine did not include reading or studying books. I found I just wanted to concentrate on "doing" and putting my acquired knowledge into practice.

The hospital gave a resident doctor solid general experience in most areas. My 10 weeks at the Royal Women's Hospital stood me in good stead at Hobart. All Melbourne graduates were highly regarded in obstetrics, so the obstetrics registrar, David "Gerry" Walters, left many decisions to us. Although he cast an eye over our decisions once made.

Despite being viewed in a superior obstetrical light to some other doctors, my introduction to the ward was a touch humiliating. The obstetrical floor was newly polished, and my stately entry ended when my shoe heel lost grip, sailing me past the sisters' station, and landing me on my bum in front of the head sister.

"Oh, mother (presumably of God), look at Dick," the head nurse called out about this Tom, Dick or Harry who had just arrived.

Very funny. So much for my impressive, confident stride.

Over my three short months in obstetrics, I noticed I had developed my easy empathy with women in labour as I had vowed to do. I enjoyed sitting and talking to them. This was a great help in appreciating the subjectivity of a woman in labour.

Obstetrics registrar Gerry Walters was son-in-law to Sir Eric Harrison, Deputy Leader of the Liberal Party to Menzies. Sir Eric was a contender for the leadership before he resigned in 1956 to become the British High Commissioner. Gerry was a good doctor and bloke, but politically he matched his father-in-law. The hospital was overrun by right-wingers and Catholics. The surgical registrar, George Mackay Smith, always known as "Mac Smith", was vehemently anti-communist. He did his best to make my life miserable, but he never succeeded, as I had found my true calling in medicine. Phil Nolan, the superintendent, made certain I did not return for a second year – especially after he saw me take to the streets for the sake of the workers.

With May approaching, the unions had decided to revive the May Day March in Hobart after a hiatus lasting a few years. I was keen to join them. I took Naomi down to the wharfies' headquarters to find out about the arrangements. As we strolled into the offices I noticed one burly bloke backing out of the room with a flagon of red wine hidden behind his back. The union office was excessively polite when I explained I was a hospital doctor and that I wanted to march.

On the day, we marched up from the wharf and onto the Queens Domain. The march then led us past the hospital. All the patients and staff were watching. I found it easy to work out who my friends were during that march. Afterwards, fellow doctor Bill Gurrtold told me he admired my courage. It polarised the resident doctors. My old quota campaign buddy

Barry Forbes, who would go on to do another 12-month stint at the hospital, said nothing. It was just in his character. Mac Smith and Phil Nolan became hostile. They jumped on me for the most minor infringement. My only triumph was a victory over Mac Smith in table tennis one night – the match felt like the East-West struggle. Of course, the West eventually won that war.

A new addition to the family

Hobart marked the first time June had lived away from her parents, and she was lonely and unhappy. Saul visited without Mary on several weekends. Without the diluting effect of her family to distract her and take the pressure off our relationship, June did not relate to me in a very friendly way, even while professing her love.

One time, I told her about a young chap who had been brought in to me at casualty. He was exhausted all the time and wanted an explanation and cure. He explained to me that he had married a slightly older woman who worked in a shop. He was a labourer and he came home dog-tired each night. They would have tea, go to bed and she would arouse him and they would make love. He said he often just wanted to go to sleep, but she wanted more and would start to caress him again. He wanted to know if this was normal. Did he need pills? Did she? What did I think? "Half your luck, mate," was on the tip of my tongue, but I didn't say it. June looked a bit sour when I told her about the case.

Ian was born on June 24, 1960. We had gone to obstetrician on a recommendation. As was the common practice, if a birth conflicted with an obstetrician's holiday plans and it was safe they brought the birth on early. The obstetrician decided on the procedure of stripping the membranes to bring on the labour. Once this procedure is done, you are committed to a caesarean if the baby is not delivered within 48 hours.

I was working in the obstetrical wards so saw everything that went on. Ian's heart rate went off, so the obstetrician applied the forceps. When the placenta didn't come out immediately, he manually teased it away from the uterus. Despite gas and oxygen, this is a very painful experience.

Ian was a delightful baby – placid and alert. One day I came in to find him kicking his legs smiling and waving his arms. I asked June what had happened. She said he was glad to see me. Of the three children we would have together, Ian was the closest to me. I have often wondered if our bond was more easily created without intervening family members. We remain close.

Hobart was a nice time with my family unit around me, but it also made clear the limitations of my relationship with June.

I remained faithful despite temptation. In the casualty ward I worked with a beautiful nurse. She frequently commented on my "skilful hands" and took every opportunity to touch me. I didn't realise what was happening until she turned up at casualty, outside her work hours, really dressed up and wearing a strong scent. It was against all the hospital rules for her to enter the hospital when she was not working. She made an offer. I was sorely tempted but would not pursue it.

One night, after a very late appendectomy, Gerry Walters and I flopped down in the surgeons' lounge with an on-call surgical honorary (blow'd if I can remember his name). I poured a cup of tea, which happened to have been left in the pot from the previous operation. It was tepid. I handed it to the honorary, who snarled: "Get me a fresh pot of tea." I was tired, paused my hand in mid-flight, and nearly let him have the tea in his face. This was like the "Tracker" Towey black tea incident at St George's College, Perth, all over again. Later, Gerry told me he could see my mind ticking, "Will I or won't I?" With great restraint, I put down the cup and made a fresh pot. Often I've wondered what my medical career would have been if I had let fly with the lukewarm tea.

It was something of a collision course with that particular honorary. Another time, a lowly resident discharged one of his regulars from the outpatients. The honorary had the patient coming back to see him week after week. I think he liked a large patient empire. The honorary tore a strip off me, telling me they were his patients and I was to say and do nothing and not interfere. Yet, I had his measure, and by the time I had left casualty we were on matey terms.

Although honoraries were originally unpaid, hospitals now paid them on a sessional basis, and many were permanent fixtures. Honoraries could bolster their income by seeing and charging for private patients in public hospitals.

Resident doctors' wages, meanwhile, remained a source of frustration. When I first arrived in Hobart, the pay was better than the mainland, but Victorian resident doctors later successfully campaigned for higher wages and better conditions. Up until that point, with their long hours, Victorian resident doctors were paid just a few pennies an hour. After the Victorian success, the Hobart doctors began to grumble about the disparity with the mainland and turned to me to lead them in a fight for wage justice. Our meetings on the issue grew hotter, with the residents sounding more militant with each meeting. One chap, called Fleming, who was staid as a stiff collar, said, "Look, I don't think we should go on strike, Perce." I was shocked he was contemplating it. I had not even mentioned striking and replied, "Well, let's wait and see what happens to our claims." I suggested we could take other actions like working to regulation, which I had seen to good effect on the tramways. In the end, our wages increased dramatically to the princely sum of £20 a week. This did not endear me to the Nolan and Mac Smith axis.

While I would later let my Communist Party membership lapse, I transferred my membership to the Hobart branch. The branch's most charming and active member worked in electronics in the city. It turned out he was a security agent, so every branch meeting was almost certainly taped.

The party characters are etched in my mind as much as any Hobart history. One member was an old wharfie who was hostile and fierce. He lived on a mountain and hated everything except the two cows he milked, and his wife of many years. She took no notice of his politics.

Another older comrade expected me to work a communist miracle on his bad case of emphysema and bronchitis. When I suggested he give up smoking straight away, he explained, as though I was a beginner, that smoking was the only thing that allowed him to cough up his phlegm. He died soon after we left Tasmania.

One chap John Nicholson, was not a party member but came along to tell us about his trips to the Soviet Union. "Johnny" was an old hop farmer from the Lachlan Valley, near New Norfolk. In the post-World War II period – sick of seeing children flogged with hop vines for working to slowly – Johnny led a campaign to end child labour in the hop fields. He showed me Tasmanian letters that used the same archaic arguments that had been used about child miners in 18th-century Britain. Johnny was vilified for the campaign, but never wavered. Nor did he ever alter his slow New Norfolk drawl. Decades later, June had a paper published about these child labour laws for *Australian Rationalist*.

A true friend, Johnny put our family up in his farmhouse when many cases of polio were presenting at the hospital. While we were all vaccinated, there was some doubt about doctors' vulnerability when treating polio patients. I would spend days at the hospital and then go to the Lachlan Valley when I got a break. We returned after the epidemic had passed.

Another character etched in my mind was Ken Dallas, a University of Tasmania economic history lecturer who was once refused a passport on the advice of ASIO. He was later granted the passport after a memo was sent to ASIO to say Menzies had "a good opinion of Dallas".

A socialist but never a communist party member, he had a passionate interest in old water wheels and folk songs. While I was in Hobart, we went on a camping trip where we investigated every water wheel along the way. On that trip, we had a three-day debate over whether the Americans should have removed Germany's fascist administration personnel from West Germany. I claimed the Americans should have instead meted out "just punishment" to the guilty fascists. Ken argued they had no option, so why not leave them in their roles. It was a good trip, only marred by Ken's "naval porridge". This is a lumpy mess of congealed porridge with raisins and God knows what else, eased down with plenty of tea.

I was rather sorry when we boarded the plane to return to Melbourne, but I had been appointed to the Royal Children's as a resident.

Immediately on our return, I got a severe dose of diarrhoea. I tried not to blame Ken's naval porridge. I was laid up at our new rented home at 22 Leonard Street, Northcote, for days. The many visitors dropping by to welcome us home were reluctant to venture too close.

Chapter 13
A resident 'necessary nuisance' at the Royal Children's

When I first worked at the Royal Children's Hospital, I had donned the "bum freezer" jacket. Now back, as a resident doctor in January 1961, I had moved up to a longer white jacket – almost like a boy suddenly in long pants.

Nurses considered us a "necessary nuisance" – so, not much improvement on being a student doctor. The nurses felt they had the experience to care for the children, while we resident doctors relied on book knowledge without much experience. When young resident doctors tried to tell the nurses what to do, this caused friction.

I had outlined my interest in neurology to the hospital administration and was placed in that ward first. I held high hopes that my medical training and psychological studies would combine perfectly.

Sadly, it was not to be. The unit was run by polar-opposite honoraries, Reginald Hooper and another surgeon. Hooper was a calm and careful surgeon who acted only when he thought it was in the child's long-term interests. His instructions were precise. His operating lists were well organised. His operating afternoons ran smoothly.

His counterpart was a British National Health Scheme refugee. His casually superior arrogance was not matched by his work ethic, skill or organisational capacity. His lack of surgical prowess meant his lists would run over time, leaving young patients fasting unnecessarily for surgeries that would have to be postponed. The ward sisters would vent on me, and the counterpart tried to blame me for his operating lists. I heaved a sigh of relief when my three months were up. I decided neurology was not for me.

My next medical three months was in the professorial unit, which was the hospital's main research unit and handled difficult and often obscure cases. It was headed by Professor Vernon Collins. He was an internationally recognised expert on baby nutrition and had written the bible on the

162

subject, *Infant Feeding*. Back then, nutrition meant infant formula and bottle feeding. As a resident doctor, I attended Collins' ward rounds and his occasional lectures. I was expected to know a baby's needs based on the calories per pound of body weight per day, as well as the ounces of fluid per day and what formulas met the protein, fats and carbohydrates requirements.

Thankfully, six mothers would soon rebel against this nonsense to form the Nursing Mothers' Association of Australia – later known as the Australian Breastfeeding Association. At best, the medical professions paid them lip-service; at worst, they were treated with hostility. But the mums won out in the end.

Despite this galling attitude towards breastfeeding mothers, my three months here were delightful after the bleakness of the neurosurgical ward. Professor Collins' assistants, doctors Arthur Clark and Alex Venables, were friendly and I worked well with them. The nursing staff took me under their wing and helped ensure that nothing occurred in the ward that I could not act upon before the professor or his assistants arrived for their ward rounds. It gave me an air of competency.

Often privy to the nurses' gossip, I was one night treated to the disastrous details of one sister's love life. She told me was involved with a carpenter who wanted to marry her and settle down, but she found him too dull.

"Perce, would you race me off and rape me?" she asked.

In an attempt at jocularity, I replied that I couldn't for the moment as it was about 9.30pm and my supper was nearly ready.

Her request is a shuddering one now, in light of the #MeToo movement and all we know about workplace sexual harassment, but back then it was a cry for help to get away from what she knew would be a loveless marriage. With her virginity gone, she had a chance to get out of the marriage. At the time, it was an attempt to take back control of her body, even if it meant giving it over to someone else. She was tapping into the early rumblings of the women's liberation movement.

This nurse invited June and me to a party, but I attended alone because June did not wish to go. She made it clear she would welcome a pass from me. I told her I was married. On the footpath of Park Street, Brunswick, just by the railway gates where the bike path now crosses over, she said, "Fuck it. It's too late isn't it?"

Years later, I went back to the "new" Royal Children's Hospital – as opposed to the new-new RCH – and met this same nurse again. She had married but had refused to have children. Now working in casualty, she was herself a love casualty.

During my months in the professorial ward, the head sister was a middle-aged woman who seemed to struggle with some elements of modern medicine but would not acknowledge her deficiencies. Estimating insulin doses and drawing up the right dose in a syringe caused her difficulty.

"Watch her," the nurse who favoured me would say. "She will leave the ward after checking the dose, and tell me to draw it up." Sure enough, this happened every time, the more junior nurse was left to recheck and draw up the syringe.

There were sad moments too. One day, just as a batch of student doctors arrived for their ward rounds, a six-year-old leukaemic child died. I raced over and attempted internal cardiac massage to revive the child, only ceasing when Alec Venables told me the boy had probably died of a cerebral haemorrhage.

Despite the occasional sorrow, the ward rounds were inspiring and enjoyable. Professor Collins had a good knowledge of general medicine and paediatrics, and he was pleased to have an enthusiastic doctor on the ward. Arthur Clark was equally as charming but lacked the authority of a professor. If he told a group of students that hypnosis could eliminate warts they did not believe him, but if Professor Collins had said so, student doctors would have written it down as gospel truth. In later years, as Professor Clark, Arthur had no trouble gaining that gravitas.

I was skilful with my hands and could insert an intravenous needle into a baby's tiny veins in a matter of seconds. At the time, we used a drop of local anaesthetic near the baby's ankle joint, then made a small cut to insert a cannula into the vein. It was fine work.

One day, with student doctors Alan Hasdell and Bob Hjorth, I played a game called "Clock me, gentlemen," which involved them timing my needle work. This game was popular among doctors in the old days when the speed at which a doctor could saw off a leg was highly valued – especially as the only anaesthetic was often a drunken stupor.

Soon after I left the ward, the technology and practice moved towards using butterfly needles on baby's scalps for intravenous therapy. These were easier to insert but could cause problems compared to the use of the long saphenous vein we used as an entry point for intravenous work.

Walking down the stairs after completing my term at the ward, Professor Collins stopped me, thanking me generously for my work. Like most Australians, I was, and still am, unable to graciously accept thanks or gifts of praise. I could only mumble the equivalent of "aw, shucks" before bounding off down the stairs.

At one of the residents' dinners, I arranged for Australian writer Alan Marshall to speak. In 1955, he had released *I Can Jump Puddles*, an autobiographical account of his country childhood with polio, and would release his second autobiographical book, *This is the Grass*, in 1962.

For my pains, I was asked to say a few words of welcome. To most of the residents, I must have seemed an enigma after this. I told of how Marshall's books made me realise what it was to be Australian – linked to people in faraway places by a commonality. I said that through a long and hard history, we had developed a culture that asserted itself again and again despite Mother England's smothering and the American smooth sell of trash. Marshall wrote about the simple life in a simple way, and this profoundly moved people, I said. I quoted a passage from *These are my People* where he describes a shearer's wedding, one of the funniest pieces ever written. I spoke of his love for the Aboriginal people and his respect for their culture.

Then Alan spoke, holding the residents spellbound for over an hour. He told stories of his life, what Melbourne was like in the 1920s, and what it was like to have polio as a child. Most thought it was the best dinner of the year.

Family time and casualty

Our new home in Leonard Street, Northcote, was a single-fronted weatherboard house that was so cold we had radiators on all night in the children's room. While I was home more than when I was at the Royal Hobart, I was still on duty at the RCH day and night, and one weekend in four. Most of the time I was too tired to initiate social outings so our social engagements centred around Saul and Mary, who always seemed to have a dinner, birthday or ceremony for us to attend.

We might have spent our weekends doing fun things as a young family but, instead, we would visit the frock shop and follow up with a lunch at Edward Street where Saul and Mary had returned to live. Despite my protests, the children were plied with sweets and cakes. Naomi and Ian learnt how to whine for sugar. I worried they would become overweight. I cannot recall going anywhere with June that was not connected to the family in some way at that time.

After leaving the professorial ward, I spent a few months in the casualty department. The system was simple. Parents of children would give their name and address at the desk. Their history would be found or a new card made out. They would then wait on hard, long benches in a large hall. The nurses distributed the cards to a handful of resident doctors. A registrar was usually the admitting officer.

Resident doctors worked their way through their pile of cards, seeing each child in turn. I thought the process ended there but later realised that doctors were being assessed and commented upon by senior doctors. The head casualty doctor was a redheaded Irish woman who praised the Catholic doctors and was scathing about the rest of us. Many clinicians were knowledgeable of their own areas but were tyrants in their clinics. Medical changes were coming in the sickness industry and many of them either did not understand them or resented them.

On weekends in casualty, a senior resident would be allocated a junior one to assist them. One weekend, I arranged to swap my weekend with another resident. The surgeon blew up when I called to tell him, declaring it the height of discourtesy. In his day, a resident was delighted to work and would even work when not on duty. He was incredulous that a resident would change their roster and miss a chance to work with an experienced surgeon of his ilk. This was typical of the training and attitude towards residents.

One of the hospital's administrators seemed to have his attitudes pickled in vinegar from the time he left his plummy private school. He favoured others from the same mould, with the same precise nasal Australian accent. He barely tolerated others. This senior doctor built his career around the Royal Children's Hospital. In a clinical setting, I only saw him go the extra mile medically when he could dispense wisdom in his own area of expertise. I had one spectacular run-in with him.

Shifts were long and, sometimes, after a full day on the wards, we would be required on night duty. On one such occasion, I was called to admit a patient at 2am. I answered, but I was so tired I fell back asleep. An hour later, an irate nurse rang. I stumbled down and took a poor history from the family. In the morning, I was still utterly fatigued and did not recall admitting the patient until I made my ward rounds that day. The administrator took me to task about the inadequate history and unsatisfactory consultation.

I could have countered with the absurdity of the roster and the risk the hospital was taking in forcing fatigued doctors to perform at this high a level. Alas, I knew it was an accepted fact of resident life. Instead, I told him I had been in a black sleep and could not rouse myself. Years later, the honoraries and the administration received a terrible jolt when hospital resident doctors demanded a 40-hour week payment plus overtime. Despite this, the hours continue to creep up. In 2020, a doctor can still work up to 16-hour days. Bill Gurr, whom I knew from Hobart, was famous for collapsing on the steps of his home on a Saturday afternoon, only to sleep through till Sunday (usually making it to the bed at some stage). The work ethic paid off. He would go on to be medical registrar at The Alfred and make the first Australasian attempt at renal replacement therapy.

After I clashed with the administrator, the year ended sourly. I sorely needed a rest and he opposed it. We had a row where his political feelings about me became apparent as he said, we were "not yet in a Communist state". I was glad to be done with the Royal Children's. Although the work was compelling, the hospital was often disorganised and sometimes distressing.

My RCH experience and the economics of my position put paid to any thought of doing a higher degree. The thought of accruing more debt made general practice look like a necessity. But to tackle that, I first needed a holiday.

Chapter 14
Buying into Private Practice

Needing a break, I set off with Geoff Sharp, my Melbourne Uni psychology department comrade. I threw some camping gear in his car and we set off north, driving one-hour on, one-hour off, and were soon up around Mildura on the Murray River. Once we hit the countryside, we both wound down. We made pitstops frequently, but our talking never stopped.

We followed the Darling River, crossed a small bridge and settled down for a beer in our destination town of Menindee. One of the regulars declared this was the "real Lawson country", another said he didn't like pig shooters looking straight at us. We asked what the fishing was like and we were told that last week there were plenty of good, big fish to be had.

"Dunno about now, the river's a bit muddy. No set lines, only use hand lines," one unfriendly local said.

We set off along a flat dusty road that was flanked by sparse mulga trees and clumps of short, probably spinifex, grass. We passed a huge frame covered in insect-proof wire, set out near a house. Later we found out the station owner slept here on hot summer nights. We camped at Wilcannia, which had a café, service station and a few houses on the Darling. Camping under the stars was the plan, so we placed our sleeping bags on the ground and tried to sleep. After bedding down for 20 minutes, Geoff lept up, grabbing his balls and screeching in pain. Bull ants had entered his sleeping bag and were clamping their nippers onto every available piece of skin. I shouldn't have laughed. Two minutes later, I was doing the same thing as both our bags were over a nest!

We travelled on. When we got to Bourke, NSW, a four-hour drive from Wilcannia, June told me there was a Coburg general practice for sale. She and her parents were excited about it as a prospect for me.

I had been looking for a practice for months while still at the Royal Children's Hospital. Looking for a medical practice was simple enough, I contacted several medical practice agents, told them I wanted to buy a practice and they presented me with a list. Sometimes the descriptions of the practices even corresponded with the truth.

The houses attached to these practices were usually overvalued. The practice descriptions were coded:

"Well-established practice owner anxious to retire" (Old practice run by a very old doctor where the vast majority of patients were now retired).

"Good will" (overestimated).

"Income" (potential rather than an actual figure).

To get a better idea of what I might have been buying into, I interviewed the doctors who ran some of the more promising practices. They were kindly, wise men who still wore dark suits and waistcoats. We usually had a chat over a cup of tea. Later I would watch the newspapers to read about the manner of their retirement.

One "reputable" city agent sent me out to Footscray. The agent earnestly told me Dr Peter Bayliss was looking for a partner to take over most of the practice's consultation and midwifery, while he devoted himself to his anaesthetics.

This was common enough in the early 1960s. General practitioners followed a particular interest, while their colleagues supported them by referring patients to them. Post-graduate training was largely unnecessary for general practitioners as they could acquire the necessary experience through their surgery. Experienced GPs could often perform quite major operations. Country practitioners were particularly adept at all-round skills across a broad range of areas. So, this idea of a GP who wanted to expand his anaesthetic skills did not sound far-fetched.

Bayliss was a huge man, forthright and hardly my style, but I listened to him carefully. He bragged as he showed me his Jaguar for which he had paid £8000 in cash. I couldn't imagine anyone carrying around that amount of "real money". He invited me to do some sessions in his rooms to find out how I liked the practice. Senior doctors with nothing to hide will offer this to prospective buyers. Again I agreed.

The first night was very quiet, so I went out and had a cup of coffee with his wife, a most unhappy woman. She was writing out account cards alone, in a huge house seated on an expensive lounge suite. She was strikingly beautiful in keeping with the Jaguar and the lounge suite, but Bayliss was nowhere to be seen. I thought, with no children, why aren't they out to the pictures or dinner? But Peter was "working," and with the words, a strange note sounded in her voice. I started to wonder who would be using him as an anaesthetist at this time of night. I finished the session, collected my cheque and went home.

A few days later I met a doctor at the Royal Children's Hospital who told me he had heard I was interested in Bayliss' practice.

"Did you know he gives anaesthetics?" the colleague said.

"Yes, this is the reason he wants someone to relieve him of his other practice," I replied. My colleague gave me an odd look. Another alarm bell was struck.

Bayliss had told me that when he started, he leased a practice across the road from where he was living now. He leased the clinic for six months, gained a good reputation and then leased an unoccupied clinic and home across the road. He took his newly acquired patients with him and terminated his lease on the old practice. The old principal – with his patients now following a new doctor – didn't even bother to come back and take over the clinic. It closed down instead. Bayliss had not paid a penny for goodwill and had gained a thriving practice. He told me he was sharp.

My alarm bell was blaring. Making an inspired assumption, I arranged to meet up with Peggy Berman at the RCH. She was still working for the abortion clinic and knew the backyard abortion scene well. I asked about Bayliss. In her best Irish accent, she said: "He's bad medicine, darling. A real butcher. Gives the anaesthetic for (one of the abortionists). Give him a miss, love. Do you no good." She knew my fear of any involvement with the wrong side of the law, a hangover from my persecution as a communist. I followed her advice. Later Bayliss in Queensland and Bert Wainer in Victoria would force abortion law reform.

In St Kilda, a doctor's wife told me her husband had a thriving practice but he was in the hospital with a heart attack. She offered for me to do a session. She said her husband had a personal following among the Jewish community, but they would be loyal to the practice. Saul and Mary had heard of him, so I went down to St Kilda to do an evening session and braced myself for the large crowd.

The wife met me there at 6pm. She was understandably distressed about her husband and a bit anxious. Most surgeries are pretty standard with locked cupboards for dangerous drugs, trolleys and a case with instruments. I sat down ready for the onslaught.

After 20 minutes, I wondered if I had missed the waiting room and went to ask the wife.

"They sometimes come in a bit late," she said, a bit embarrassed.

Not a patient turned up for the whole three hours. She gave me my cheque for £3 and asked if I was still interested? I said I would think it over.

Surgeries, where the patient lists had been run down to nothing, were common. A friend of mine went to inspect Dr Ziggy Atlas' practice. Ziggy was a salesman to his bootlaces. When my friend worked a session without any patients for two hours, he replied to the prospective buyer, that he ought to be "glad to get a night off occasionally."

Standing in Bourke on the phone, I was quite excited at the sound of this practice that the agent had told June about. I was so anxious to get back it ruined, the rest of the holiday for Geoff. Geoff and I camped at the Murray then drove straight on to Melbourne. Like a racehorse on the straight, I smelled home.

My instinct was right. The practice at 78 Bell Street, Coburg proved ideal and well located. South of Bell Street were the pre-World War II housing settlements where established families and older residents lived. But north of Sydney Road were the burgeoning suburbs of Fawkner and Merlynston. Beyond them were establishing suburbs of Broadmeadows, Glenroy and Craigieburn. These post-World War II homes were filled with young families and couples. The community was a good mix in need of a good doctor.

The house was a large, solid brick house with an interesting layout. It would be adequate for Naomi, Ian and a third child, as June was expecting again. The language used in doctor's surgery contracts did not change greatly over the years, but contract idiosyncrasies were often surprising. For instance, the vendor could not remove their nameplate from the building for at least six months. The vendor could make copies of patient cards at any time at no cost. Any new practice the vendor started had to be more than two miles for the buyer. The price included flywire screens, the oven and other fittings. The good doctor would provide a price list of furniture and instruments should I wish to buy any of it.

The present doctor, Ted Wellsted, confirmed the good mix of pensioners, repatriation pensioners, young couples having babies and a lot of children as patients. He showed me his yearly expenses and income and it looked good. The only problem was the price, it tallied up to £14,000 – £3500 of which was goodwill. I would need to find a way to pay for it.

Under the terms, I would pay a deposit of £3000, with yearly repayments increasing from £250 to £1000 a year until the end of the seventh year when the balance would be paid. There was interest too.

It was too good to refuse, but given my struggles with money, I was anxious about going into debt. My largest debt before this was to Jack of £400 who funded my final year of university and that was already paid back. Saul and Mary generously offered their house of surety to the bank so that I might get the initial £3000 deposit. Other wealthy family friends of Saul and Mary offered to stand at guarantor, but the bank never accepted them. I rang the affable agent Roger Van Assche, who came out in a rush to get me to sign the papers. This I did, and then came the moment which nearly wrecked the venture.

"Well," said Van Assche, "Could I have an advance on the deposit? Say £1000, roughly my fee, a widow's mite, ha-ha."

Van Assche's fee was in addition to what I had already paid, and I had not budgeted for it.

"Look," I said, "I just haven't got that much in the bank at the moment."

"Well, let's say £500."

"Sorry," I said "I haven't got that."

"What about £100?" said the optimistic agent.

"Sorry."

"Say £50?"

"Make it £25 and I'll make it a deal."

I still have the receipt for £25 from Van Assche where I paid a deposit on the proposed deposit of a deposit on a deposit of the initial deposit. Van Assche gave me a very curious smile as he went out the door.

It is common practice when a medical practice is changing hands for a handover period – one week before the new doctor works at the surgery and is introduced to his new patients, and one week after he takes over; the old doctor stays for a week. Ted suggested I get paid as a locum for a week beforehand from February 24. I was happy about this as I could use that money to buy his equipment. The week passed pleasantly, and everything was as Ted said it was, including the finances. Patients were upset to lose him, but, in time, they became my loyal personal following.

The only minor disagreement was caused by Mrs Wellsted who overestimated the value of nearly all the equipment, some of it by almost double. Ted on hearing the complaint reduced the amount and things went smoothly.

All the relevant papers were signed, and on Sunday night June and I drove over to look over the premises. We let ourselves in, and on walking into the kitchen, found Ted and his wife drinking a bottle of champagne. They quickly left, but I wondered what they were saying to each other, as they had once been like us, moving into this practice anew. Had it been a good life for them? Or were they selling because their life in practice had been burned out? June and I wandered around deciding on where things were to go and where Naomi and Ian were to sleep. Then we went back to Northcote to continue packing.

On Monday, March 1, 1962, I started as a solo general practitioner in my own medical practice. My debts before now were to Jack (£400), Ramsay's bookshop (£100), Tim Loh (5 shillings) and Bert Anderson and Vivian Voss from Perth (£15 each). With a stroke of a pen, I owed Ted Wellsted £14,000, plus interest, not mention Van Assche's fee. The enormity of the debt obscured its reality. As I couldn't fully comprehend the sum, I didn't worry on a day-to-day basis about it, but it hung over my head like a black cloud when I tried to think of the future.

With a typical working-class attitude of being personally responsible for debts, I saw I had no hope of holidays or frivolous spending. I made mental resolves to put so much each week aside for all wages, power supplies. It was a very strict budget.

I was uncertain about how to run a practice. The accounting seemed quite difficult. The administration of the history cards and medical aspects were quite straight forward. Ted's secretary/nurse seemed quite efficient, so I kept her on for a week while I advertised for another. I noted she had a curious intimate relation with Ted and he referred a lot to her.

Some secretaries not only run the practice but because of their intimate knowledge of the doctor's work, moods, dislikes and likes, run the doctors. Many second marriages are to doctor's secretaries. Later, it came as no surprise to me to learn that a colleague in a three-doctor practice a mile away ran off with the practice secretary to Queensland, leaving his wife and children behind. Marcia knew Ted Wellsted and every patient in the practice. She could assess a call's urgency, knew Ted's location at any given time and knew when he needed to be rescued from patients who talked too long in the surgery. She was slim, well-dressed and had a pseudo-high-pitched accent that is the articular trademark of the "better" secretaries.

Chapter 15
Dr Rogers GP

The night before I opened my doors, I could hardly sleep. I pondered whether it would be possible to pay my debts. Was I wise to start in solo private with only two years' hospital experience behind me? What if I missed something important? By the time morning came I was so tired, I didn't think I'd be able to start anyway.

At 8am, I opened the front door to the surgery and found two people waiting.

"Good morning doctor. Here is your paper and milk," one said.

I could only mumble a sleepy "aw thanks". My dressing gown had lost its cord and – without pyjamas on underneath – I needed one hand to keep it closed while I used my other hand to flip the newspaper under my armpit and grab the two bottles of milk. Great impression, I thought, but at least two patients had turned up. I didn't even stop to think that they might be sick. They, in turn, let other patients in after them while I got dressed.

At 8.30am Marcia arrived, brisk and efficient, and I heard her inform everyone that Dr Wellsted was taking a long, well-earned rest and I was taking over for a while. Unbeknown to me, Ted Wellsted had told everyone I was a specialist in children's diseases and the erroneous word had spread around Coburg. The going rate for a consultation was a guinea, the equivalent of 21 shillings.

Now dressed, I came up the passageway to hear the busy conversation in the waiting room. To my astonishment it was full. Marcia had the first patient already in the surgery so I straightened my new tie and walked in.

The first patient was a Mrs L, who told me she had a cough and burst out crying. Her husband was home from the tuberculosis sanatorium. Although not infectious, he could not return to his work as a chef. She had five children, one with Down syndrome, and didn't know how she would survive if she fell ill and couldn't work. And now she had a cough.

I listened. After her examination to exclude tuberculosis, I gave her some medicine. As she went to pay at reception, I told her not to worry about the fee. She should spend the charge on food for her family. The consultation had taken 40 minutes and I had a debt the size of Sydney Harbour.

God, I thought, I'm going to sink fast. The waiting room was standing room only, more a testament to my slowness in finishing up with Mrs L than my popularity.

My next patient was an elderly woman who insisted on filling me in on the details of all her illnesses and operations, just in case it was not on the card.

"Dr Wellsted was always in a hurry, you see," she said.

I gently terminated the consultation when she started to tell me the full horror of her late husband's terminal illness. As she was a pensioner, the government paid eight shillings for me to see her and, in my first hour, I earned that paltry sum.

The waiting room conversation had turned from pleasant to chilling. Marcia came in to say there were many patients to see and I might want to pick up the pace a bit and see more than two patients an hour. After that, I used the excuse of the waiting room to terminate conversations about my background, the birth of their second child or how Dr Wellsted had saved their life with an immediate hysterectomy. Still, I could only get through about four in an hour. At 1pm, I finished for lunch. Marcia handed me a handful of names and addresses for house calls. The next surgery would start at 2pm. I had better hurry, Marcia said. What in the hell had I been doing all the morning? I had seven house calls to make and rushed out to scoff a sandwich, drink some tea and say hello to June, Naomi and Ian.

Finding my way around the suburbs was a challenge, and after two house calls, it was 1.55pm.

The phone started to ring "Where is the doctor? I rang at nine this morning ....." Marcia explained and pacified with talk of emergencies and promises I would be there soon. She brought me a coffee into the office so I wouldn't waste time going down to the kitchen. I drank this on the run and was thankful there were only a few patients in the waiting room. I finished by 4pm when Marcia handed me another coffee and a list of three more house calls to make. Some of the callers from the morning had been phoning again to ask where I was. She suggested I do them first. Thankfully, traffic in 1962 was light. I was able to park conveniently to most houses, which helped considerably. Later I would come to know every little lane and shortcut in Coburg. On this day, I hardly knew a street.

House calls were only for people who were bedridden or too sick to come to the surgery. One resented that I had not arrived in the morning and told me I was not measuring up to my predecessor.

"If you rang in the morning he would be here before lunch. He was always in a hurry."

Wellstead had spent the minimum of time with a patient to keep on top of his schedule. I drove from one house to another examining, prescribing and hoping there would be no more.

After finishing the house calls, Marcia met me in the driveway to remind it was after 5pm and she had waited for me to return. Why hadn't I rung in to get the afternoon calls? There were three more to do. I took the list, backed out into Bell Street and visited three more houses.

It was 6.30pm before I sat down to tea, utterly fatigued, to see my family. The evening clinic was advertised to run from 7pm to 8pm. After tea, I found four people waiting to be seen. By the time it was 7pm, the consulting room was almost full.

I had hoped for no more than an hour or two at the most in the evenings, but a curious thing happened. The evening engendered an intimacy which kept people talking for ages about things quite away from their complaint. At 9pm, I was still working and the waiting room still seemed quite full. Those waiting let in anyone who came along. The evening hour of practice was a myth. At 10.30pm, there were only three people left, and at 11pm, I said goodnight to the last patient and closed the door.

Up until then, I had been buoyed for so many challenges and new faces, and I had been energised by the diagnostic chase. As soon as I closed the door, I collapsed on the waiting room bench, hoping no one would see me. After a while, I turned the lights out and walked down the passage to the lounge room where June was reading.

"How long do you think you can keep this up?" was the greeting.

The question was reasonable enough. I should have answered that night or a month later when it was apparent that I felt the burden of responsibility. I felt compelled to respond to any pain or discomfort. It is an unwritten law of medicine to respond to this pressure of necessity. Yet, I never answered that question. How could I say I just have to continue regardless? I made a cup of tea, picked up a book and sat down. Back then, after a consulting session, I found it difficult to impossible to switch off – thinking about possible errors, emergencies that might arise and the patients' problems.

Quickly, I realised I could nominate the diseases a person might have just through my intimate knowledge of how they lived, their age, lifestyle, diet, housing and so on.

Unsettling births

Although exhausted, I had no hope of a good night's sleep that night. After tossing in bed for two hours, I was almost relieved when the phone rang. It was the Sacred Heart Hospital labour ward, now the John Fawkner Private Hospital in Coburg. Mrs B was ready for delivery.

I had put my clothes out ready for any night emergency. In 1962, doctors did their own night work and most of them did all their weekday work too, so I followed suit. No wonder private general practitioners died early.

We had bought a secondhand car. Mrs Fowler of Fowlers Vacola bottling outfitters was the previous owner, and the secondhand salesman said she had the car for eight years, drove it to church and shopping and nowhere else. It was an unusual story for secondhand salesmen to tell. I bought the car. It had only done 4000 miles and was a very good buy.

Thankfully, the engine started at 3am and I raced down to the hospital. I found Mrs B in the second stage with the head crowning the perineum. I scrubbed up, had the trolley pushed next to me, placed Mrs B in the left lateral position, infiltrated the perineum with a local anaesthetic, cut an episiotomy and delivered the baby.

The babe was shown to Mrs B, but she was not allowed to touch it. The baby boy was then taken away to be weighed, bundled up and then brought back for a quick cuddle before it was put to bed in the nursery. This was the usual practice. Babies were kept in the nursery for a minimum of 24 hours so a mother could rest after a tiring birth. But Mrs B was not tired; she was elated after her short labour. She wanted to see her baby and was in good spirits. She saw him in the cot before he was whisked off to the nursery. I met this same boy 19 years later as a strapping six-foot Carlton footballer. He recognised me, but I couldn't see any resemblance to the baby I had delivered in 1962.

After congratulating her, I told her the hospital would ring her husband who was waiting at home. I checked the firmness of her fundus, the amount of bleeding and her blood pressure and went home. I thought this was a good normal delivery. The labour ward staff seemed to approve too.

Despite the excitement, I crawled back into bed and slept until I was woken by Naomi and Ian who wanted to get up. June made a practice of reading late into the night and disliked rising early. It fell to me to get the children's and my breakfast.

I put on the kettle and went outside to pick up the paper and milk from the front door where I found people waiting for the doors to open. After the exhaustion of the first day and night, I felt a little resentment that they should be intruding on my time so early. The phone started ringing so breakfast was rushed and I kept answering it and the door until Marcia arrived at 8.30am. In between, I helped Naomi and Ian dress, saw that they had plenty of toast, and tried to get June out of bed. The children were still finding the house new and loved playing in the yard.

The morning's work started as it had the day before. A heavy morning surgery, morning house calls, afternoon surgery, afternoon house calls. At night, I had a call, this time from St Elmo's Hospital, Brunswick, saying another woman was ready for delivery. As Marcia had left at 5pm, I asked a patient to answer the phones. The patient was delighted to be close to the "drama of medicine" and wished me luck. No one has ever worked out why most babies are delivered in the middle of the night or at mealtimes.

St Elmo's Hospital was a curious place in Moreland Road, near the railway line and now replaced by a downmarket hotel. The operating theatre was on the first floor and there was no lift. If a patient could not walk up to surgery, the matron would heave them up in her massive arms and carry them upstairs, placing them on the operating table. At least the post-operative wards were on the first floor.

Untrained as a midwife, the matron usually employed very competent midwives to manage the labour ward. She had a habit of interfering in the ward, much to the senior midwife's annoyance. The matron knew very little about obstetrics but would make pronouncements about labouring women that were absurdly wrong.

"She just came into the second stage as you walked through the door," she once told me. The woman was barely two-finger dilated and was hours away from the second stage.

On this occasion though, the woman was well into her second stage. The head was crowning and the baby was born before I could cut an episiotomy. The woman, whom I had not seen before, appeared very tired. She flopped back on the bed when the nurses tried to show her the baby. The baby was taken to the nursery. Again, I congratulated the mother, checking everything. The sister then said something that gave me a whack in the pit of my stomach.

"She got quite distressed in the first stage and we had to give her quite a bit of analgesia. Would you mind signing the book?"

I went over and found the woman had been given pethidine plus sodium amytal (also known as truth serum). No wonder she was tired. The babe was a little flat but breathed after he was rubbed on the back. I felt very uncomfortable about signing for a drug I hadn't ordered. I asked that I be called in future if any of my patients needed drugs. "You don't want to be disturbed every time a mother needs an analgesic do you?"

I nodded in reply.

"Look," she said. "I'll tell you what to do. Leave your orders on a card and we'll just follow out the instructions and save ringing you."

She showed me the hospital card system. Each doctor had a favourite drug to be given at different stages of labour. This method saved the doctor time and trouble. It almost meant he didn't have to attend the women during lengthy labours as midwives carried out their instructions. It probably suited doctors who did not like to see a woman in labour, it tended to frighten some of them. The qualities which allow a couple to handle labour – like courage, trust, love, morale – are outside the pharmacopoeia and cannot be prescribed with a pen.

The doctors and labour ward staff colluded to ensure the doctors only arrived just as the head was about to be born. It was an assisted birth if they were on time and an unassisted one if they were not on time.

Pavlov to the rescue

Going back to Bell Street in the car, I tried to work out why I was dissatisfied with the two deliveries. One of the major reasons was that the women had known Dr Wellsted and were disappointed he was not there. I decided I would get to know all the midwifery patients, even those whose deliveries were imminent. Also, I would spend time with women while they were in labour. Two early decisions, but that was a start.

When I got back to the surgery everyone still waiting in the surgery wanted to know how things had gone. Were they both well? Was it a boy or a girl? Of all the details, I could never remember the sex, so I solved this by committing the baby's name to memory. The remaining patients were happy to be seen quickly so I finished at an early 10.45am. I was so used to feeling tired now that it felt normal.

June was reading when I came in but became animated when she heard I had delivered a baby. She was nearly seven months pregnant with Silvia. After two traumatic experiences with our first two, she was hoping this would be better. She was arming herself with books on childbirth.

I had bought a book which applied the Russian Pavlov's methods and his physiological principles to childbirth at the International Bookshop. Pavlov had previously been the inspiration for my rat experiments at Melbourne University. It was an interesting concept, but after glancing at it I had ignored it.

The book was in June's pile of books to read, so I picked it up – *Painless Childbirth through Psychoprophylaxis*. What on earth was it talking about, painless? It was a bit jargonistic, but I persisted as I was familiar with Pavlov's theories and dissatisfied with childbirth to date in private hospitals. I started to read the book with fresh eyes.

June was delighted and enthusiastically showed me what she thought were the suggested breathing and abdominal massage techniques. She directed me to specific pages where she had already read important passages.

If I was going to do this, it was imperative that I got to know all the women giving birth quickly, so I decided to hold a pregnancy class. As I was working out the details, the Sacred Heart labour ward called to say another woman was ready for delivery and admonished me for not visiting the first of my patients, who had given birth at 4am. I had completely forgotten her. As I set off, again in the middle of the night, I wondered how on earth I could apply "painless childbirth" techniques to a place like the Sacred Heart Hospital.

The young woman had come into the hospital early with mild contractions as she was having her first child. She arrived in the late afternoon, but now her contractions were growing stronger. She was frightened despite knowing analgesics would offer pain relief. I remembered seeing her in the surgery that morning.

Under the guise of taking her pulse, I sat down next to the bed and held her hand and wrist. This simple act, I would come to realise, gave warmth and comfort to any woman distressed in labour. Labour ward staff were brisk, efficient and even ready to criticise a woman's effort in childbirth. In 1962, no one comforted labouring women; they were placed in a room and told to ring the buzzer if they were worried. Later I would encourage husbands to keep close contact with their wives while they gave birth.

I began to quietly explain what was going to happen. How the babe's head was opening up the cervix, how it would come down through the vagina, and then stretch up the opening until the head was born. I suggested that with each contraction she breathe up with the abdomen, and this would make the contraction easier.

She relaxed. We talked about her house, where she had worked, her plans for a family, and how her husband was waiting at her mother's to hear the news. It occurred to me that he would be the ideal person to be sitting here talking to her.

The sisters were buzzing in and out of the room. Every time they came in I felt I had to break off relating to the woman to restore a sense of loyalty to the staff. An odd feeling that by being kind to the woman I was breaking some unspoken pact with the hospital staff.

When the sister asked me if I wanted a cup of tea, I had to leave the woman alone for a few minutes. From the tea room, I could hear her distress with the next contraction. I gulped my tea down and went back to restore her breathing rhythm, all the while talking to her in between contractions.

It had always seemed to me that women in a left lateral position while delivering their babies were very uncomfortable. When this woman's babe was ready, I suggested she remain on her back in the dorsal position. When the head was coming out I told her to breathe with her abdomen, not push as the perineum was too thin. The sisters urged the episiotomy scissors on me saying "otherwise she will tear." I tried to deliver the head without cutting and did so. I noted the perineum had a slight graze which did not need stitching.

Around 9pm, I headed home, elated about the delivery but disturbed to think my days would have to be spent in consulting and my nights in delivering babies. I wondered how I could possibly spend hours sitting next to women as they laboured.

That morning I sent a letter about pregnancy exercise classes to all my midwifery patients. As Wednesday afternoons and evenings were free, I would hold them then.

On the same morning, I had to advertise for a receptionist as Marcia decided to go to work for Ted Wellstead, who had set up his practice just over the agreed restrictive limit. I later wondered how many patients she redirected to his new practice during her week with me. But proximity to a medical practice counts in the end, and I didn't lose too many patients.

The morning passed quickly, and after my morning calls and lunch, I was relieved to find I had an afternoon and an evening off.

Despite my packed working days and broken sleep, I was keyed up and keen to do something. Rest seemed a waste leisure time, so we drove over to Saul and Mary's frock shop. They were pleased to see us and wanted to hear about my first couple of days. Saul pretended indifference to the practice's financial aspects. His attitude was soon echoed by his daughter. Mary was interested in the details and whether I could meet all my debts. We sat in a small back room that was so stacked with old books, receipts and cardboard boxes. The children had to sit on an adult's knee to fit in.

Despite their pleas to stay for tea, we went home, bathed the children and fed them. I found I could not eat and went straight to bed, sleeping through until it was time to get up to the children in the morning. They were used to the house but insisted on round after round of toast always swimming in butter.

Tea and sympathy

Every morning was greeted with buzzing doorbells and ringing telephones. After becoming accustomed to the haze of starting a new practice, I began to get to know the area, my patients and their personalities.

The Woi Wurrung people originally occupied the land, but disease and farming dwindled their numbers and forced them off the land. From 1851, Coburg was known for Pentridge Prison.

My clinic at 78 Bell Street was a few doors down from the bluestone house at 82 Bell Street, where the Coburg Historical Society made its home. I had another patient at another old bluestone farmhouse, a single elderly lady, and she remembered her father entertaining Henry Lawson in her home.

Built on the area loosely bounded by Sydney and Moreland roads and Nicholson and Bell streets, across Bell Street from my practice was one of Victoria's first soldier settlement housing estates. I felt sympathetic towards the former WWI soldiers and their widows, who were mostly pensioners and always pitifully glad to see me. In 1962, 40 years or more after being built, many widows were living in cold, rundown homes untouched by a handyman since the husband had died years ago. When I visited those pensioners they would frequently be alone, huddled by a single bar radiator in the kitchen. They stayed in this room most of the time, drinking tea and eating Boston buns. After checking their blood pressure and any medication, they often asked me to put the bin out or post some letters.

They had lived on pensions for years and the affluence of post-World War II had passed them by. For some, a trip down to the Sydney Road shops was a highlight as the contact confirmed their humanity, although they probably bought little with their meagre funds. Their children had grown up to cars, new homes, refrigerators and furniture. These socially mobile children settled in distant thriving new suburbs on Melbourne's fringes in suburbs like Doncaster, Greensborough and Ivanhoe. Some of the pensioners never learned how to drive, stayed home and held onto their possessions rather than buying more.

Back then, there were no social workers at the then Coburg City Council. Meals on Wheels and the local senior citizens' clubs were the only social supports. I began seeing some pensioners weekly, others fortnightly. I became a social worker, friend, visitor and doctor to a lot of the elderly men and women.

I couldn't help getting a sense of their unrelieved toil. From the Great Depression up until their present day, they had managed and continued to manage through difficult times.

Their dark furniture was kept as proof that their struggle was worthwhile. I noticed they were mostly women and could see a pattern emerging. Their husbands would retire, repair the house, paint it and in a year or two die. Was retirement a death sentence? Or did work empty a man of life and push him out just before he died? Sons and daughters would visit on Sundays, Mother's Day and Christmas. They usually called the doctor on arrival. I was never certain of their motives. Was it to atone for the guilt of desertion or because they were shocked by their mother's neglected state?

"Doctor, we have just come over to see Mum and we all think she is looking terrible. Could you come and see her?" came the mid-morning call.

"Well, look I was just there last Friday (Monday, Tuesday etc) and she really is no different. It might be better if you could pop over and see her more frequently?" I would reply.

"We really would like to but we live so far away."

Left alone by her children from one Mother's Day to the next and her children demonstrate their filial concern by calling the doctor?

Then came the blackmail and guilting trick: "But if you won't come I will have to ring another doctor." Naturally, I capitulated even though I had already seen Mrs so-and-so only that week. I tried to fit in my family meal around the urgent house call.

"Doctor, we have to go home soon and we would like to talk to you about Mum, so could you come soon? We all think she can't manage and want you to put her in a home."

I especially resented the "call another doctor" line because I had grown to know and be friendly with their mothers, and they wanted to make big life decisions – like putting her in a nursing home – with some ring-in doctor. With indecent haste, they wanted to break their mother's medical care.

The nursing home was the final solution. These women had lived in their homes for perhaps 40 years. They had brought babies into these houses, had survived motherhood, suffered through the Depression, farewelled some of their men to war, and through death or departure, watched everyone leave their home. The house was a part of them. Every room had its memories; the backyard had special memories of the children at play. Surely these older people had the right to preserve the richness of the past rather than being pushed into a home that could only promise them poverty in the future.

My policy was to avoid tranquillisers at all costs and, where possible, sedatives at night. Old people do not need as much sleep as young active people and it is only under institutional conditions that they are required to sleep to a routine.

Nursing homes for the infirm elderly only become necessary when someone is disabled by disease or disability. There are a large number of old people who are capable of operating in a limited environment – it might be just their kitchen and bedroom – and they are quite happy to do so. I encouraged them to stay at home. A granny flat is probably the best answer for older active or semi-active old people who *do* wish to leave their homes. Failing that, a collection of flats where the generations are mixed works well.

With this in mind, Easter and Mother's Day were times I endeavoured to be away from home, taking off to the beach sometimes, but often I could not get away.

The pensioners took up a lot of my time. For years, I kept my 1963 call-book. This was an extract from April 19, when I made 23 house calls.

Mrs C. She and her husband kept an immaculate house and garden. She struggled to keep her weight and blood pressure down – both without success.

Mrs H. She lived in a huge house with her daughters and family. Every room was crammed with old beautiful furniture. Rows and rows of leather-covered books lined shelves. Every time I went there I noticed a faint smell of sherry on everyone's breath.

Mrs W. She was shocked when her husband had a heart attack and died one day. She seemed a frail woman but survived his death with a sensitive strength that astonished her family. They wanted me to give sedatives to give her a good sleep. The last thing a grieving person wants is an artificial sleep. They want, in fact need, to grieve.

Mr and Mrs C. This couple lived in a one-bedroom flat in the middle of a projected freeway. The husband was a shell of a man, but by dint of glue-ing the marriage together with gallons of tea and Boston buns, they coped with their collective hypertension and increasing senility.

Mrs A. A dynamic woman who lived with her daughter until her house was bulldozed to make way for a shopping centre car park. She later developed carcinoma of the pancreas and, after a painful end, died in another daughter's house. I still have the letter her daughter wrote thanking me for coming day or night to give her poor mum an injection to ease her suffering.

A couple with different surnames were drunk every time I visited. The house was filthy. I patched up their numerous sores, ulcers and rashes with vitamin injections plus medication, ready for their next alcoholic binge.

Reading the list still evokes in me that desperate sense of urgency, knowing the pensioners were waiting washed and dressed because this was the "Doctor's Day." If I failed to visit them, their disappointment was palpable, a phone call placed. Frequently I was met with a plaintive response; "I thought you must have been cross with me."

In a few months, I had grouped the houses that I visited geographically – a bit like the old milkman delivered milk. Due to particular historical circumstances, a whole street could have pensioners' houses. I took some pride in thinking everyone in the street was my patient. I had unwittingly fallen into the greatest trap for doctors of feeling you are indispensable, so I continued rushing year after year until the inevitable happened and I became rundown.

The fight for husbands and hair

Ted Wellstead was a capable doctor and, seeing as he had only moved down Bell Street, I felt certain most of his midwifery patients would have followed him, but my midwifery antenatal classes gave me a reputation in the district, and I rapidly built up a large midwifery following.

In my Wednesday afternoon classes, I taught women breathing, elementary anatomy, physiology and obstetrics. I started to get results.

The hardest battle was to get dad-to-be in the room. Stymied by nursing staff who were against husbands attending their wife's labour and the delivery, I just started to bring them in. Soon, I was instructing all the couples to ring me before they went into the hospital, and I met them there when they arrived. When the women were first admitted, I wrote on the women's charts – as an order – that the husbands were to stay.

Keeping husbands in the labour wards was much harder than I had imagined. They were regarded as a nuisance and, in some hospitals, as perverts.

"There is something wrong with a husband who wants to see his wife give birth," was a familiar cry.

The husbands were made to feel most unwelcome. The staff insisted the husbands gown up and stand on the far side of the bed. They were excluded from any rounds of tea and sustenance.

They were sent out of the room on the slightest excuse.

In retrospect, the nurses' reasons for sending them out of the room sound ridiculous. When a woman passed urine, the husband was sent out of the room. When I did a pelvic examination, he was sent out of the room. Initially, it was a minor victory to have him in the room, so I conceded these minor exclusions.

One difficult birth was for a woman called Lorraine at the Sacred Heart Hospital. I thought a caesar was likely and called in RWH chief obstetrician Don Lawson, who brought Kevin McCaul with him, aforementioned RWH anaesthetist champion of women's birthing rights. Don was a humane obstetrician who understood the minimalist approach to medical intervention in childbirth but also knew when and how to act in the best interest of the patient and their child. Lorraine had been going along with some difficulty until the second stage. The head did not descend despite adequate contractions and good strong pushing.

Don felt he could get the head out with forceps, and after McCaul administered an epidural, Don applied the forceps and pulled. They got the head easily enough, but the body was a challenge.

Eventually, the baby was delivered. With Lorraine reassured of the baby's health, Kevin, Don and I went outside. I had asked her husband Tony to step outside when it was clear the babe wasn't coming out using the method. After the baby was born, I told Tony to go back into his wife and meet his new son, but the sister told him to wait.

I had had enough. I told the sister he was to go in, and that was a doctor's order.

She was furious. The nurses were a bit frightened and quiet. Tony walked into the labour ward and embraced his wife and smiled at his son. The atmosphere in the ward was icy, but I went in with warm congratulations. I spoke to them both about the birth and the struggle to have Tony enter the ward after the birth.

As I left Don said, "Well, that was a victory." It was, but I went back to the surgery in a rage against the inhumanity of midwifery staff and particular that sister at Sacred Heart Hospital.

I recall a story told to me about a woman who was not a patient. When her husband was told he could not go into the labour ward with her, she replied with tremendous courage, "Well if he goes, so do I."

Hospitals were attempting to eject husbands so forcefully that I made it became a necessary part of the antenatal educational program to discuss tactics to stridently deal with the rigidity of hospitals. Husbands were told not to confront the staff directly but say the doctor had told them to stay and let me argue with the staff. Couples became too upset when they fought with the staff over not only a husband's right to stay with his wife but also a wife's refusal of enemas, shaving or analgesics. Whereas I simply had to write my orders in the patient's chart and these were not to be disobeyed.

For a time, I didn't have the confidence to dispense with shaving pubic hair, showering and enemas for the women, but I gradually realised how unnecessary these habits were, and by 1964, I was ordering that these procedures be avoided.

Still, it was a struggle. A delightful woman, who wore a calliper on one leg, came into labour with her second child at Essendon Community Hospital. She rang before going in, so I met her at the hospital, settled her in, saw her breathing was under way, saw her husband was present and would be remaining and went back to the surgery to sleep until she was ready for delivery. About 11.30pm, I was woken by the sister-in-charge, a Sister True, to say the mother was in distress and needed analgesia. I expressed surprise and said I would come over but to hold off giving her anything. When I got to the labour ward about 15 minutes later, the mother was in tears and quite dopey. The husband was angry and the rhythm of the labour had gone to pieces. After a lot of talking and tears, I got the story.

Sister True had come in, stated I had ordered analgesics and proceeded, despite the couple's protests, to give her an injection in the buttocks. Soon after, she felt dizzy, angry and was unable to do her breathing. I confronted Sister True and demanded to know why she had given the mother an injection when I had given specific orders. She was quite truculent and said, in her opinion, she needed sedation and told me to sign the drug book. I called the matron to say I wanted Sister True sacked. She replied, "This is a very serious charge, doctor, and I can't do anything about this tonight. Could you let me have a report in the morning?"

I stayed with the patient all night and got her breathing going again. She did well and produced a healthy girl. The three of us ended up joking and admiring the girl. Sister True came in and out of the ward without a word.

My report was filed but I thought nothing would come of it until I met a Sister Thomas at Sacred Heart labour ward months later. Largely as a result of my report, she said it was revealed that Sister True was a pethidine addict and this was her way of getting supplies. Half or some to the patient and the rest to herself.

In the early days of using psychoprophylaxis, the women I trained did not realise they had achieved a revolution in childbirth. With the support of their husbands, they breathed through their labour and thought everyone had a baby this way. Returning to the post-natal wards, they realised they were the odd one out when other mothers asked how many stitches and injections they needed. An Italian patient in the 10-bed post-natal ward at Sacred Heart drew the curtain around us to ask whether she should have stitches like everyone else and had something gone wrong with her.

Women who had used the technique often came back to me for their second or third baby, but anxious. After talking to the other mums they had convinced themselves they had merely been lucky last time.

Rarely were they right about this, although not always. One woman was pregnant with her fifth child. She was a devoted supporter of psychoprophlaxis, having had her second, third and fourth child using this method with me. She was somewhat apprehensive with the fifth child, but I reassured that her track record and statistics meant she had little to worry about.

She was admitted to the Royal Women's early one Sunday afternoon and settled down to steady regular contractions. About 6pm, the babe's head was still high, so I rang a consultant colleague and suggested with this sort of obstetrical labour we would be delivering her by caesarean section. He felt after only a few hours labour it was too early to call it for a caesar and suggested we wait. Knowing the mother and having witnessed her four previous labours, I felt something was obstructing the head.

She laboured on for another six hours, and still, the head had not descended one centimetre.

We took her to the theatre. Despite four previous babes all of good age, all delivered vaginally, the head of this babe was firmly jammed in the brim of the pelvis and in a posterior position of the occiput. While a woman is pregnant there is time to assess and know with a degree of certainty you are right in your judgements. For the woman, she has time to grow accustomed to the physiological changes in her body. But, during birthing, it is a time of obstetrical uncertainty; decisions are made quickly and on balance. This uncertainty is worse for women as their body is changing rapidly and the outcomes are unknown until her baby is born.

After a damaging birth experience, women can view their subsequent pregnancy with horror. To regain her confidence, she needs to experience the onset of labour, successfully cope with it and feel on top of her contractions, and finally give birth.

One evening a woman came into my surgery telling me she had heard I was "good with obstetric cases." She was about 25 weeks pregnant and hated the idea. During her first labour, in a fairly typical birth for 1961, she had been given repeated doses of analgesics, an episiotomy and forceps. No wonder she was terrified. When I examined her, I could immediately feel two heads growing. Until that moment, she had not known she was expecting twins. She was now trembling.

Still, with encouragement, she attended the classes, learned the breathing techniques and started to understand something of her own body. Her husband worked as a security guard in a large Broadmeadows factory and the idea of him attending the labour, or taking paternity leave, was a bit much for him. He felt completely out of his depth at the consultations and was reluctant when I suggested he attend a husbands' night at the surgery. Once he understood, he became supportive and enthusiastic for the "Rogers' way". His wife remained fearful of the impending labour and our conversations would run along these lines.

"Look, doctor, I understand all that you're trying to do and I can do the breathing, and I know about the cervix opening and the head coming down, but I'm still scared stiff."

"All right," I'd say. "You stay scared but continue to practice the breathing until you can do it automatically and understand as much as you can about your labour and I'm certain you'll gain your confidence during the labour."

"We'll see. I tell you now I don't believe it," was her standard reply.

As she was expecting twins, I sent her to the hospital early to await her contractions. While she was resting they began. After a short time with good contractions and well-controlled breathing, she pushed out the first baby. She simply refused to believe it and I had to trace the cord down from the babe where it disappeared into the vagina before she would accept a birth had occurred. The second twin was delivered a few minutes later. Somewhat inappropriately, she turned to the nun assisting with the birth and asked what real labour pain was like. She didn't believe she had been through "real" labour.

While June did not attend my classes while pregnant, she read the book and practised the psychoprophylaxis technique. June went into labour and was admitted to the Queen Victoria Hospital where Dr Alwyn Long, who had delivered Naomi, was to assist with the birth. Alwyn was agreeable for me to attend the birth, but I was told June would be a while longer so I finished off the work I was doing before heading to the hospital. Alas, I arrived just after the birth.

On May 7, 1962, Sylvie was born in a quick delivery with no pathology. After the trauma of Ian's birth, June said Sylvie's birth was much easier. June and Sylvie were home quickly and Sylvie slotted straight into the household. She was a very affable baby, very pleasant and placid. As she grew older she started to learn the piano and became very talented musically. She eventually moved to Port Fairy, where she has played local gigs regularly, mostly playing the guitar but more recently taking up the harp.

Poor hospitals and milk

In those days, my patients were admitted to wards in peripheral hospitals. The hospitals' sizes and equipment varied, but the procedure was much the same. Women were put into bed and left alone to labour with instructions to ring the bell if they needed anything. Even if the atmosphere was friendly and encouraging – which frequently it was not – the delivery was essentially a hospital delivery, not a family birth. No matter how clinically accomplished these births were, the isolation the women suffered was distressing.

Some hospitals were so poorly equipped they should not have been allowed to conduct deliveries. As a weekend locum, I was called to Vaucluse Hospital in Moreland Road, Brunswick. Any doctor can call in for assistance on any procedure or operation where they think they need help. The doctor who does the calling in is the principal and takes the lead, the other doctor is called the "second". At Vaucluse, I arrived to find the principal attempting to deliver a babe by forceps, with the woman lying perpendicular across the bed on her back, legs up and supported by stirrups but the rest of her body flopping over the side. Every time the principal tried to pull the babe out, the woman slid across and then nearly off the bed. She was deeply unconscious and blue. A nurse was stupidly pouring ether directly onto the woman's mask, rendering her near death through lack of oxygen. I got the woman looking pink by ceasing the ether and giving her pure oxygen.

In the early 1960s, the practice was to feed women in labour. Having listened to the teaching of anaesthetist Kevin McCaul, I introduced the idea of abstinence to my patients. The Vaucluse Hospital staff regarded the practice of fasting as almost criminal for labouring women, but the critical circumstances surrounding this woman showed the necessity of the policy. When a woman comes into labour, food remains in the stomach for the full length of the labour. It is as if every ounce of blood and energy is diverted to the uterus, and her effort of expelling the baby, there is no energy for digestion. Everything else is shut down for the duration. If stomachs are full of food, it can be vomited up. There was no suction handy, and with the woman lying flat on her back and deeply unconscious, it could have been fatal.

Now with oxygen to revive her, I braced the woman to stop her from flying off the bed, and the baby was delivered.

The hospital was inadequately equipped and uninformed and so had transformed a straightforward obstetrical manoeuvre into an obstetrical hazard.

When I began to assist women in their deliveries at the Royal Women's Hospital, I began to realise how inadequate these peripheral and suburban hospitals were. Fortunately, three of the peripheral hospitals have ceased to accept midwifery bookings and some have closed.

A woman might escape the labour ward unscathed but then her problems in the postpartum period. First, she was separated from the babe. The babe was taken to the nursery for 24 hours and fed complementary feeds. At the time of writing, the Oxford definition of complementary was "forming a complement, completing, perfecting," but how can formula complement anything if the baby is not put to the breast first? This was disastrous for mother-and-baby bonding time, often causing the mother considerable disappointment and anguish. It also interfered severely with establishing the mother's milk supply. The usual milk given was diluted sweetened condensed milk, which rapidly accustomed the baby to a sweet taste. Instead of bonding with her baby, the mother mostly spent a miserable night away from her baby, her husband and her home.

The mother and baby were only reunited after 24 hours. At one hospital, I vividly remember seeing the "baby express". This was a long trolley with upper and lower decks, where each baby was separated into little bays. Every three hours the babies would be loaded onto this trolley and taken to their respective mothers. Mostly, they were screaming with hunger. If the hunger screams grew too much in the nursery, they were given a bottle of sweetened condensed milk until feed time. Mothers were not encouraged to come to the nursery and staff were too busy to take a baby to its mother every time it cried for a feed.

Under these circumstances, mothers had great difficulty in establishing their milk supply – no wonder. The hospital system was actively preventing many mothers from successfully breastfeeding their babes, and with breast-feeding, demand leads to more supply.

"Rooming in" – where a baby sleeps next to the mother in a cot – was not an acceptable hospital practice. Demand feeding was considered positively harmful. Many times I argued with hospital staff over the effect their actions were having on milk supply.

On one occasion, I went to the Preston and Northcote Community Hospital (PANCH) where I had some five prenatal patients. Everyone was in tears following a badgering from a Sister O'Connor. She was a middle-aged, rigid woman. She had no idea about breastfeeding, yet had laid down the law to mothers having their third and fourth babies. One woman was a Nursing Mothers' Association counsellor at the time, an artistic, highly intelligent woman with a rather small baby who had difficulty sucking and tired easily. Despite this woman's obvious competence and track record, Sister O'Connor did her utmost to prevent her from breastfeeding her baby.

The tears were testament to the sisters' power in those days. Yet, the mother persisted, the babe put on weight on the breast. Sister O'Connor had to admit defeat.

Chapter 16
Missing money and mistresses

While I was becoming deeply involved in my practice, my children were growing up, and I was hardly ever there. June had decided to do a diploma of education. She completed the diploma and started teaching at Princes Hill High School. Our life together was going from bad to worse.

As I was the only interested party in the bedroom, June suggested I should get a flat nearby and take a mistress. When she first suggested it, I think she felt she was being urbanely European. I rejected the suggestion at first, but it played on my mind. I began assessing the potential prospects for the new role in my life.

Finding a sexual partner is difficult for a doctor. As a doctor, you know hundreds of people quite intimately, but making a patient your lover in the early 1960s would see you rightly struck off, the Medical Board of Australia. Over time, the rules changed and a former patient could become a partner in certain circumstances, but back then it was impossible. Consulting patients took up 80 per cent of my waking life so opportunities for a sexual alliance were almost nil. This is one of the many reasons doctors marry their medical secretaries.

When Marcia left for Ted Wellsted's practice, I employed various secretaries and, for one reason or another, all left after a time. I did not seek them out as mistresses.

Around the spring of 1963, I employed a Mrs Veronica Brown. With me and most patients, she was quick, pleasant and bright. She was married with two boys. She worked well and stayed with me for some months. On occasion, I was puzzled at the small amounts of cash banked.

"Oh yes, things are a bit slow," Mrs Brown would respond when asked about this. "I've noticed they are not paying."

I noticed some irregularities with her account filing but did not worry beyond mentioning the importance of accuracy.

One Saturday, when Mrs Brown was on her weekend, a patient came in, presented her account and asked for a duplicate receipt. I took the invoice from her, noted it was for £8, then got out her card, but there was a discrepancy.

"You have paid £5 and I can give you a receipt for that," I said. "No, I paid the girl £8," she said. "I thought she was fiddling with that duplicate receipt a bit." She added that Mrs Brown had a rude manner, which I had heard about from other patients. I wrote the patient a receipt for the £8 and asked her to leave her account. I began to check what had been paid in the receipt book.

Mrs Brown was diddling the books – hundreds of pounds were missing. She was giving the patient the correct original receipt and then altering the duplicate to reflect a few pounds less. Then she was marking off the full amount as "paid" on the account card. I had to take action.

On Monday, we started off normally. After surgery, I called her in, where my accountant Len Alexander was seated with me.

"Mrs Brown, you have been cheating me for some months," I began.

"Someone who doesn't like you very much showed me this receipt and this is a list of all the receipts you have altered," I said.

She turned white and then red. She started to shake. She strenuously denied everything, even when presented with altered receipts. We were locked like this argument for some time.

"OK I will call a detective I know and he can sort it out," I said to break the impasse.

In mind, I had Ken "Crusher" Webb, a friend from the professional running group I was in. He was at Carlton CIB and was a part-time movie stunt man, although I did not mention his name or his movie career at the time.

At this, she stopped.

"Yes, I did it. I suppose this means the sack."

"Too right it does," I said.

Len had worked out how much she owed the surgery, which was a great deal more than I owed her in holiday pay. I told her to go but neglected to check the Monday morning's takings. She has siphoned off £20 in two hours.

Three weeks later, I had a call from a social worker at Prince Henry's psychiatric ward where Mrs Brown had been admitted. The social worker said Mrs Brown had delusions that I was going to have her put in jail for theft. I told the social worker they were not unfounded delusions, but I did not intend taking action.

Mrs Brown's departure meant I needed to spend another Saturday interviewing receptionist candidates. Only one was immediately suitable, and as I could read her writing she got the job. By that autumn afternoon, Belinda had entered my life. It is not her real name, but I have no desire to cause her any harm whatsoever for these would become tumultuous times.

Belinda had been married for five years, was about 27 years and had been a dental nurse.

Her marriage was faulty. Her husband spent more time drinking beer with his male friends than he did with Belinda. I think in hindsight, he was probably homosexual, no doubt married to the wrong person. In five years of married life, she claimed they had never had intercourse. At first, when they had the time to try, and he was relaxed, his mother would drop in. After a while, they stopped trying.

She was a tall thin woman who was bright, competent and energetic. Her pleasant and efficient demeanour kept the surgery running well and it was a friendly place. Belinda knew where everything was and could trace a person on a telephone in seconds. Patients would wait, without complaint, for hours, particularly if I had to attend a delivery.

More importantly, she started to show concern for me.

If I came in tired from delivering a baby, she would put the patients off so I could rest. Belinda made me coffee and shared my anger at the hospitals and their practices, and she supported my humanist approach to medicine. Everything between us was strictly proper but I felt the connection.

I was grateful for Belinda's concern and care, and in about March 1965 we began a clandestine affair.

A murky world exposed

In 1965, I had a call from Peggy. She wanted a "yarn" about something. I asked her to come to meet me at my car in front of the Royal Children's Hospital.

Peggy was working for abortionist Dr James Troup in East Melbourne. She had worked for several doctors in this field since 1954. Along with reception duties, her other main duty was to courier bribery money from the doctors to homicide police officers, who offered tip-offs and protection from raids.

At that time abortion was illegal, so the industry was ripe for crooked cops. There was also a growing campaign to end the criminality of abortions.

Medical disasters were common enough, but the police corruption, standover tactics and extortion didn't help the case for continuing to charge doctors.

Peggy paid the money to homicide officers Frederick John Adam, John Edward Matthews, Martin Robert Jacobson and John "Jack" Ralph Ford.

Peggy met me in my car out the front of the Royal Children's. She told me she was involved with Ford, who she said was increasingly abusive and violent towards her.

"I've been seeing Ford for quite a while and he's bad medicine." It was her favoured term for a bad egg.

Ford was a gambler with significant racing debts.

Peggy explained how Troup was protected by Masonic police because he was a Mason, while Catholic cops protected other abortionists. There was a sectarian division within the police force then, even in terms of who they took kickbacks from.

Ford and Adam were particularly greedy and kept asking for more and more money. Peggy realised if Troup paid it, the clinic would go broke, so she gave Ford $200 a month of her own money.

I arranged for Peggy to meet with a civil rights lawyer (who later became a big mucker in the Labor Party), a Slater and Gordon lawyer and me at Jimmy Watson's bar in Carlton.

After much to-ing and fro-ing, we decided Peggy should write a thorough account declaring all the details of corruption in Victoria's murky abortion world, including Peggy's own role. She would include where she met Ford, when and how much she paid each crooked copper, and why she believed the extortion costs had inflated. We sent it to every politician in Victoria and waited. Silence. The letter was never discussed publicly and she was never contacted about it.

Peggy and Troup were arrested in 1968 and all money was off the table if it did not buy protection from the raids on the clinic.

Evan Whitton of *The Truth* got hold of the statement, and found that Peggy, Troup and abortionist campaigner Dr Bertram Wainer were ready to talk and name names. Peggy would go on to wear a wire to entrap the crooked cops and, in December 1969, *The Truth* got the scoop.

By January 1970, the Victorian Government was finally acting. So began the Board of Inquiry into Allegations Against Members of the Victorian Police Force in Connection with Illegal Abortion Practices in the State of Victoria. It would produce two volumes, the first by Commissioner William

Kaye in 1970 and the second in 1978 by Justice Barry Beach. Seven police were named. Ford and Matthews were jailed for five years a piece and Jacobson three years. Adam was acquitted and died soon after. Peggy was never jailed. After surviving breast and pelvis cancer, she died in 2002. Her son, Peter Berman, is now a judge. He was a law clerk during the inquiry.

In 1969, Justice Cliff Menhennit found that abortion was lawfully justified where it was "necessary to preserve the physical or mental health of the woman concerned, provided that the danger involved in the abortion did not outweigh the danger which the abortion was designed to prevent."

Doctors didn't know what exactly that would mean in reality, and the price of abortions went up astronomically – from $100 to $500. We believed we could still be arrested, and with no tip-offs from corrupt police, the risks were greater.

Wanting to test the law, the abortionist campaigner Dr Wainer let it be known to police that he would be performing an abortion. Advising them of the time of the abortion, he said he would stand at his surgery door and wait for the police. The police didn't turn up. That threw open the doors for abortions in Victoria, as they could be performed without fear. I performed abortions myself but only for my own patients – no ring-ins.

The French ally

One bitterly cold Saturday morning, in 1964, a Mrs Andree Frame called as I was finishing the morning surgery. I was tired, looking forward to a cup of tea and was barely interested in taking the call.

She started by saying she was delighted to hear I was using psychoprophylaxis. She had worked with Pierre Vellay in France and started the first psychoprophylatic childbirth clinic outside Russia with Ferdinand Lamaze after which the method took its name. Vellay had written *Childbirth Without Pain*. The book was banned and seized at customs in Australia. It showed photos of women giving birth with babies' heads crowning the perineum. This inspirational book caused an outcry, yet here on the phone was a woman who had worked with the author and she wanted to meet me.

Despite my fatigue, I invited her to the surgery, and in 15 minutes the charming Mrs Frame entered my life. This French woman would spearhead tremendous changes in childbirth for Australian women. Mrs Frame had knowledge, courage and a real appreciation of the finesse required in dealing with the conservative forces in the medical profession. From the time of our meeting, until her death, we remained firm friends. She bequeathed me all the letters she had received from grateful women about their birth experiences.

Our initial conversation was an excited sharing of experiences and faith. Faith in the ability of women to give birth without the intervention of meddlesome doctors. I recounted my painful labour ward experiences where hospital staff were obstinate and mothers' wishes were ignored or worse. She described Pierre Vellay's clinic. We discussed the challenges facing us: midwifery staff attitudes towards women; getting husbands into labour wards; the stupidity of shaving; and episiotomies. Most importantly, we spoke of the experience of childbirth as a continuation of an act of love.

Mrs Frame asked me whether I would be an adviser to the newly formed Association for the Advancement of Painless Childbirth (AAPC – later the Childbirth Education Association). Readily, I agreed. She told me physiotherapists were very interested in the training program, although few midwives were interested so far. Years later, many physiotherapists concerned themselves too much with the athletics of childbirth, which led them to concede antenatal training to enlightened midwives with whom most of the training occurs today.

Mrs Frame invited June and me to a dinner in a few weeks. Little did I know that the people around that table would change the climate of birthing in Victoria and later Australia. I was the only man. Lady Phyllis Cilento, the mother of film star Diana, was present. This self-assured woman stated her commonsense opinions on childbirth and parenting. She stated them like every other person had the same view. While it *was* commonsense, she failed to grasp the struggle every day to instil this commonsense into the culture of the medical profession. It would take years of struggle.

We ended the evening with someone demonstrating easier positions for pushing in the second stage of labour. The following year, Baroness Fiona von Thyssen would become its patron.

At the first official AAPC meeting, I was again the only male and doctor present. I recall speaking about the labour ward routine and the enormous difficulty in changing this. Older midwives couldn't cope with the concept, but the younger ones were responding well. I told them of my success at converting a Catholic nun who was a sister and midwife at the Sacred Heart Hospital, to the humane principles behind psychoprophylaxis. She transferred to Geelong Hospital, introduced it there, left the religious order and had four children of her own.

I told them how some women who had trained in the method did not realise the centuries of superstition and fear they had overcome. First-time mothers often refused to believe that not all births were like their own pain and drug-free experience. Many women had become advocates of antenatal training to their friends.

Once the conference was over, I realised all the speakers spoke in generalities or anecdotes. We had no convincing studies or objective data to demonstrate this antenatal method to hardened and conservative medical "experts".

They needed medical advisors, and both I and gynaecologist and obstetrician Carl Wood stepped up. Carl would co-author *The A to Z of Pregnancy* with AAPC co-founder Dimity Reed. He would also go on to become a pioneer of in-vitro fertilisation treatment.

I looked over any articles in journals comparing the method to what was common practice in hospitals. Most articles compared the results of questionnaires. Women would assess their own degree of pain on a five-point scale. It is hardly necessary to point out how unsatisfactory this is for comparing objective criteria. If a woman is under an anaesthetic when her baby is born, she won't feel any pain, but she won't remember the birth either. I needed an analysis method that would allow me to compare psychoprophylactic childbirth to the common practice of hospitals.

I sought out many obstetricians' opinions on my study. Don Lawson showed interest but said it would be difficult, almost impossible.

"As soon as you select anything you think is objective in obstetrics, it starts to run away in the sand," Don said.

He suggested that the real effort should be in helping women cope with young babies. This was possibly true, but I was only trying to improve childbirth procedures and practice. Infant care and training would have to wait.

Another obstetrician suggested I needed 1000 deliveries for a reasonable analysis sample. It would take 10 to 15 years for a GP to deliver 1000 babies. Families, and I, could not wait for 1000 cases, I needed to find another way.

Chapter 17
The holy trinity

Pathology is the science of disease processes. It is at once a descriptive and explanatory science. Understanding this seemed to underpin any medical practice. In private practice, I was constantly reminded of the aphorism coined by medical giant Osler, whom I had discovered while studying medicine. Put simply, the aphorism is: "As is your pathology so is your practice." Osler's aphorism stands as tall as any stated by the ancients. I felt an urgency to act upon it, but to study pathology as a post-graduate required a special effort.

In another leap into the dark, I approached the Melbourne University pathology department in 1963 to ask if I could be a demonstrator. To my surprise, Associate Professor George Christie was delighted to have someone with practical experience in the department. He would later go on to become Professor of Pathology.

Belinda arranged for a physiotherapist to take my birth classes on Wednesday afternoons so I could attend the Melbourne University sessions.

In 1963, I fronted up to demonstrate histopathology to the students, which is the study of disease tissue on microscopic slides. I was excited to be once again in the stream of ideas and scared that my knowledge and ideas would not be enough. After a few weeks, I could confidently and accurately field most questions the students bowled at me.

The staff were friendly and helpful and invited me to the staff discussion and slide presentations held also in the afternoons. On one occasion I was asked to lead the discussion on acute tonsillitis. For seven years, I was thrilled to work for the pathology department.

The breadth and knowledge of people like John Hurley and Ross Anderson were amazing. John was a former RAAF medical officer, then reader at Melbourne University, but he later became Emeritus Professor of the pathology department. Ross was a founder of neuropathology in Australia and later became the department's chairman. They might disagree, but I found their thinking dialectical. Nothing was forever; always the opposite could be true. They were constantly questioning. I felt it was a privilege to have a parasitic role in the department, feeding on their knowledge.

I recall one discussion in which they – one or other or both – questioned the infectious theory of diseases. They simply said the exact mechanisms of how infections caused acute pneumonia had not been demonstrated. Their questioning, sceptical approach lives with me still.

After two years, I asked if I could do some pathological tutoring. This was a position usually reserved for pathologists in hospitals. Doctors who had made pathology their life's work. But I argued pathology was part of general practice and I used it as the basis of my general practice. Hopefully to the benefit of my patients.

By way of example, I told them of a woman patient, aged 26, who came to me after noticing an unusual and small amount of mid-cycle blood. I had given a tutorial on the diseases of the uterus some weeks before. Although it felt more cautious than necessary, I suggested I should do a diagnostic dilatation and curettage. This entailed scraping the uterus for tissue and sending this off for pathological analysis.

The suggestion was complicated from the outset as the woman was a virgin and was naturally reluctant to contemplate procedures which meant rupturing her hymen. Thankfully she agreed. The results found carcinoma of the endometrium or lining of the uterus. It led to the removal of her uterus, but she lived. Whenever I have seen her since, she has reminded me of this, but I always say it was her courage and pathology that did it. Working at Melbourne University taught me a lot of about pathology. While working there, I evolved the personal dictum of "practice, study, teach – the holy trinity". A dictum I have tried to stick to, sometimes successfully.

Taking a break

With all my tutoring, independent research, running the general practice and Belinda, in late September 1965, I needed a break.

June and I did not usually holiday together, and this time was no different. She was busy with work, study and career. With both of us working, the children – who by this stage were two, five and seven – were sometimes in the care of childminders. We also had a housekeeper.

We were living such independent lives we barely saw each other. After surgery, I would put a piece of steak on the grill or go out to a café for a meal.

To get away, I arranged for leave from the pathology department and for a locum to look after the surgery. I caught a plane for Sydney to meet a woman doctor friend with whom I had had a dalliance in Far North Queensland while on a previous holiday. Over dinner, we discussed how I should spend my break. She suggested the Northern Territory and that I should contact Ella Stack in Darwin. She would set me on the right path. I booked a motel and flew to Darwin.

Ella was a dynamic woman who seemed to know everything and everyone in Darwin. Nine years later, she was Darwin's deputy mayor when Cyclone Tracey struck, and the following year she became the mayor charged with rebuilding the city. She always was a powerhouse of energy. After I got off the plane, I headed straight for her. She told me there was a boat headed for a Melville Island mission leaving soon and I could jump on it. Within minutes, I was in a taxi headed for the wharf and was introduced to the crew. They put out a chair on the deck for me, and the captain welcomed me with a beer.

In two rushed days I had gone from Melbourne, via Sydney, to Darwin, and now I was motoring on a lugger boat, sipping beer in the sun, enjoying the sound of the waves and the cool breeze off the ocean.

The lugger called into an Aboriginal settlement and Catholic mission on Bathurst Island. The Mantiyupwi Clan are the traditional owners of the Wurrumiyanga community. The Wurrumiyanga are distinguished among other things by their burial methods, most famously the Pukumani burial poles which are installed at the burial site. Although I don't remember seeing them on this visit.

We landed in the dark, unloaded the fortnightly supplies, and went up to the mission dining room to eat with the order. The Missionaries of the Sacred Heart were a very friendly bunch, who to a man were enthusiastic and practical, although their mission to convert the locals seemed unlikely to me.

That night, the mission was called out to give the last rites to a Melville Island man, at his family's request, and the lugger crew followed on.

Bathurst Island is separated from Melville Island by Apsley Strait which is only a few hundred metres wide for most of its length. The channel's tide flowed in and out twice a day, and at that time, varied in height by 20 metres from low tide to high tide. I am unsure what global warming has done to the tide now. Back then, if the tide was running, crossing the strait was much more difficult than if the tide was slack. At that time, the tide had slackened, so we sped across in the dingy in a few minutes. We walked towards the crying to find the body lying on the ground wrapped up in a blanket surrounded by about 12 Aboriginal people wailing, both singly and sometimes in chorus. The firelight was reflected on their glistening faces. Only when one of the dozen camp dogs raced in to snap at the body did the mourning stop. The offending dog was rewarded with a shrill curse and a hit on the head with a stout stick, which seemed to be kept handy for the purpose.

Against this chorus of wailing, barking and cuffing, a priest calmly donned his stole and started Latin incantations, liberally sprinkling water from a bottle around and over the body. Once finished, he said a few words to the mourners.

"Have you had enough?" the priest asked. I would have gladly stayed but took my guidance from him. We crossed back to the mission. I was given a room, a bed and, in the morning, a huge breakfast. All offers of payment were refused and an open invitation to return "anytime" was pressed on me.

The lugger's captain waited for the tide to run north. By positioning the lugger in the middle of the channel with the motors running slowly we made good time to the next settlement, this time on Melville Island's north-west corner.

Pirlangimpi was a settlement for young Aboriginal people usually referred there by the Darwin Courts.

The priest in charge was a Father John Leary, a red-bearded, red-faced Irishman who ran a very just, but fairly tight, ship. He and about 20 Pirlangimpi community members met me when I got off the boat. Father Leary asked me a few questions, and I told him I was on holidays and was returning with the lugger. Without pausing, he asked me why I wasn't staying on the island until the lugger came back in roughly 10 days? I needed no second invitation and so began one of the highlights of my life.

Again, I was given a spartan but adequate room and got about in my holiday dress of shorts and sandals. Joining Father Leary and me at mealtimes was an Englishman who was trying to grow cashew nuts on the island and a married couple volunteering on the settlement. We all ate in a small fly-proof dining room. Two older Aboriginal girls were the cooks, and they always seemed to have great smiles on their faces and giggled a lot.

At lunch that day, Father Leary asked me if I would like to do some fishing as the cool store needed replenishing. Recalling my love of fishing even as a child freezing on the Geraldton Wharf, I headed out with others in two motorised dinghies that anchored over a shallow portion of Apsley Strait. From the shallows, we let the boats drift over a large hole in the centre, which was 50 to 100 feet deep. The fish seemed to be waiting for the privilege of jumping onto my hook. Everyone in the two boats hauled in fish. At the tug of the line, we brought up some enormous fish. So deep was the hole that when the fish were brought to the surface their swim bladders expanded with gases under the altered pressure and popped through their mouths – a sort of fishy bends. This, I later discovered, is known as barotrauma and occurs when a fish is hauled out of the water from more than 30 feet. We caught grouper, snapper, dewfish, cod and other varieties I couldn't name at weights up to 20 pounds.

The next morning Father Leary told me a group of Aboriginal people had invited me to collect oysters on the reef. We all went down in the back of a small utility truck and came across beds after bed of huge oysters. These were broken off and collected in kerosene tins – the most delicious oysters I had eaten. I have a photo of the Aboriginal people around a fire at twilight cooking some of their oysters. It captures some of the magic of the place but does show how well the Aboriginal people blended into the setting. It was theirs and it was right.

For three days we ate oyster stew, oyster patties and oyster salad.

Father Leary told me some of the senior men wanted to take me out spearing barramundi at night. They carried guns in case we saw a crocodile. At dusk, we set out in two canoes with outboard motors and travelled away from Apsley Strait down a side waterway which was lined with mangrove trees. We cut the motors and glided along under the overhanging leaves using the roots and trunks to push the boats along. One man shone a torch on the bank and spotted the outline of a large fish, motionless, near a submerged root. The leader gave me a three-pronged spear and told me to aim about six inches below, where I imagined the fish to be. Over the centuries, the Aboriginal people had worked out the necessary correction to the refractive error of the water.

I aimed, lunged and caught the fish on one prong. Not for me the triumphant lifting of a wriggling barramundi lunch. I was told to keep pressing it into the bank while a nervous young lad went over the side to grab the fish. I thought this very brave as the bank was lined with crocodile holes. He missed the fish but soon after we saw on the surface two red beads which glowed in the torchlight. I was handed a rifle. The ecological reality of crocodile shooting was not then an issue, so I fired and shot at the three crocodiles, and I believe struck them. I may say, they are the only crocodiles I will be shooting in my lifetime.

We chugged through the night along the broad, moonlit waterways and tied up where we began, welcomed home by half the settlement.

After 10 days of bushwalking and fishing, I became aware of how carefully these Aboriginal people walked through the bush – it was like watching a dance. Each foot was carefully placed, then the other lifted and glided into the next position. The action is relaxed and graceful, and despite the apparent lack of pace, that style allows the Aboriginal people to cover the ground quickly.

On the day I left, I inspected the old ruins of a soldier settlement. The bricks were still in remarkable repair despite lying there since 1828. As with all forts, I sensed the loneliness of those manning the battlements looking for an enemy that never came. These buildings were indeed decaying edifices to man's constant paranoia.

I returned to Melbourne feeling fresh and excited to see my family again and bearing gifts. On the day of my return, I answered a call from a wife whose husband had collapsed on the toilet. I told her I thought he had a cerebrovascular incident. I had treated him for hypertension for years. When I arrived about five minutes later, his breathing and paralysis confirmed my suspicions. We waited until the ambulance arrived.

Back home, the excitement of my return had dampened.

Dad was back working seemed to be the attitude and interest was low in my trip and my life other than one to two comments and questions.

On Monday, Belinda returned to work and wanted to know everything – where I stayed, what I did, who I met. I relived the holiday with her and not my family.

The patients wanted details too and parroted media platitudes on Australia's poor treatment of Aboriginal people over the decades.

While I was on Melville Island, the coup aimed at the rising Communist Party of Indonesia – Partai Komunis Indonesia (PKI) – had taken place on September 30 and October 1, 1965. In this incident, the PKI was blamed for the assassination of six Indonesian generals. In the military power vacuum, General Suharto stepped in, declared the PKI had instigated the coup and set about purging the communists. An estimated 500,000 people were killed.

The papers were full of the massacres. Indonesian people were denouncing others for their left-wing views and those denounced were shot out of hand. The extent of the CIA's involvement was not realised until years later, but it reeked of American meddling. Later we would know that the US ambassador at the time, Marshall Green, acted as the CIA's architect for right-wing coups in foreign countries. He presented his diplomatic credentials to the Indonesian Government in June – just months before the blood bath – and to the Australian Government in 1973. His arrival was an ominous sign anywhere, as Edward Gough Whitlam discovered when Governor-General Sir John Kerr orchestrated his own bloodless coup.

Deceiving dalliance

Back at work, I was working as hard as ever, and June was as distant as ever. She told me very little of her plans, the children, or what was happening at Princes Hill High School. These discussions she reserved for her parents, particularly Saul.

Belinda was waiting when I returned, and once my wife made it clear there would be no improvement in our marital life, Belinda and I resumed our relationship.

I hated the clandestine nature of affairs and, although there was no one else in my life, within a short time, I broke it off with Belinda. If my marriage was going to fail, I wanted it to fail on its own merit, not because of another woman. She took this very badly, developed a migraine, felt faint and lay down sobbing on my marital bed.

Eventually, June came in and I fessed up to the affair but told her I wanted it to stop. A life of deception was not for me, even if our marriage was failing, I told her. June claimed she was shocked. Even now, I cannot understand it. She offered me no comfort in bed, no warmth in the house, stated she was not going to be a cook, told me I should have married someone else and our casual conversations were down to bedrock. She had told me to find a mistress and I had. Where was the element of surprise?

Between the tears and the shock, I decided "bugger the lot of them" and went for a run around Princes Park. Running provided me with headspace. I determined that I should move my family to another house so, if June and I did separate, I would have the surgery to work in and use for a home.

I returned home to find Saul, Mary and June all distraught.

"Why, but why?" cried her mother.

Through their rose-tinted glasses, the Factors saw June as a perfect wife and mother. How could I explain to a doting mother that her daughter was inadequate as a marriage partner for me? I did try though, but Mary kept saying: "But why when we have been so good to you?"

Many times I have thought of why this situation was doomed. Yes, my in-laws had assisted to help me buy the practice, but they also disrupted my sense of family. By claiming a close relationship with my children, without the responsibility for their upkeep, Mary and Saul effectively pushed me aside as a father. By Saul maintaining his very special relationship with this daughter, he was usurping my role as my wife's main companion. For my part, I could not return to the dark and financially struggling times I had come from. I was compelled to make my medical practice my priority to support myself and my family, but this kept me from them too. I supported June too in her career choice as a teacher, but – in 1965 – I felt she neglected her dual role of providing a home for our children and myself.

The solution to separate was simple. Easy to say. When one breaks an intimate relationship, trust is shattered and bitterness is generated. In an intimate relationship, two people bare their inner being because they like or perhaps love each other; to ultimately reject one's inner core and deem it unworthy of that affection is crushing. When you cover up your rejected core, the seeds of bitterness are sown, and it is easy to adopt a defensive-aggressive stance to protect yourself.

Over the next months, we looked for a house to put one suburb between the surgery and our new house. We settled on a house in Ivanhoe, which I thought was inconveniently designed, but June liked it. I had the foresight to put this house in my name, having a gut feeling that the surgery – which had been put in June's name – was going to be the source of a lot of heartburn.

The eldest two children went to Ivanhoe Primary and Sylvie continued at Coburg Kindergarten. I took her every day. June picked her up at lunchtime. Moving only meant I saw less and less of June. My day started at 9am and I rarely finished my evening surgery before 10pm. Then there were the hospitals to visit. This stretched life between surgery and home. It lasted about a year before I could stand it no longer.

Proving it

My practice was busy with obstetrics patients, but I somehow felt compelled to get Australian medical practitioners, nurses and midwives to take psychoprophylaxis in childbirth seriously. The only way to get them to change was to show them hard evidence.

Politically, at the time, hostility towards psychoprophylaxis in childbirth was intense.

It could be argued that the book I based my obstetric work on *Painless Childbirth through Psychoprophylaxis*, was written out of political and economic necessity in 1954. Post-World War II Russia saw the economy in the doldrums, medicine and medical practitioners in short supply, and the nation's population needed to rebuild. Put simply, Russia needed a cheaper way to have babies, but it would have been useless to suggest women have babies without drugs if it did not offer a way to cope with the pain.

French obstetrician Ferdinand Lamaze had brought the method over from Russia to France. He was said to have broken down and wept on viewing the humane way Russian women were giving birth. He and Vellay established a Paris clinic with Union of Metallurgists of the Seine and found themselves in the centre of a national controversy between the right and left of politics. Both men were brought before the Council of the Order of Physicians and were twice cleared. In 1954, Pope Pius XII blessed the method, and there was an instant acceptance of psychoprophylaxis throughout the Catholic world. It took a French National Assembly another two years to eventually decree it was an acceptable method of childbirth in France.

Politically, in 1960s Australia, hospitals and medical practitioners were as hostile as the French. They resisted any change which they thought might be a threat to their power in the labour ward. Parent groups supported the method but had only impressions and anecdotes to argue the case. Neither of these cut any ice with hard-nosed doctors and nurses. Women were yet to realise their power as consumers.

I had been often urged to evaluate what I had been doing, but how do you quantify the bonding of a family through education, training and the birth experience? This is nigh on impossible to quantify in a hard-headed medical way.

By 1965, I had 120 deliveries for which adequate hospital records existed, and I started analysing my delivery data. This was not the 1000 births some had suggested I needed, but it was a sizable cohort.

I employed a young woman I knew called Maria Varrenti whom I had met during my university days. Maria collected the results of 100 birth cases from a large public hospital. Other than my patients, none were trained in psychoprophylaxis. Maria proved a most skilful negotiator with hospital administrations.

We could have matched the two data groups by age and number of births etc, but I was working in a busy practice and did not have a team of researchers at my disposal. I did not feel this criticism was enough to abandon the study.

I set out the comparative indices I intended to use and all the information on huge sheets of paper. I would compare the length of labour; the amount of analgesics given; whether forceps were used; episiotomies cut; whether resuscitation was necessary; and whether a caesarean section was the method of delivery. I tried to correlate these where I felt they were mutually dependent. It was an enormous amount of work, taking close to two years to complete.

Maria and I discussed the results and more over cups of coffee. She was a very intelligent daughter of an Italian migrant couple. She took on the hostile hospital environment and interviewed, analysed and collated material that alone would have taken me years to do. She shared my enthusiasm for the work and for what was being revealed. This intellectual compatibility led to the beginning of an affair.

By 1967, I submitted the article to Carl Wood, one of the medical advisers of AAPC who would also go on to become an in-vitro fertilisation guru. Carl was organising the 1967 international conference of obstetrics and gynaecology. He insisted I present the paper at the September conference.

I went up to Sydney and met an extraordinary variety of people. The vast majority were men. Only the Soviet Union's delegation had roughly the same proportion of men as women. I tried to attend as many sessions as possible, but conference fatigue took over after a couple of days. I went to one lecture by a Russian who I thought was delivering the talk in his native tongue. It was later pointed out that she was speaking in English.

I gave my lecture on a Thursday morning to a crowded smaller hall in the Regent Hotel. I showed slides presenting my results and discussed, in limited terms, the role of the husband.

After the talk, a Charles University professor from Prague congratulated me and told me his results were very similar. He invited me to visit Czechoslovakia as it was then. A Leningrad doctor told me he was interested in what I had said and was surprised I had heard of Pavlov. No Australian doctors came up to me afterwards

On every comparative scale, the women trained in the psychoprophylactic method were superior – the outcome was better for the woman every time. In modern times, natural childbirth with minimal pain and no obstetrical interference seemed an obvious preferred outcome, but back then it was a revelation.

Family tethers

When I returned to Melbourne, my affair with Maria, was definitely on, and I was officially separated from June.

Maria and I came from culturally different backgrounds but were both strong personalities. She had married a man so she could leave home. She then divorced and remarried and divorced the same man before meeting me. She said planning weddings relieved the boredom of returning home to her parents.

Belinda was distraught at me taking up with Maria and I had to let her go. She eventually remarried. After losing a good secretary, I then had a series of others, eventually settling on a woman called Charlotte, who was strongly anti-abortion, until she became pregnant to her fiancé. She said she had to rethink her stance, but I suggested she merely get married early and tell everyone the baby was early.

When my family had moved out of the surgery's house to Ivanhoe, June arranged for John and Glenys Thurgood, whom she knew through Princes Hill High School, to move in. He was a radical teacher produced by decades of reactionary Australian governments. Glenys and John were very kind and gave me breakfast in return for paying little rent.

With nowhere to live, I camped at the surgery, showering there and sleeping on the examination bed. My clothes were kept in the boot of my car and my other meals were taken in cafés. This was a diabolical situation. I needed a place to bring my children, so I rented a flat in Carlton at 20 Bowen Crescent, close to my beloved running track around Princes Park.

Although I was not sleeping at the Ivanhoe family home, I saw more of my children, aged five, seven and nine, than ever before. I saw them at the dedicated times of afternoons on Wednesdays and Saturdays, and that time was not diluted by Saul and Mary.

After 10 years of a fairly restrictive marriage, I was now free but felt tethered to my children, and I welcomed their claim. Our afternoons in the flat were among my happiest times during my "gay bachelor" existence.

The kids would stay for tea, and Naomi, Sylvie and I would dance at the flat in Carlton. I would play chess with Ian. It would become obvious when I would be losing because Naomi would say, "Did you start off on the wrong foot again, Dad?" (Very funny!) Ian was about 10 years old at the time. I ended up joining a long line of Ian's defeated chess adversaries. He became the nation's first Australian-raised chess grandmaster, competing in 14 Chess Olympiads, as Australia's number one player.

I would take the children out for drives in the country, and once we camped in the bush overnight. We lit fires, boiled billies and played football. I felt close to my children at these times.

One year, my sister Rona and I took Ian to show him all the places I had worked at out West. Places like Bulyee welcomed me as if I had never been away. Every morning on that trip, Ian would wake me with a chessboard. He was training like any Olympic champion might.

On Christmas morning, 1968, I travelled with presents to a Sorrento beach house where the children and June were staying. Arriving before they woke, June asked me to stay. The three children were then awake and insisted I stay. As Saul and Mary were coming down, I stayed for breakfast and left.

Sadly, I underestimated the wrench I would experience in leaving my children when I left the marital home. While relieved to be away from the Factors, my anguish at being away from my children hurt.

Back at the Princes Hill flat that I had rented, I frequently had nightmares about leaving the children that left me in an anxious sweat. In a recurring nightmare, I ascended scaffolding to rescue one or other of my children. They were perched precariously close to the edge. As I stepped out closer, the child moved closer and closer to the edge. I'm sure I woke up screaming, but I couldn't stop the dreams.

Ending with Maria

Tired and torn apart, sometimes I became impotent. Maria thought I was rejecting her, and this led to a bitter onslaught. My perception of myself and what it was to be a man – always at the ready – took a beating during this time. The men's liberation movement had not yet found me, and the strict rules of masculinity were wholeheartedly accepted.

After Glenys and John moved out of the back of the surgery, Maria moved in with her two young girls, Elly and Lizzie, for a few weeks. Maria wanted me to live there too, but I could no longer live so close to the surgery.

In 1968, Maria and I moved into a house at Brown Street, Heidelberg, which had previously been her marital home. She was not working and was grateful for the support I gave her, which allowed her to stay home and care for her two daughters.

It was not to last. A blended family and two strong personalities could never work. It was an awful, bickering time. Before the year was out, we had parted ways. It was the beginning of a dry, lonely and mucky, mucky time.

Chapter 18
Medical Officer of Health

Back in 1963 I was running my private practice from early morning to late at night, while working at the university's pathology department and raising a family. Some would say that was enough. But in that same year I took on another job. At once fascinating and full of humanity, this work would continue well into the 1970s.

It began when a health inspector I knew from Coburg City Council came into my clinic and asked me to apply for the role of medical officer of health for the city. The inspector's name was Frank Ford. We had worked on some infectious disease issues in the past. Frank later became the mayor of Northcote City Council and had a street named after him.

The job paid £600, but after a few years this rose to $1000 with decimal currency and inflation. Frank and I worked with the chief health inspector, Matt Howden, along with a third man whose name I don't recall.

A local doctor was unhappy with my appointment and wrote to the council proclaiming I was unfit to hold the chief medical officer's position because I was a communist. Thirteen years after losing my first professional job in the public service and I was still being dogged for my political beliefs. The GP was a very staid conservative who just wanted to follow centuries-old British traditions rather than live in the present. But I was battle-hardened against such types, as there were so many of them found in obstetrics. Frank Ford, to his credit, said my beliefs would not stop me fulfilling my duties. The local doctor maintained a grudge.

The medical officer's job was to follow up all infectious diseases in Coburg and to give immunisation injections. The other role was to investigate any production and transportation issues related to food and water in the city.

This job came with significant "rights of entry" powers, which meant that I could inspect a building and its contents at any time. Occasionally, this led me to sensitive materials, like the time I was given the site plans to Pentridge Prison.

The plans came to me in 1966, after a boy got sick when he swam in the Merri Creek, next to the jail. This led to an outbreak of gastroenteritis in the community. I suspected raw sewage was pouring from a prison outlet straight into the creek. We contacted the prison administration and they invited Matt Howden and me to investigate and make recommendations. While doing so, I was handed the plans and layout to the prison, which included drains – a traditional route of escape for prisoners throughout the centuries. What some inmates would have given to get a hold of those drawings!

The prison's original sewerage set-up was basic to say the least. Old quarry rocks were used to "filter" the discharge, which flowed over the rocks. The solid matter remained on or near the rocks before it dried out and dispersed. While the prison's sewerage system had been updated and attached to the Melbourne Metropolitan Board of Works mains, there was still a glitch – not all parts of the prison had toilets – and offenders working the prison farm had to make do with a bucket. One young inmate admitted emptying a toilet bucket of excreta into the storm water drain, which discharged into the creek.

The prison governor decreed all farm worker waste should be deposited into earth pits treated with lime until a new toilet block could be built. As a result of the investigation, the MMBW also had to divert some sections of the stormwater drains into a pond, which was part of the old quarry and original sewerage plant.

The prison never asked for the plans and I never offered them back.

The health inspectors and I became good friends with the Pentridge authorities, especially as the prison was close to the council and my surgery. Prison warders were occasionally patients, and when the prison doctor went on holidays or was indisposed, I was called in to see sick prisoners or warders.

On one occasion, in about 1970, I was called in to see a prisoner. He was lying on a stretcher with his arms locked to his sides, as rigid as a board. I'd never seen a case like it.

"Oh God, he looks pretty crook," I told the warder. The guard asked me what I thought they should do.

"I think he ought to go into hospital," I said.

The bugger lying on the stretcher then winked at me. Though I knew I'd been duped, I sent him off to hospital just the same. Hospital is a bit

215

of a relief from being locked up in a cell for 16 hours a day. This prisoner needed a holiday.

Another patient was a guard terrified of going inside a cell occupied by Ronald Ryan, who was to become the last person legally hanged in Victoria, in 1967. Ryan had shot and killed a Pentridge guard during an escape from the prison in 1965. The guard I was treating suffered extreme anxiety, so I prescribed some time off to settle his nerves.

The font of the problem

When there was an outbreak of infectious hepatitis in the area in 1966, I traced the worst of it to a school in Pascoe Vale – the Blessed Oliver Plunkett Roman Catholic school. All but four cases had occurred in the junior school.

The parish priest, Father Thomas Keogh, was angry at our visit and declared to me: "They are all bigots down at the council." He claimed our visit was sectarianism rather than a health assessment.

Using our powers of entry, we investigated. During mealtimes, the children did not seem to be sharing anything in a way that I considered a health risk. At playtime, I looked for other clues as to the mode of transmission. At the bell, every one of the children rushed from the classroom to the toilet and then had a drink from the tap, each one using their hand to clear off the last person's spit before putting their mouth around the bubble-top nozzle.

Frank Ford and I inspected the toilets. They were filthy. With no toilet paper, the kids were taking the dags from their bums and streaking them on the walls. There was no soap. At best, the kids were rinsing their hands before using those same hands to "clear off" the germs from the bubble tap. Gotcha.

It turned out that Father Keogh was at loggerheads with the caretaker. After the source of the problem was found, toilet paper and soap were restored.

Knowing the source of the hepatitis spread was not enough. I felt that the bubble tap designs were faulty, and could lead to outbreaks elsewhere. I set about designing a new tap to prevent the drinker from putting their mouth directly on the nozzle. It seemed to me that if you had to turn your head and cheek to the side, this would be achieved. My design was a beauty. Frank Ford had a contact at a plumbing company, John McIlwraith Industries. The company thanked me for my design but came up with a better one – with a square guard that rounded from the base of the nozzle in a wave motion. In a worldwide public health gesture, the company never patented the design, which I thought was rather good of them. The company made millions of these new taps, and other designs soon followed.

The McIlwraith design is in the article I wrote for the *Medical Journal of Australia*. More than 70 letters poured in, from 20 different countries, requesting my research. One South Australian politician thanked me for my contribution to public health, and hospitals including the Royal Adelaide Children's Hospital (now the Women's and Children's Hospital) asked for copies of my research.

My local nemesis, the doctor who had complained about my appointment, was not impressed. I went to a local Australian Medical Association meeting, where he was heard to say, dubiously, "He thinks he's got the answer to infectious hepatitis …".

All I could do was roll my eyes at his closed-minded attitude.

Childcare changes for the better

As part of my role as medical officer of health, I needed to inspect childcare centres for cleanliness and ensure the correct child-to-carer ratios were in place. Courtesy of the bush telegraph, once I had been to one centre, word would travel from one centre to the next: "He's on the prowl." By the time I arrived at the next centre, it would be spotless after the forewarning.

Early in my Coburg council career, I had a notice of infectious hepatitis, this time in a childcare centre in Bell Street. This was run by a Mrs Goulburn, who was in her late 50s. She had three or four centres in the municipality, employing girls aged 15 or 16 years old.

"No, you can't come in," said the young girl who answered the door to chief inspector Matt Howden and me.

"Let us in or I'll bring the police around," I replied. "I have the right to enter any premise if I think there is a threat to the health of the community."

"Well," said the girl, "I have to ring Mrs Goulburn."

"You ring her," I said.

The situation was resolved, and we were let in. The place was filthy. There was a smell about the building. There were dirty nappies in corners. There were 28 kids in the centre, but in the fridge there was only a loaf of bread, half a pumpkin and some peanut butter.

"This place is closed down. I'm closing it down," I ordered.

That night, the mayor Salvatore "Sam" Gandolfo, came to see me in the clinic.

"Look," he began, "Mrs Goulburn is a friend of mine. She is doing a real service to the people. Mothers leave their children there so they can go to work."

I understood their plight, but I had to hold firm. "I'm prepared to go back," I told him. "Whenever she cleans it up, I'll go back and give it the okay."

He replied: "Could you go back in two days?"

I told him I would give Mrs Goulburn one day. But no, the mayor insisted, she would need two days to do the job properly.

When I went back, the childcare centre was immaculate. It had been repainted and the staff had clean uniforms on. It was an incredible turnaround.

This incident got me to thinking the council could, and should, have been running childcare centres. Without the need to return a profit, they could operate efficiently and would adhere to stricter health measures than private centres.

The idea was to build a centre for a certain number of children and, if more children turned up on the day than the centre could cope with, the overflow could go to vetted families registered to offer family day care. This way, mothers could have faith that their child would have somewhere to be cared for while they worked or studied.

In 1968, I started the Coburg Day Nursery Fund Committee to raise money to do it. A few people attended the first meeting, including one lady knitting socks. I calculated the value of socks if we sold them to pay for the centre. It would take until 2080 to open at that rate.

At the Victorian Professional Cross Country Club, I came into contact with ultra-marathon runner George Perdon – a world and Australian record holder for running the 30 miles and 150 miles. In 1969, I asked him to run around Coburg for 24 hours to help us raise money for the childcare centre. We set up a caravan and set out a course around Coburg. The Alfred Hospital would do blood analysis – the glucose, blood elements, red and white blood cell counts and neutrophils. I was most concerned to ensure he remained hydrated.

In search of sponsors, I rang Carlton & United Breweries. I said to them: "Do you know your business supplies all the fluid replacements for professional runners in Victoria?" Which was true. After every run, the blokes would scull one beer after another. Alas, the company'syearly allocation for donations had just been used up.

Without a blush, I rang a local dairy to tell them that professional runners drank milk to replace their fluids after a run. Again, the cupboard was bare – the dairy's budget for donations was already spent.

I also tried my luck with the Coburg Chamber of Commerce to no avail. Fortune refused to smile on us. We did not raise one penny.

Undeterred, George, then aged 43, ran the route. Starting out in 36-degree heat, he completed 143 miles in 24 hours, nearly setting a world record.

I did produce an interesting paper on the impact of an endurance performance in long-distance running, using the samples of blood and urine taken from George during the run. In fact, these jabs and expulsions cost poor George the world record for a 24-hour run at the time.

Analysing the data collected, I discovered his heart rate went from 24 beats per minute before the run to 42 beats by the 117-mile mark, with similar results for blood pressure. I had other findings related to the heat generated and expended in his body and the amount of fluid he took in compared to his output. He drank an orange juice mixture, a glucose mixture and Sustagen. George took in 7.28 litres of this fluid, but his total urinary output was much less, only 1.71 litres. He lost 11.5 pounds (5.2 kilograms), which is the equivalent of 5.52 litres, so the total loss in litres over the 24-hour period was approximately 11.09 litres, plus the insensible loss from respiration.

The paper was presented at an international sports medicine conference in Melbourne. The organisation asked me to submit it to a journal, which I did, but I never followed up whether it was published. George came along to the presentation but sat in the crowd. One bloke, being a bit of a smart arse, asked in a nasally voice, "What motivation would a man have for running 24 hours?"

To which I replied: "Ask George. He's here."

George stood up and answered: "Well, I thought it would be a help. Perce asked me if I would run 24 hours, and I said, 'what's it for?' He said to get a childcare centre. So, I did. I ran the 24."

George got a standing ovation. It was well deserved. I thought he was just marvellous – a very modest man.

We continued to dream of having the childcare centre. It became a reality when Labor's Gough Whitlam came to power and, in 1973, introduced the Australian Assistance Plan, designed to support urban and rural projects for a social good. The Coburg Children's Centre was built with a grant of $80,000 – and a lot of knitted socks – in Bell Street, Coburg, not far from the town hall and my old surgery.

Responding to poverty

Whenever there was a case of an infectious disease in the Coburg area, I was required to attend to ensure the individual family was safe and of no risk to the community. In 1972, I received a notice that there was an Italian man in Fairfield Infectious Diseases Hospital whose address was listed as Coburg.

The family had started their journey in Switzerland and come to Australia on a boat from Marseilles. On the way, the father had developed typhoid fever, which was common in the 1960s among migrants travelling on boats.

They had already suffered so much on the journey, and the wife and three children were staying at a house in Railway Parade, Coburg. It was a bitterly cold winter's day when I arrived with chief health inspector Matt Howden at the house.

The door was opened by a child aged about seven years old. She had a thin dress and an oversized jumper, which was in desperate need of a wash. In her hand she held half a loaf of bread, and as we were speaking to her, she was breaking off pieces to give to the younger two siblings. It was the only food in the house. It was a terrible sight to behold.

"What's happened? Where is your mum?" I asked.

As we were reassuring the girl we meant no harm, the mother arrived. Returning from visiting her husband in Fairfield, she was frightened at the sight of authorities in her home. We assured her that we were only there to take a look, and check that no one else had typhoid.

"Where are your warm clothes?" I asked.

"Oh, we haven't gotten any," she replied.

"What about blankets?" I asked.

She pointed me to threadbare covers on the beds in the next room. The rundown house was rented to the family based on their future work and payment opportunities. It was at the very lowest end of the rental market. The situation was dire. All I could think was "you poor bastards". I could not bear the thought of the poverty of this family.

I knew a Mr and Mrs Sinclair in nearby Baxter Street, so I knocked on

220

their door to ask if they might take some soup around for the family. This is what people did in the Depression years. I remembered my mother in Geraldton always having soup ready for people who turned up hungry at the door. The Sinclairs had been through the Depression and were happy to provide big bowls of soup for the kids and mother that night. They brought other food too.

The Herald newspaper was running a blanket appeal at the time, so I thought they might do something for this family in such clear need. I called a reporter and he agreed to run a specific appeal.

To bring a bit of gravitas to the story, I called the Italian consulate in Melbourne and spoke to the consulate-general.

"You've got a compatriot here who's really suffering. What about coming out?" I said.

"Oh no, we haven't got time do that. I've got to go to a reception," he replied.

"That's bad luck," I said, "because *The Herald*'s coming to take the photos."

"Well, look, I might be about to fit that in. What time is it?" The consular officials were suddenly in like Flynn – heading out for the photo, and making a contribution to the fund for the family in distress.

The Herald ran the picture and story, and within 24 hours the family's home was choc-a-block with clothes, food, whitegoods and Christ knows what else. The house owner even gave them six months rent-free. Money poured in too. The reporter had done a terrific job.

The response overwhelmed the family and me.

The father was soon out of hospital and, through the generosity of Melburnians, the family had enough money to open a fish and chip shop in Broadmeadows.

Contact tracing

During the worldwide COVID-19 pandemic that began in 2020, Australians got to know their state and federal chief health officers quite well. While health officers tended to advise governments behind the scenes, these officials were front and centre during the pandemic.

When criticism rose about contact tracing and the virus seeping out of quarantine hotels, I felt for Victoria's chief health officer, Professor Brett Sutton.

Contact tracing is one of the hardest parts of the job. In 1972, we had one case of cholera in which a man arrived by plane while infected. Coburg's health department was given the job of tracing all his contacts and following them up. In 24 hours, he had made contact with 70 people. We got in touch with as many of these people as we could, and they were all well, but it was a difficult task.

In local government at that time, a medical officer's position was sort of elastic – the more you wanted to do, the more you could find to do. The more I investigated, the more I found.

In my life, I have found that you can always do something more. You can always fit one more task in. Having taken on the role of medical officer of health on top of my duties as local GP, I was still an advisor to the Childbirth Education Association. Along with my psychoprophylaxis classes, I also had my Melbourne University work, and would later complete an arts degree. To unwind at night, I played folk records and drank red wine in the quiet of the evening.

I think it was my training as a doctor that drove me to do more. I was very conscious of the obligation in medicine to respond. If somebody says, "Look, I've got a pain in the gut," then no matter what time of day it is, a doctor will respond. That sense of obligation affected me.

My year-in-review reports to the council covered everything from immunisations and infectious diseases to baby births and deaths, as well as the childcare centre and a family planning centre. It was busy but rewarding work. Despite the impost on my time, I continued with it until 1975, when I took a leave of absence and later resigned. I had found a new way to live and work – this time in New Guinea.

Chapter 19
Lonely but enriching times

On the homefront, after leaving Maria and still missing my chlidren, 1968 was a tough time for me.

Around this time, I was once offered a chance to go to Antarctica for work but turned it down because I could not bear to be away from my children for months on end as was required.

Briefly, I rented a different flat in the same block in Bowen Crescent but then moved to a flat in Stranger Street, that odd little street between Park Street and Brunswick Road that affords northbound Royal Parade drivers a right-hand turn into Brunswick Road. I lived in Stranger Street for 12 months from the end of 1968.

To reduce my stress and fill my time, I did a hell of a lot of running. Having started when I felt lumpish at the tramways, in 1953, I was running around Princes Park four to five times a week until the point of exhaustion or cramp. I found the last 200 metres were always the ones that killed you. After an evening run, I would return to drink red wine and listen to records.

Running became a rhythm in the day, and then an addiction. With running you first have to get your breathing regular and concentrate on your stride. Once you have your rhythm up, the longer you can do it, the fitter you are. I would get into the zone and run.

It was during these runs that I met Ken "Crusher" Webb, the aforementioned Carlton police detective, in 1962. I was running at Princes Park when he jogged up beside me. We got to chatting and he asked if I would like to join the Victorian Professional Cross Country Club. He said if you won a race you could win £20, which was all the encouragement I needed.

Ken was a slim bloke who worked as an actor and stuntman. Famously, he was the double for Mick Jagger when the Rolling Stones singer played Ned Kelly in the 1970 film of the same name. So, for the film, the policeman stuntman was hanged in Old Melbourne Gaol. Even though his neck was protected, he said it was "bloody awful", as every part of his body ached from the hangman's drop. He was sore for a long time afterwards.

In another sideline, Ken was in charge of a boys' home. He took the boys out running, which wasn't always that successful. He was also a professional wrestler and would emerge in the ring with a rose between his teeth. A real character.

The cross-country running club ran on roads in Melbourne suburbs. They ran pretty fast and I had to pick up my pace a bit. Many of them were detectives battling with their weight and trying to get fit. I was able to keep up with them and eventually won the Leo Shanahan-sponsored National Studley Park Championship, a race over 10,000 metres. I also got a second in an eight-mile and a 20-mile race.

In 1967, I was awarded the Most Meritorious run in a marathon. The prize was for the runner who completed the Beach Road marathon in the most valiant fashion – no matter how painful. And it was very painful. I completed the 20 miles, leaving from St Kilda, without too much trouble, but a marathon is 26 miles and the last four felt nearly impossible.

I went out in good time, turned around, and was coming back when I hit a wall. Unfortunately, that metaphorical wall was just outside a pub, and someone offered me a beer, which I had to refuse. How I ached for that beer. I could barely keep my legs going, but I dared not stop able to walk or run.

I collapsed at the finish line and was awarded a silver plate for my agony. The trophy has two spelling mistakes, including one calling my run "meretricious", which is essentially calling me a prostitute. My fellow runners were good athletes but terrible spellers.

In 1968, I was entered in the Grampian Stakes Two-Mile race at the Stawell Gift, but had to withdraw as Ian was in Fairfield Hospital after an asthma attack.

Studious times

Around this time, my secretary, Beryl, left to have her baby. I was again on the hunt for a new helper. As I was still working in the pathology department, I thought there might be someone suitable at the university, so I advertised on the student noticeboards. It was this fateful action that saw Mary MacDonald walk into my life in about November, 1969.

Mary was studying law. She seemed perfect: professional, proficient and attractive to boot. She was very bright and seemed interested in intellectual pursuits. She wanted to work full-time and said she would fit in her university work around the surgery.

Mary and I worked alongside each other professionally, but I was attracted to her. Though I found her delightful, I did not broach the possibility of a relationship.

Earlier in 1969, during my emotionally lonely time, I fancied myself a law degree and enrolled at Melbourne University. To weed out timewasters, the university required me to enrol in two arts subjects before I could take up a place in law. I enrolled in British history and politics subjects. I realised almost instantly that I loved studying arts subjects. Mary, who had by now changed to the arts faculty, convinced me that I would find the intellectual stimulus I was seeking in humanities subjects. I abandoned my law pursuits for Australian history, English and sociology. I graduated from arts in 1979.

One of my favourite pieces of study was an analysis of Victorian parliamentary debates. I was aware that the Australian Labor Party had its roots in the Queensland shearers' strike of 1891, but I wanted to know whether there was any influence on its formation in parliament. I found that in order to claim a seat in the Victorian Legislative Council, you needed an income of £1000 a year or £10,000 in land. You also needed to be in the colony before 1848. These rules were designed to exclude working people. The taxation system favoured those of the same ilk as those on the council. The Legislative Assembly was more egalitarian, made up of professionals and small farmers and men who arrived post-1848 and made their fortunes.

I analysed the debates to see whether they voted as a bloc on some issues. I found townspeople often voted together, but the debates and alliances were hard to follow. Alhough I enjoyed it and received a good mark, I don't believe I discovered anything much.

In the tropics

After two years helping in the pathology department, I was made a tutor at Melbourne University. A few years later, in 1969, the University of Papua New Guinea, then in its infancy, made a request for a Melbourne University lecturer to provide a 10-week lecture series on cancers. While I had rejected Antarctica as too long away from Naomi, Ian and Sylvie, 10 weeks would be bearable.

My trip to Port Moresby in 1970 gave me the work-travel bug. It was an unbelievable experience. I stayed in a donga, a portable hut-type room, and bought a motor scooter to get around.

Continuing with my running, I sweated like a pig as I ran around the PNG university's oval. I soon found my students wanted to train with me. I can't tell you how much I enjoyed my 10 weeks here. The trouble is, I've enjoyed everywhere I've worked.

Two weeks after I arrived, the fourth-year medical students went on strike. They were objecting to their timetable, which allowed 10 hours of psychology lectures but only four hours of pathology. They wanted more pathology. The students asked me to speak on their behalf at a meeting of staff.

"Six hours of psychology is more than enough," I told the psychology lecturer. "I was a psychologist. I graduated in Western Australia. I know it, and I taught in Melbourne at the psych department. And it's not worth teaching."

The psychology lecturer burst into tears.

I thought it best to shut up at this point. In the end, the students got an extra two hours of pathology and a bit less psychology.

My students in Port Moresby were a mixed bag. There was one ecclesiastical gentleman who was a trainee and wanted to do medicine to enhance his contribution to society.

One bloke, Eli, whose surname escapes me, was so shy that he couldn't look at me when he was addressing me. I asked him to prepare his paper on inflammation and he read it without once looking up. Years later, in 1976, I returned to find he had passed his exams and taken higher medicine exams in Australia. He asked me to accompany him on his ward rounds. Looking me in the eye, he carefully described the pathology of each patient. It was a proud moment for us both. He also took me to meet his parents and family at their village in Pari. Just south of Port Moresby, Pari has huts on stilts over the water. His mother had betel-stained teeth and his father shook my hand, thanking me for my role in his son's education.

I had known Pari well. Nearing the end of my 10-week lecture series in 1970, the university's foundation Dean of Medicine, Professor Ian Maddocks, asked me out to dinner at his place. He too lived there over the water and I could hear the fishing boats coming in underneath the hut. Ian was a very nice bloke. An advocate of world peace, he was the vice-president of the International Physicians for Prevention of Nuclear War when it received the Nobel Prize for Peace in 1985. He asked me to stay on in PNG, but I had my practice in Melbourne.

At the end of my 10 weeks, I sold my scooter to a right-winger I knew. He complained bitterly that the security police were following him around – as they had followed me around. He really resented it, but I had come to expect it.

Chapter 20
My hand is willingly forced

Returning to Melbourne, I took up again at 20 Bowen Crescent before buying house at 115 Arnold Street, Carlton, in mid-1971. The house had a colourful history and was once owned by diamond merchant William Dunkling. Subsequent to his ownership, during World War II, the house became an illegal brothel. I bought it for $27,000. My mate and neighbour, Ken Turnbull told me I paid $5000 too much for it. In 1998, I sold it for $600,000, but it is now worth over $2.5 million.

I was fast asleep at Arnold Street one early November night in 1971 when the phone rang. It was Mary.

"Could you come and get us? My father is kicking us out of the house," she said.

Mary's father was booting her out of the family home, along with her two brothers, Tony and Roger. Their father was quite mad, and a bit of a dill. He had been in the public service for decades and became paranoid when the public service started hiring graduates rather than those, like him, who had simply finished high school. The government wanted to increase the intellectual capacity of the public service. The young guns were being promoted up the ladder and he felt he was being left behind. After going on sick leave, he wanted to be free of all encumbrances, and so, he kicked his children out. Mary's poor mother had no idea what was happening. Eventually the father left the house, leaving Mary's mother behind. She was wheelchair-bound, with multiple sclerosis.

Mary and her brothers had nowhere to go. I offered up my house in Arnold Street. It was dingy and unrenovated then, but it had enough space for extras.

The move into my house changed the dynamic between us. Mary and I could no longer hide our relationship. It was out in the open. The brothers quickly moved out, and Mary and I were officially a couple.

Saving the heart of Melbourne

Mary and I had been living together a little over a fortnight, still in November 1971, when the Country Roads Board announced that the state government would be building a freeway – in a straight line – through our front bedroom.

My place was not the only property under threat. In 1969, the CRB and the Melbourne Metropolitan Board of Works had released the Melbourne Transportation Plan, which showed 510km of freeways, all pointing like a dagger at the heart of Melbourne. It was now planning to act on it. Motorists would be able to drive from the Eastern Freeway (then called the F-19), to the Tullamarine Freeway.

The Carlton Association was incensed. It knew how to take up a fight. The association had formed in 1969, when the state housing department wanted to bulldoze homes in Lee Street, as part of a "slum clearance". In their place, there would be high-rise flats. The association eventually won, after the Builders Labourers' Federation, under Norm Gallagher, slapped a black ban on any union man demolishing and building dwellings on the site. While Normy Gallagher was sent to jail for thieving building materials, it is my firm belief that the motivation for the Royal Commission into the BLF was sparked by black bans he placed on many projects. Some of these bans saved entire neighbourhoods, and some of the state's most precious buildings.

At a public meeting with the Country Roads Board, the board's man was asked how the route was chosen.

"I just took a pencil and drew a line through," he replied.

"Well," I replied, standing up, "you are a public servant and we are the public. So I am telling you to go back and take a rubber and rub out that line, because we the public are not going to have our houses bulldozed by you or anyone else."

As a result, I was made the Carlton Association's environment spokesperson. I later became the president of the United Melbourne Freeway Action (UMFAG). Created in December 1971, our group was determined to fend off the road daggers pointed at the heart of Melbourne and save the residents' homes.

We were contacted by people from all over Melbourne and Geelong, all butting heads with the government over its poor road planning. There were spotfires everywhere, including one that would have seen homes near Merri

Creek bulldozed for yet another freeway. We approached each home owner and they stood firm against having their homes sold.

UMFAG called a massive public meeting at the Melbourne Town Hall. People came from all over, outraged by this plan that threatened so many homes, including my own on Arnold Street. One bloke from Monash University said he could stop the freeway development by hiring tanks from the army.

Always at these meetings the Country Roads Board sent along public servant spies to these meetings to hear what we were saying. At another meeting, one local, Tom Canning, said, "I know who they are." He walked down and pointed them out: "Boomp, boomp." Chairing the meeting, I was worried the angry residents would lynch the spies, so I moved the discussion on.

Facing a state election and backlash, the Hamer government cut the freeway miles in half in 1973. For us, it was a great victory.

In 1974, I went with a deputation to the Whitlam government's transport minister, Charlie Jones. He promised there would be no more federal funds for freeways. But this was an empty political promise.

This trip was the straw that broke my presidential back. When I returned I thought it was "silly" to spend so much time on this. I submitted my resignation.

Our protests were legendary, and we used a telephone tree to mobilise people. Looking down the list, the name Lensky popped out at me. I thought, "How does a Russian name end up on this list?" Little did I know how much that name, and the person it belonged to, would mean to me in years to come.

In 1975, the state government began cutting a swathe through Yarra Bend, tearing up parkland to build the Eastern Freeway. This road now funnels traffic into congested Alexandra Parade. The government promised, and set aside, a light rail reserve down the centre of the freeway – the softener to reduce public angst about losing parkland. The rail reserve remains, but the light rail promise remains unfulfilled.

Mother Mary

Mary wanted children very badly, but I said I would not have children with her unless we were married. So, we tied the knot in 1972. After the carry-on of my last nuptials, I wanted a low-key wedding, and Mary agreed. We married in her mother's backyard in Preston.

We sought IVF assistance through the Royal Women's. I cared very deeply for Mary. I wanted her to be happy.

One nagging worry with Mary, though, was her ability to fabricate stories. She had a vivid imagination, which she could call on at a whim. I realised this after we married.

We were out to dinner and got talking to the people at the next table. They asked whether we had any children.

"Yes, we've got three children," Mary lied in an instant.

I was quietly flabbergasted.

She then went on an elaborate fantasy about our three fictitious children. Before long, I said I thought we needed to go.

Later, I asked: "Why in the hell did you make up that story?"

"Oh, it doesn't matter, we'll never meet them again," she replied.

On another occasion in the surgery, I bought a cake from Coles supermarket for a staff member's birthday (by this time I had others working for me). It was quite obviously a store-bought cake with elaborate icing. A relation of Mary's came to the surgery and Mary asked them to try the cake – she had "made it" that afternoon, she said. She was sometimes away with the fairies.

By 1973, Mary was pregnant with a boy but, exceedingly premature when he was born at 24 weeks, he died. It was an emotionally devastating time.

Mary became pregnant again, this time with a boy we called Jolyon. We were very careful during that pregnancy. He was born just a couple of weeks early on May 6, 1975, at the Royal Women's Hospital.

Medicare boom

Mary remained my secretary but worked less and less. I also employed two others, and a typist. One of them was a real intriguer who always had a complaint and often buggered up everything. I had to ask her to leave.

The extra staff were needed to cope with the workload created by my reputation in psychoprophylaxis in childbirth and by the Whitlam government's introduction of the universal healthcare system. Initially called Medibank (now Medicare), it began on July 1, 1975, and the work flooded in. Thank goodness I had already given up my role at UMFAG!

Universal healthcare removed the financial barrier to patients seeing a doctor. It was great for picking up lots of ailments that might otherwise develop into serious health issues, but it was overwhelming for doctors. Patients would ring day and night, and expect a visit. My already busy patient load increased by a further 10 per cent. It was great if you could keep up or if you were interested in making more money, but it was too much for a solo practitioner.

Each line of my pocketbook diary was now filled with calls and house calls – up to 40 on one particular day. I was running from the minute I was up. How I wish I'd kept those diaries.

When universal healthcare was first introduced, I contacted the then Minister for Social Security, Bill Hayden, and told him about the issue of overstretching doctors and leaving them at the "free" beck and call of patients. He sent down a man to do some research, and I took him on my rounds. He could not believe it. Although he never specifically acted on my case, after this time, doctors were encouraged to form clinics together so that they might share the night-call load. The solo practitioner was on the way out.

Meanwhile, my reputation for psychoprophylaxis in childbirth was also growing. Women came from all over, including one woman from Malaysia who had contacted the Childbirth Education Association in Britain seeking a doctor who could assist in Australia. Married to a very rich Chinese bloke, this woman was incredible. Her hair was immaculate. She gave birth, and it was a very good birth. She just breathed away. It was hard work, but she still did very well – with not one hair on her head out of place for the entire birth. I do not know how she did it.

Afterwards, she came to me about the fee.

"Look, if there's any difficulty with the fee, don't worry," I told her. "Don't pay me. Or just pay a portion of it."

She replied: "Oh, no, no, no … It's nothing."

Perplexed, I asked what she meant.

"I expected a fee four times this," she answered.

I replied that my fee was £10 or £15 and that I was happy to receive it. At the time, a city birth might have cost in the hundreds of pounds. She wanted to pay more, but I declined.

Chapter 21
Tropics Mark II

My chaotic workload continued until I heard from friends about another interesting opportunity in PNG. After visiting for an interview, I was appointed as the medical officer for the PNG University of Technology in Lae. It looked a fascinating place and it was an incredible time to be there. The country was finding its feet and building up its institutions. Australia had only granted the country its independence on September 16, 1975. I would start my new job there on January 1, 1976.

The University of Technology was originally in Port Moresby but shifted to Lae, the country's second largest city, on the northern coast in 1967. The university wanted to bolster its medical sciences teaching, although it now defers to the University of PNG for medical teaching.

By now, Mary had added an extra "a" to her name to make her the more exotic Marya. But for ease of recognition, I will continue to call her Mary. Perhaps the name change reflected her restlessness too. We realised we needed more leisure time together, and the Melbourne clinic workload was too much in the long term. I could always arrange for a locum to look after the surgery. It was time for a change, and Mary and I grabbed hold of Lae with both hands.

Lae was very, very hot, with rows and rows of houses. Everything grows green in PNG; even the fence posts sprout if you leave them in the ground too long.

Academic life was free flowing. So too were other aspects of work and play. The 1960s had continued unabashed into the 1970s, and the interchange of sexual partners was extensive.

When Mary and I were invited to dinner with university folk, a chap and his wife tried to promote the advantages of open marriages. I thought that was a crappy idea and told him so. He continued to defend it. His wife was a runner who met up with an English runner on an oval every night. Eventually, they fell into bed. The running partner left campus for England

and the wife followed him. That left her husband with three children on campus.

The man regarded me as a father confessor and continued to write to me after we parted in Lae. When he took a job in America, his runaway wife returned to him there. She then denounced him for cruelty and domestic violence and took out a court order, telling him to leave the house. She took the kids back to England and he was left with nothing. So much for the so-called advantages of open marriages.

My philosophy has always been that if one of my partners wants to leave, they can go with my blessing. I hate the subterfuge of affairs, even though I did participate in them while married to June. I would have nothing to do with open marriages – you are either married or you are not.

Drinking was a big part of the social scene in Lae, but I was not up for much of that. I once read a book set in Africa which argued that the planters could only maintain their sanity as long as they did not drink so much as a peg of gin before the sun went down. I can only wholeheartedly agree.

The people on the campus were extraordinary. The bacteriology lecturer lived across the road from us and he took a shine to us. He asked me lots of questions. I soon realised he knew nothing about anything to do with bacteriology or anything else – and he was a senior lecturer.

Before I knew him well enough, he told me he wanted to start a pathology laboratory in Lae.

"Yeah, good idea, do it. I'll help you if you like," I said.

He employed two Swiss women pathologists to do the blood analysis and he would pretend to understand it. He was taking samples from all over PNG, processing them and sending out bills. He was making a fortune as the only pathology clinic assessing bloods, urine – and God knows what else – in PNG.

He asked me to do a lecture on the lungs for his students. The next day I saw he was showing slides on cells. They were plant cells, not human cells. The cell structure is quite different. He was simply teaching students the wrong information.

I could not stomach it. His actions were appalling. I cut all associations with him.

The university eventually asked him to justify the amount of time he spent away from campus at the pathology clinic. There was a disciplinary hearing.

I realised he was probably a fraud and checked his original degree with a university in New Zealand, where he claimed to have studied. It had never heard of him. This man had failed so many students, both literally and figuratively, by giving them incorrect information. I gave evidence and the administration sacked him quietly.

Mary became pregnant with Guy in early November. I decided I could trust no one else to deliver this baby more than myself. Finally, I would be in attendance for the birth of one of my children. Guy was born eight weeks premature, on April 19, 1977, in a breech delivery at the ANGAU General Hospital. ANGAU stands for the Australian New Guinea Administrative Unit – the civil administration unit responsible for PNG from World War II.

For some reason, despite all the complications, Guy was an easy delivery. Even though he was prem, we took him home straight away – thanks to the PNG climate, it was like we were all living in a humidicrib.

Mary found it hard to bond with baby Guy, and struggled with breastfeeding. Though her feeding did become well established, he later went on a bottle and thrived. Guy had a high-pitched prem cry that was ear-shattering. He was a difficult baby to appease and I did most of his parenting, while our young housekeeper really liked him and helped care for him also. Like Jolyon, Guy was a sweet baby and grew to be a sweet child and adult.

In my last year, I volunteered to work in the hospital on night duty on Fridays. It was unbelievably busy and I never stopped running all night. At any one stage, there would be 50 people waiting to see the doctor. The patience of the patients was astronomical.

Being in PNG did have its drawbacks. In December, 1976, my mother died at Mount Henry Hospital in Perth. She had been widowed twice, but was well cared for in her later years. I could not get back for the funeral. My strong focus was on Mary and her baby in utero.

In 1977, Naomi, Ian and Sylvie, aged about 18, 16 and 14, visited me in PNG and stayed for a few weeks. They were maturing and were quite independent. We explored the highlands and spent time in the picturesque Madang region before returning to Lae, from where they returned home to Melbourne.

Ian was already ranked third in the world as a junior chess player. The University of Technology chess community organised a competition for him, and he took on a dozen players at the same time. He beat all but one of them. Ian said he lost because the winner had a chess set with pieces in black and a dark grey colour. They looked almost identical and Ian couldn't tell which pieces were his. Ian was a hit in Lae.

On my 50th birthday, in 1977, I ran 50 laps around the university's campus oval. I invited everyone to run their age as a contribution to the health of the community. We had about 120 people on the oval, with the youngest a little kid of about four running (and walking) four laps. One senior lecturer, aged 70, did 70 laps. Afterwards I put on orange juice and cake. It was a lovely birthday and brought the campus together.

At the end of my two-year term in December 1977, we returned to Melbourne. Although I was offered a senior lecturer position in Lae, I had to decline as the lease on my surgery was up and I needed to get back to the relieve the locum I had hired to look after the practice.

Taking my practice back, I discovered that the locum I had left in charge was trying to pull a swifty. Sometimes when you hire a locum, they are trying to get their experience up before they start out on their own. They are not supposed to poach your patients. When they start up, they need to be more than two miles (or five kilometres) from the original practice. In this case, the rival doctor decided 400 yards was far enough. To add insult to injury, she took my telephone number and redirected all my patients to her.

I rang the Australian Medical Association to complain.

"Tell her not to be so bloody stupid," I said. "This is something I can report to the ethics committee."

The AMA was bruising for a fight: "Report it. We've got to stop this sort of behaviour," they told me.

I replied: "No, I'll ring her solicitor."

I then told the solicitor: "Look, I've been in touch with the AMA. They want me to report her to the ethics committee. Ring her up and tell her not to be bloody stupid. Return my telephone number and sort this out. She can stay where she is. I don't mind a bit of competition."

And she did. She ended up being a big wig in the union movement.

Chapter 22
Politically fuelled

When we returned to life in Carlton in 1977, it was a very active time politically for me. Two seismic shifts in thinking occurred and I am pleased I was part of both of them. Both show that it only takes a small group of good people to bring about widespread change.

Settling back into Arnold Street, I immersed myself in the neighbourhood again. The freeway fighting had continued without me, and would continue for decades more, with bad decisions still being made.

One day in early 1978, I met with two of my neighbours in the street. One was Dr Frank Burden, a Monash professor of chemistry, who lived two doors down. He was in his garden and we had been yarning over the front fence. The other neighbour was Margaret Fallshaw, who had stopped to chat on her way home. Margaret's husband, Robert, was a stalwart Liberal candidate for the seat of Melbourne. She had a strong interest in health and was advisor to the Nursing Mothers' Association. Years later, she asked me to join the advisory group. As we were all neighbours, our children played together.

On this occasion, our talk turned to leaded petrol – an issue that had been percolating in the background of the freeways struggles. While West Germany and Japan had already banned lead from petrol, the Australian the car industry maintained the additive was required to stop "knocking" in engines.

Frank was telling me about a UK study of vegetables grown at various distances from Britain's M6 motorway. The study found high lead concentration levels. I made a quick calculation that an estimated that 600 tonnes of lead hung over Melbourne and Sydney each year – a total of 1200 tonnes over both cities. While my quick calculations suggested that 600 tonnes of lead was emitted into the atmosphere every year in Sydney and in Melbourne, the real figure, I later learned, was much higher. In 1978 alone, there was 1554 tonnes of the toxin over Victoria and 2075 tonnes over NSW.

I had also read about higher-than-normal levels of learning difficulties among children in Mount Isa, where there was a lead smelter. We were all aware that studies were emerging worldwide showing that lead, even in low quantities, was a poison in the body that affected the nervous system and childhood development. Studies indicated that lead competed selectively with calcium absorption in the body and bones. Children were most at risk because of their brain's developmental stage. (And children, being children, were also more likely to ingest lead from the environment.) Those who lived close to traffic were at highest risk from airborne lead particles.

There, over the fence, we decided to do something about it, by starting the National Association for a Lead-Free Environment (NALFE). Frank brought the science to the table; I brought the health impacts of lead; and Margaret brought the political entree into the Liberal Party. We would need an audience with the presiding Liberal Hamer government if we were going to effect change.

On October 24, 1978, at the Melbourne University graduate student lounge we held the inaugural National Association for a Lead-Free Environment public meeting. Frank spoke about how lead from vehicle emissions was landing on everything, including our fruit and vegetables. We were ingesting it. I spoke about the dangers of lead to the body, particularly for children. Margaret roused the crowd into action. The wheels were rolling on our campaign to remove lead from petrol.

We encouraged parents to have blood tests for themselves and their children. Likewise, we asked them to test their children's baby teeth and hair. The results were alarming. Lead was so high in one Collingwood family's blood that they sold up and moved to the suburbs to be away from freeways and traffic.

Frank was great during this time, not least because he had access to a mass spectrometer – a tool that, among other things, could measure lead levels in the environment. He began taking samples of fruit and vegetables at various distances from freeways and main roads. He found that lead levels in dust in Melbourne classrooms had an average of 1200 parts per million, with similar levels in private homes. (The areas studied were free of lead paint, emphasising the point that exhaust emissions were the likely culprit.) Frank estimated that two finger licks of dust (after lunch, for example) would be enough for a person to reach the maximum daily dose of lead considered safe.

One of the most shocking finds came out of a five-year study by Professor

Lloyd Smythe at the University of New South Wales. This estimated that 22 per cent of Sydney school children had excessively high levels of lead in their blood. Nearly one in four had levels that could cause harms such as overactivity, antisocial problems, blood formation and learning difficulties. Smythe too found that petrol was the main culprit.

Collingwood City Council conducted its own research and compared its inner-city children's teeth with that of children in Sherbrooke, an eastern fringe suburb of Melbourne. It found that lead absorption was 30 per cent higher in the baby teeth of the Collingwood children compared to their outer-suburbs counterparts of the same age.

Findings on lead were pumped out all over the world, and the campaign grew. Our letter writing and public meetings grew in volume, and Frank continued testing.

In late 1979, Margaret arranged a meeting with Rob Maclellan, then Victorian Minister for Transport. Neither Frank nor I were permitted to speak beyond pleasantries, but Margaret took up the gauntlet. She was dynamic and compelling. She won over Maclellan, and we deputised him to convince transport ministers nationally to put an end to leaded petrol.

To keep up the pressure, the campaign continued outside the halls of power. A good mate of mine, Bob Semens, was a senior lecturer at the Melbourne State College (which later merged with Melbourne University as the Melbourne Teachers' College). He wrote to school principals and invited hundreds of teachers to a meeting.

Everywhere we spoke, we asked people to talk to their neighbours to raise the alarm about lead levels. With most of our meetings at Melbourne Uni, the campaign was focussed on the middle classes, who we felt could be best alerted and activated.

Rats in the ranks

As momentum built, NALFE teamed up with the environmental group Friends of the Earth and its convener, Andrew Herington. On one occasion we were meeting at the Fitzroy Town Hall in the lower committee room. It was a dingy downstairs room with a single table and brown vinyl chairs. Around the table sat Frank, Margaret and I, along with three others: Andrew, with his Jesus beard; a man who twitched frequently; and a woman who was breastfeeding her baby.

Unannounced, down the stairs came nine strangers – seven besuited men and two women dressed to the nines. One of the men was a Dr Green. He was an environmental science "doctor". I never knew his first name ,even though he attended all our public meetings to dispute the science on the harmful effects of lead. He tried to say it was not a risk to children. Nonsense.

Green asked if the men in suits could address the meeting. We obliged. The first speaker introduced himself as representing oil refineries.

"If you win and get lead out of petrol," he began, "it's going to cost us millions upon millions to put catalytic converters into our refineries. It's not only what is going to happen to the cars, but it's going to push the price of petrol up."

Then the next speaker was from the car industry.

"It's going to increase the price of cars because we'll have to change the cars and put catalytic converters into the car engines," he said.

We politely responded to both of them with a "That's interesting".

The next chap was from the tyre industry, who said words to the effect that the sky was going to fall in if lead was not kept in petrol. The women accompanying these men didn't say a word. The party of suits went back up the stairs and I haven't seen hide nor hair of them since.

Collectively, they were worth billions, even back then, but I've never been able to work out how they knew we were meeting in that dingy room.

'Trouble with the law'

This wasn't the first time in my political life that I had smelled a rat.

A few of us from UMFAG once went out for a drink after a meeting. Among this group was a bloke we suspected was an ASIO spy. He asked me to stay back for another beer. I thought it an odd request, but I agreed.

"I was talking to a few people from the Melbourne Metropolitan Board of Works who are concerned with the development of freeways," the bloke said.

"They said, 'That Dr Rogers, he's in a bit of trouble with the law.' I just thought I'd let you know," he said.

The threat was clear – I was being warned to back off. At the time I was indeed facing legal trouble, though I had done nothing illegal. And while I did not need reminding of it, it was clear that someone was keeping tabs on me.

The source of the legal trouble came from a procedure back in 1974, when a woman came to see me as a patient. I had helped her deliver her two babies. But since her last baby, she felt her marriage was on the rocks. She thought her husband was going to leave her. I asked if she was sure, even with two children. She seemed certain. She said her prolapsed uterus was coming down and I said we could at least fix that. I considered whether the problem might be affecting the couple's sex life. I sent her to gynaecologist and surgeon, Dr Bruce Sutherland, who stitched the uterus into position to stop it descending through to the vagina. After the operation, the woman came to me see me. She said she didn't want to have any more children, didn't like the pill, and wanted her fallopian tubes tied.

"I don't think that is a very good idea," I told her. "You are only 26. If your husband does leave, you might find someone else, and you and he might want children from that marriage?"

We discussed an intrauterine device called a Graefenberg's ring, and I said these had improved over the years. She agreed to it.

When you insert an IUD, you first place a "seeker" into the cervical canal to ascertain where to insert the dilators. The uterus was not located as I expected it to be and the seeker went through the tissue and pierced her uterine artery. Worried that the seeker had gone too far, I withdrew it. There was a spot of blood on it.

"I'm not happy. Wake her up," I said. The anaesthetist argued that it could be a minor issue, but my gut told me differently. She was put into a bed and I told the nurses to watch her carefully with regular blood pressure and pulse rates taken. It was a Saturday morning and I waited at home. When I called I was told she was doing fine. At about 2.30pm, I called again. The nurse said her pulse was up slightly.

Immediately, I called a surgeon I knew. He opened her up and found the uterine wall was gone – her uterine muscles had gone to mush. We had to do a hysterectomy.

The woman recovered and came to see me at the clinic.

"What happened? They would not tell me in the hospital," she said. I fessed up to the sorry tale. I felt dreadful for her, but I believe in telling the truth. She thanked me for telling her.

I later had a call from the surgeon who assisted me: "Perce, you know you are going to get sued."

It was a dreadful incident but not uncommon among obstetricians. The legal action had begun while I was in New Guinea with Mary. When I returned, I was served to appear in the Supreme Court. I contacted by the AMA and they asked whether I was insured. It was one of the hundreds of papers I had not signed, so I was uninsured. The AMA assisted me with a lawyer.

When I attended court, in November, 1979, the lawyer from the other side told blatant lies, accusing me of putting a rusty dilator inside the woman. I had not.

My lawyer was a young bloke who questioned the couple. The husband told a pack of lies, claiming they had a "good marriage," but my lawyer caught him out. The husband was squirming now and the judge was starting to get a bit annoyed. The judge suggested we have a conference to see if we can settle it.

The lawyer came in and said, "We are winning."

I was aghast.

"What do you mean 'winning'? She's lost her uterus," I replied.

He said if we kept going for 10 days, we would win. I sensed that this was probably true.

"How much is your fee per day?" I asked.

It was $4000 a day. It was a quick calculation – a $40,000 bill for a possible win.

"How much are they asking to settle?" I asked.

It was $20,000.

"She's lost the uterus. Give her the $20,000 if she's asking for it," I said.

He replied: "I think you're making a big mistake."

I told him he might think that but I wasn't budging. "Settle it now," I said.

All the while, I wondered how the Melbourne Metropolitan Board of Works could have known about this case before it went public.

Birthing a birth centre

After returning from PNG, amid the legal worries and the NALFE campaigning, I sold my general practice and, in 1978, enrolled in a diploma of obstetrics at Melbourne University.

In the exam, I was given a pregnant woman to assess. She was about two weeks over her due date, but her baby's head was quite high up. I could find nothing wrong with her but, initially, I was not sure what to advise. I took her blood pressure, and it was very high – 180/30. I thought the baby should have dropped lower. I had previously done work on blood pressure during childbirth because I felt there was a lot of bunkum said about blood pressure. I called for a new sphygmomanometer and, sure enough, the first one had been faulty – the woman's blood pressure was normal.

When faced with the examiners, I said this woman was, "a puzzle and a problem". Why was her baby still so high up, and what should be done about it? I mentioned the faulty sphygmomanometer and suggested it was a ploy to weed out some students. They took umbrage at that and I thought I had blown it. It went from bad to bloody awful. They were firing questions at me. I suggested the baby's head might be slightly deflexed (bent, or curved the wrong way), which could explain why the baby was not coming into position. Sure enough, one of the examiners went to check, and the head was deflexed. I recommended that the woman get out of bed and walk around. I thought that might help.

Apparently, it did. I was one of only 30 per cent who passed. It was one of the hardest things I have ever done.

To support my family while I studied, I returned to work as a locum in Blyth Street, Brunswick, with another doctor – Peter MacCallum, son of the cancer centre co-founder of the same name. I also worked at a health centre in Kensington, while keeping my obstetrical practice, which I ran from a practice I had at home.

In 1978, after years of delivering babies and while I was still studying my diploma of obstetrics, I was asked to join the Royal Women's Hospital as an honorary obstetrician. I was attached to a clinic within the hospital headed up by Dr Michael Kloss. He was a generous and very humane obstetrician. Born in Poland, he had come to Australia after World War II without any English, and, like me, had had lived in Geraldton before going to Mullewa for work. While I had worked at the wheat bins, he had driven a tractor on a station. He had realised, as I did, that if he did not crack on with getting his degree, he would miss out, so took his savings and enrolled in medicine at Melbourne University. He worked his way through his degree as I had.

As an honorary obstetrician, I introduced what others would come to call "Percy's Pillow" – a large, firm wedge of a pillow placed behind a labouring woman. This allowed the woman to be comfortable reclining and, when she needed to move, the pillow would be adjusted or flipped around to help her give birth in whatever position she preferred.

In May 1979, the Childbirth Education Association, of which I was a life member and remained an advisor, held the Birth and Being midwifery conference in Melbourne. It was a catalyst for change in obstetrics, with speakers from around the world all pushing for a kinder childbirth and mothering experience. Speakers included authors, academics and doctors who were mother and baby pioneers – these included Sheila Kitzinger, Suzanne Arms and Dr John Kennell. One speaker was from a birth centre in the UK and another from a privately operated centre in New York.

This was a lightning rod moment for those of us working in this field. Margaret Peters was deputy of nursing at the Royal Women's at the time and she drew us together. She campaigned hard with the hospital administration to turn Ward 54 into the RWH Family Birth Centre. Here, fathers and family members could attend and be part of this natural process in a home-like environment. The group that Margaret drew together formed the Friends of the Family Birth Centre. I employed a woman to help with the administration required to organise it.

Around the same time, the Queen Victoria Hospital, in Lonsdale Street, was also starting its own family birthing centre. Spearheaded by Carl Wood, who had supported my research into psychoprophylaxis, it advertised the service before the RWH one.

Both hospitals wanted to claim the mantle of the first family birth centre. We were all waiting for the first couple to agree to have their baby in the birth centre, and waiting for women to go into labour. But babies come when they are ready.

The first family birth centre birth

Sarah was a quietly spoken woman who came to me when she was pregnant with her first child, and I had assisted her. In late 1979, pregnant with her second child, she invited me to lunch with her and her husband, Greg.

Back then, pregnant couples had to decide whether to accept the brutality of institutional birthing or try for a new-style homebirth with a midwife. There was a lot of chatter among couples as they decided. Sarah and Greg were a gentle couple and wanted to shun that brutality at childbirth. In the course of lunch, they told me they were planning a homebirth. They had attended classes and met dedicated people who assisted at homebirths.

I listened, but could not agree with having a baby at home instead of in a hospital. I told them that for years I had struggled to alter hospitals' attitudes to childbirth. Families like theirs needed to have their babies in hospitals and help transform them from within, not abandon them for a homebirth which was fraught with danger.

The hospital equipment and buildings did not belong to the nursing, medical and administration staff, I said. They belonged to the women who used them through their taxes. I explained that private homes were not built for births. They did not have, nor could homebirth practitioners bring, the equipment needed to deal with an obstetrical emergency. It was necessary, I said, for women to be given the chance of a decent birth, a family birth, inside a hospital.

They asked if such a hospital existed, and I described the Family Birth Centre at the RWH. In effect, they would stay in a motel room, but outside the door would be the state's best mother-and-baby doctors, nurses and the equipment that could be called upon if needed. Nurses had volunteered to work in the Family Birth Centre because they believed in the principles of a humane birth. These nurses felt they could not express their warmth of feelings towards their patients in the traditional hospital setting.

Sarah and Greg agreed to visit and investigate the Family Birth Centre. When they were there it was still being painted and furnished with couches and other touches to give it a more homely feel. They cancelled the homebirth.

Afterwards, I told them that it was their responsibility to become informed about the birth process so they could make informed decisions about the birth of their baby. It was the hospital staff's responsibility to ensure that if anything untoward happened, they took appropriate steps to ensure Sarah's and their baby's safety. They attended the birth centre's classes as well as my classes.

On October 17, 1979, around 6am, Sarah went into labour about five days after her due date, which conveniently allowed the paint to dry on the birth centre walls. Around 7am, Sarah and Greg were ready to come to the hospital when they hit a hurdle – Sarah was wearing socks for the birth that were pale blue and white. Knowing I was a Carlton supporter, she made a show of finding a pair of navy blue and white socks for Carlton, jokingly suggesting I might refuse to assist if she was wearing any other team colours. So, she dug around to find some old running socks in the correct navy blue and white.

Then there was another hold-up on the way to the hospital. Back in Carlton in those days, everyone stopped for a cappuccino at Genevieve's in Faraday Street – and contractions or not, this couple were determined to be no exception. So, with a caffeinated pitstop thrown in, they finally got to the birth centre around midday.

The nursing staff watched Greg and Sarah with much fondness. Not only were they the first to use the new Ward 54, they were also clearly a loving couple.

After a couple of hours, I went in to ask how they were doing. Greg raised his head in surprise and said, "Oh, fine Perce." I got the impression I was not needed and, after assessing the progress, and some pleasantries about football, I departed. Two hours later, the birthing centre called to say Sarah was in the early second stage. I rushed back to the hospital to find things moving along quickly. Greg was arranging his camera to record the birth. Sarah made jokes with the staff, and there was more small talk about football. The birth was progressing nicely.

Within a matter of two or three pushes, the baby's head appeared and then I asked Sarah to start panting. She alternately pushed and panted, gradually easing the baby's head through the perineum. It was a model delivery. The nursing sister said to me, "It was just like Beethoven's 9th Symphony." I thought she was going to throw her arms around me in a most unprofessional way, so I retreated.

With the baby breathing straight away, we put the bub on Sarah's abdomen. As soon as the umbilical cord stopped pulsating, it was cut. The babe was put to the breast and started sucking. Rarely have I seen a happier, more united family. It was a moment to savour – the first birth in a family birthing centre anywhere in Australia.

Between 10 and 20 of my patients had their babies at the RWH Family Birth Centre before I headed off in late December, 1979, for a new adventure. I left the birthing centre in the capable hands of nurse Margaret Peters, and obstetricians Michael Kloss and John Neil. The campaign for humane births in hospitals was won.

Chapter 23
Cocos (Keeling) Islands –
Hell in a Heavenly Place

When we came back to Melbourne at the end of 1977, Mary could not settle. She befriended a woman called Jenny, who was a bit mad and convinced Mary that she was being restricted and oppressed by having a family and a husband. (It was during the height of the 1970s feminist movement and to be expected.)

Mary's feminist friend said that she had to battle for her rights as a woman and that it was her right to do as she wanted. Under this kind of influence, Mary wanted to leave the family because she felt it was limiting her. I cannot say I saw it the same way. We had tried hard to have a family, and this could and should have been a warm, happy place for us both.

"Well, if you wish to leave, you leave," I told her, matter-of-factly. "Don't be held by the bonds of convention, as it were."

Mary stayed, but was unhappy and searching for something else. With life at home and at work something of a challenge, we went on this way until one day in 1979. A job was on offer in a tropical paradise – the Cocos (Keeling) Islands, where I could work at the hospital. Mary was dead keen on the idea of this exotic experience. I thought it would be good to get the kids away from the city pollution, and it would be good for our family.

Cocos (Keeling) Islands has a fascinating history as Australia's most remote territory. It is a far-flung speck in the Indian Ocean, half-way to Sri Lanka. Named after the seafaring Captain William Keeling, who "discovered" the Cocos Atoll in 1609, it has 26 small islands, but the two main islands are Home and West.

In 1827, Captain John Clunies-Ross, a Scottish trader, laid claim to the islands. The Clunies-Ross family brought 120 indentured Malayan labourers to work the land. Queen Victoria eventually granted the islands to the Clunies-Ross family and their descendants, making the head of the family the governor. The islands became an important military flashpoint during

World War II, and later the Americans used it for decades as an airstrip between its Diego Garcia base in the Indian Ocean, south of India, and Guam in the Pacific. So, there were usually US soldiers around. Eventually, Australia purchased all but the Clunies-Ross family home and some acreage around it and assumed control in 1978. The Department of Home Affairs administrated the island, but I would work under the auspices of the Department of Health.

Before I left, I had a call from Dr Barry Christophers, the world authority on Professor Frederic Wood Jones – a brilliant pioneer in the study of flora and fauna. Barry explained how, in 1910, Wood Jones wrote the definitive book *Corals and Atolls: A History and Description of the Keeling-Cocos Islands.* He called me a "lucky duck" for getting a chance to go to this remote paradise. He piqued my interest further in the islands when he told me about Wood Jones and his career, which included training as a doctor in England before studying mummies in Egypt. (Barry himself was a Melbourne GP and long-time president of the Victorian Council for Aboriginal Rights.) *Corals and Atolls* is a rare book and, on my return, Barry gave me a copy. It is among my most treasured possessions.

I would later find that one of the many natural wonders of the Cocos (Keeling) Islands was a freshwater "lens" that sat above the saltwater of the lagoon. No wonder Wood Jones was fascinated by the place.

Cocos (Keeling) Islands was to be an adventure.

We had a two-week holiday in Perth before heading to the islands. On January 1, 1980, we spent a hot day at the Perth Zoo with Guy and Jolyon, having spent a few days living off the Home Affairs and Commonwealth tab. We were enthusiastic about our new life to come.

On arriving in Cocos, at 2am, my counterpart John McCarthy met us at the airstrip. I would replace him at the hospital. When we got in his car, the windscreen was so salt-encrusted I could hardly tell the difference between the road and the surf. He rushed us to our West Island house with our luggage (the bulk of our belongings would arrive by boat) and, in between his quick tour, handed over his medical cases to me. He had a deadline of one hour, as he had to get back to the airstrip for the return charter flight back to Perth. He told me I was bound to enjoy my time on the islands, while letting me know of some of the issues I might encounter. Along the way, he pointed out the local "watering hole", a club, which was the social scene centre.

Mary and the boys settled in, and we all had a good feeling about the place. In the morning I made my immortal toasted sandwiches for the first time on Cocos, and we wandered into town to meet the administrator, Charles Buffett, amid a sea of other faces.

Shopping for basics, we realised with a start that the cost of living was very high on the islands, and our wealth was wanting. With food stuffs especially expensive, we feared we would soon be broke if we spent money this way all the time. On this happy thought, I started work, attending to three patients, all with ear infections. It was apparent that the relationship between the nursing staff and the previous doctor was quite poor, and I set about fixing that situation.

In the afternoon, after we failed to get the boys to have a snooze, we went for a drive. On West Island, there were only two places to drive – north and south. In the north, we heard the cargo ship *Tropic Star* coming into the jetty, but our sea freight was not onboard. We then swam in the turquoise Indian Ocean at Trannies Beach. The boys took to the water like ducks.

After having servants in PNG, Mary and I decided we wanted to run our own show in Cocos. Apart from anything else, servants made us feel like strangers in our own home. As I had in share houses, I devised a demarcation of duties: Mary would do the clothes; me the dishes. I would make breakfast; she would make the evening meal. Astoundingly, this meal was sometimes crayfish, as Mary could buy a large cray for just $4 ($17 in today's money) and a small one for $3 ($13).

A few days after we arrived, we travelled to the south end of West Island. The locals invited us to a barbecue, but I was on call so we travelled back. By now it was getting dark, and driving through encroaching jungle palms was quite eerie at night. The scene was topped off with crabs attempting to throw themselves under the car wheels as we swerved to miss the ones we saw in time.

The islands' owners, the Clunies-Ross family, lived on Home Island. To get to them I would take a barge, unloading supplies and other goods under conditions that would not be acceptable to the Maritime Union of Australia. There was no safety gear whatsoever. Here, on my first visit to Home Island, I met Daphne, wife of John Clunies-Ross, and the last of the Clunies-Ross women to reside in the family's historic Oceania House. She seemed as lonely as any wife could be and told me about how she had brightened the house when it had been quite gloomy.

We soon found that the scenery on both islands was magical, especially the sunsets, and the water activities great for our children. We prised off clams from sea coral and caught crabs for our supper. The waters were alive with colourful coral fish and non-dangerous sea worms. The boys loved floating in blow-up boats. It all went well until one day when we saw a school of sharks, presumably attracted by the smell and the noise. We hurried out. During this time, we realised how fiercely independent Jolyon was, even when faced with dangers – a parents' worst nightmare.

From the sea, yacht crews would arrive with all kinds of ailments and viruses and some came with dubious cargo. The Malay community on the island was most at risk of getting these infections as they had little immune resistance to any viruses. Sometimes, a larger ship would arrive with a crew who all appeared to be suffering from the same virus. One time, I arranged for a plane to take two seamen to Perth, believing their condition needed treatment beyond my scope on the islands. In truth, I now believe they were mostly just sick of seafaring and wanted a Perth holiday.

The West Island had the hospital while Home Island had the Malays' clinic. The hospital was a long fibrocement building with a dispensary, a consulting room, a waiting room, a delivery-cum-dental room and a toilet. To bring the place up to scratch for the impending United Nations' committee visit later that year, a nurses' flat was being added and an extra ward with a dark room for X-rays. The X-ray machine was 18 years old, illegal and probably radioactive. I put in for a new one, and got one quickly. In fact, most medical supplies came quickly. I even asked for a family birth centre to be built onto the hospital, and within weeks, an annex was erected.

The hospital was well equipped with bandages, splints and drugs for day-to-day problems, but I felt that in the event of a catastrophe, which could happen at any time – be it a plane crash, car crash, cyclone, fire or epidemic – we were woefully underprepared. I arranged for supplies to be taken to the club, which was the spot we were all to go in the event of a disaster. It was supposedly built to withstand a cyclone, although I never saw it tested.

Without our own lab, I had to send specimens to Perth for analysis. Parasites were common, and some children had hookworm and whipworm. Ear infections were also common among divers (but not swimmers).

The charter flight took the samples. In the dark of some nights, at 3am, a siren would sound to tell everyone to clear the airstrip. Fat use that was at 3am. After an hour, once we were all sleeping again, the siren sounded again to clear the strip for take-off.

A little Cocos chaos

While on our island adventure, Mary and I decided we would try for a baby girl – although Jolyon said he would rather a cat. In a family conference it was agreed that both were possible.

In the meantime, Mary and I got involved in the local radio station. She became a part-time volunteer announcer. As she became more heavily involved with the radio station, Mary dreamed of being an ABC journalist. It was also around this time that she again began to claim that her family, and I, were oppressing and restricting her. The reprieve had only lasted a few months.

My first radio show was *Health in the Tropics*, where I discussed the effects of heat on man. Later, Mary and I shared a spot in which we played music and chatted. On the day of my first radio show, I also bought an inflatable boat for $950, so I became a skipper and a radio host on the same day.

Both Mary and I began to lose any excess weight we had put on. Mary shed many kilos and became lithe and lean and even more beautiful, although I later worried she might get scurvy.

Despite my initial fears about spending too much, with a pay rise in my first month, we began to realise we could save money on the island, as there was little to spend our money on. Sometimes food stuffs ran low in the stores. August looked like a starvation month when, three days after the last charter and a fortnight before the next, the store ran out of milk, eggs, fruit, vegetables, flour and other staples. It took some strongly worded telexes to the Department of Home Affairs to bring additional supplies in a Hercules. It was touch and go, but after seven days of agitating, another plane arrived with supplies, including beer.

Other things were also frustrating. The new school principal and teachers were delayed until March, which put a dampener on Jolyon's start at school.

We continued to get letters from home, and I was especially pleased to hear about Sylvie's great results in her studies.

While our attempts to have another baby were without success, we were kept busy enough with our too little ones. Though they woke early and were a handful, I found both boys most charming, engaging, vibrant and funny. They would generously make us peanut butter sandwiches.

It was chaotic at times. I remember once Guy climbed up on a chair and then the bench, and began scoffing a bottle of antibiotic Bactrim. It was half gone before we noticed it.

On another day, Guy was so quiet that Mary came in from pegging the washing out to find he had run himself a bath in the kitchen sink, with water spilling on the floor and into the lounge room, just missing the carpet.

Once on my return from work, I became irritated by the house being in disarray: clothes unsorted; dishes piled up. With Mary's role at the radio station, we needed help at home. We relented and decided to employ a Malay woman twice a week. In our desperation to get Jolyon to start learning to read, we employed a Seventh Day Adventist woman to teach him two mornings a week. She was already teaching her own children, so we were hopeful of a good outcome.

By the time the actual schoolteachers arrived, they created a new problem for us – Jolyon hated going to school. We could hardly blame him. The primary teacher was arrogant, hard and petulant to the point of appearing to hate children.

There were frequent visitors to the islands from the government. In about May, the then Minister for Defence, James Killen, and a rear admiral came to visit. There was at the time discussion about turning the islands into an Australian military base. Those men were not coming for a swim.

A foreign affairs official came up too to look at the hospital. After that, in June, a dentist and ophthalmologist arrived to check the teeth and eyes of the Malays.

Sometimes, medicine provided high drama. In August, an American serviceman was found on the runway after he crashed his motorbike in the night. I was wrenched from my Sunday bed to race down, where I found him still alive – just. I got him into the hospital, got a drip into him and found he had hyperthermia and an irregular heartbeat. He would not regain consciousness. My assessment was that he had a severe brain injury, with possible subdural bleeding and a depressed temporal bone fracture. His pupils were pinpoints. To get a surgical team to Cocos could take 14 hours, so I decided the US Orion aircraft was needed to take him to Perth, along with medical staff to keep him alive. For the next few hours, the nurse and I stood watch over him, taking note of every breath, clearing every vomit and watching the drip. He made it to Perth's Sir Charles Gairdner Hospital casualty, but his brain was destroyed. As far as I know, he returned to the US a vegetable. We had done all we could.

On my way home, I flew the Orion. The pilot had me up front in the cockpit with him in the other seat. He let me take the lever and move it up and down. I felt the Orion do the same. Then the pilot said, "I think you've got the hang of it, so I'll just go make a coffee." I told him to stay right where he was. He was actually controlling the Orion with his feet.

The hairiest thing I ever had to do on the islands was climb aboard a ship with 20,000 sheep. A man had come down with a mystery illness and I needed to examine him. We went out to the ship in a small boat and they lowered down Jacob's ladder, a rope ladder with wooden rungs. The waves were coming up and the official boat I was on rose and fell with them. The crew said I would just have to make a jump for it. I leapt for the rope and hung on. After about 300 steps the ship's crew pulled me on board at the top. The stench that struck me was unbelievable. The smell from 20,000 sheep – all shitting in a confined space – was absolutely foul.

We adjourned to the captain's cabin, where everyone except myself had rum – it was 10.30 in the morning. Along with the rum, the captain kept a single rose in his cabin to help drown out the smell of the sheep.

After going through the pathology and history of the ill crewman, I could not work out what was going on. I said I would need him to come back to the hospital for observation and further investigation. The crew got him on a stretcher and lowered him down on a rope. Then I needed to climb down Jacob's ladder again. When I got to the bottom, the launch was coming up alongside and the waves were right up. Someone yelled at me to jump. I thanked God all my insurances were up to date and leapt for my life onto the deck.

Back on the island, the administrator Charles Buffett had put a surgical team on standby in Sydney. They would fly the moment I gave the word. The problem was, I still could not convince myself of the crewman's diagnosis – and he was getting better and better by the minute.

"You bugger," I thought. "You were putting it on to get off the ship."

Charles was unimpressed when I told him.

"What am I going to tell Sydney?" he asked.

"I say we tell them we've cured him," I replied. And that's exactly what we did. The patient left on the next charter flight to Perth.

Emergency staff were not always so well prepared. Late one night in September, I got a call from the air-traffic tower to say three New Zealander yachties had capsized their dinghy in the lagoon, but only one had been found. I arranged for the hospital theatre to be prepared, and picked up an Oxy-Viva resuscitator. At the jetty, I found Dennis, who had been fishing when he heard cries for help. He rang the three other men who were all on call for such emergencies. The trio had been drinking and were so drunk they barely knew what to do. (I rarely drank much because I was on call all the time.) Dennis was beside himself with anger at them. One of them was even driving the launch that was looking for the missing men – in the wrong area. Fortunately, the two missing Kiwis were found and were not too drunk, so got a hot shower and hot drink and survived a night in hospital. I discovered a few things about those three officials that night but, primarily, I found out they could not be relied upon in a real crisis. Charles Buffett was livid at the yachties and demanded they come to see him first thing in the morning. The yachties however hightailed it out of Cocos at dawn. When they got to Geraldton, the yachties were found to be carrying a quantity of drugs. Arrests were made.

Back in July, a new couple, Deidre and Chris, had arrived. We had met them through other friends on the islands. She was a marvellous painter who worked 12 hours a day. He was a well-read, active bloke with a good knowledge of the islands. He was also a keen landscape gardener and worked as an air-traffic controller.

While I felt close to Mary at this time, I had sensed for some time that Chris had been paying her a lot of attention. It caused friction between me and Chris. Sometimes I saw him fighting with Deidre, including one time when he complained she spent too much time on her paintings and too little on him. I thought the paintings were a better investment.

It was a difficult time because, while we had some of our best conversations with Deidre and Chris, by late September I had gone off him in large lumps. I felt he could easily turn malicious, even if he initiated the problem he was being malicious about.

Meantime, our laissez-faire, democratic attitude to parenting Jolyon and Guy was not producing good results. Jolyon was subject to outbursts of mania that were hard to bring under control. While the children had freedoms, they sometimes strayed too far. I once found Jolyon on the road with a broken kite and Guy out on the airstrip. Another time I came in to find Jolyon sitting on a chair, sipping alcoholic cider.

"I'm going to drink this waiting for the [Cocos Keeling] Olympics to start," he said. Fortunately, he had not drunk too much. And, in his defence, they were a great deal of fun.

Approaching the end of our first year on the islands, we were weighing up whether to continue for another year. Reasons to stay included the pollution of Melbourne versus the beauty of the sunsets and the beaches. Mary also had an important role in the community, which she relished. But the schooling on Cocos was inadequate, and Jolyon needed a good school.

My sense that life back in Carlton was calling was only heightened by Chris's presence around our house. I couldn't help but notice how much time he was spending with Mary. The Malays had begun to gossip about it. Both our housekeeper, Mus, and I felt Chris was spending too much time alone with Mary. It was clear he was keen on her. One night, listening to records, he tried to strongly embrace Mary while dancing. She rejected him. Later, when we went to Chris and Deidre's place, Chris followed Mary to the toilet every time she went. When I tried to offer assistance, Mary told me she would ask for help if she needed it. Chris was really starting to give me the shits. The situation was a tinderbox.

Election night, rejection night

On the night of the 1980 federal election, October 18, I was still hopeful of a Labor Party win, led by Bill Hayden. But as the results came in, it was clear the situation was grim – Malcolm Fraser would be elected for a third term.

We drank bottles of wine with Chris and Deidre. Emboldened by the booze, and morose about the election loss, I decided to tackle the one thing I could – our relationship with the other couple. I felt the air needed to be cleared.

It was plain to me that Mary had a strong attachment to Chris.

"Is there something going on here that I don't know about?" I said to Chris and Mary.

Mary and Chris fumbled about at this without a direct answer, so I continued on. I told Chris and Deidre we liked their company but I knew Chris was attracted to Mary. Sly visits to my home while I was out were not on, I told Chris. This needed to be played out in the open so everyone could see the game Chris was playing.

Deidre was aghast: "What's this? Is it true, Chris?"

Chris was trapped. If he said no, he would let Mary down. If he said yes, he would be letting his wife down. Deidre continued to nail Chris until he had to admit they were having an affair.

"Oh, yes," Chris replied simply.

That, I had not expected.

"What? What the hell's going on?" I asked Mary. "Are you having an affair?"

Mary held her head in her hands, and kept repeating: "This is so embarrassing."

The floor fell away from below me.

The break-up

From then on, I repeated to Mary what I had already told her in Carlton: "If you want to go, go."

We had many deep discussions about marriage, attraction, the need for change and constancy.

Things began to unravel. Mary told me she was in love with Chris but that he had not made her an offer, so she could not make up her mind about whether to stay or go. I could not play second fiddle, nor could I stand in her way. I told her I needed to reassess my feelings of unreserved love for her.

A week after the election rejection revelation, I told her I would take the boys back to Melbourne. We would not be extending our visit by another year. I said she could do as she felt she must. At night, she could convince me she was still with me, totally, but in the morning the thought of leaving Chris made her vomit and tremble.

When I saw Chris on the side of the road, I refused to wave to him, an unforgivable action on the island. Mary called me petty. She was siding with Chris. We were in a crisis. I told her I was warder only to our two boys, not to her.

I withdrew my love for her. It was clear she had chosen Chris, even though he would not commit to her. I could do no more.

The one bright moment in this time was the aforementioned Cocos (Keeling) Islands' Olympics. Jolyon ran and won the flag race and came second in the 25-yard sprint, both for five-year-olds. Despite warning the locals for weeks to warm up before a race, I failed to do so and pulled a hamstring five steps in. Mary thought I had had a heart attack. With all that had been going on in our lives, there was no doubt my heart was aching.

Getting out of Cocos

Before the marriage breakdown, I had planned to stay another year. Now that Mary and I were through, I found I could not even bear to complete my first year. Mary had slowly withdrawn from the boys' care and it was clear I would have custody. She did not object. My main concern was now the boys. I would take them back to Melbourne. Their mother could do as she pleased and make her own arrangements. That said, there were times when we were affectionate and caring for each other, even under the strained circumstances.

But the overall situation was intolerable. Mary was planning her life with Chris, yet we were living in our home socially, as if we were a married couple.

When I could take no more, I booked a flight back for November 18 at 10.30pm – one month after the election night revelation. My tenant and her child would need to move out of Arnold Street early – something she did not appreciate, but she agreed.

Looking back, I think the break-up was on the cards from the minute we had children. At the time, I convinced myself that intellectuals should not have children. All suffered. This thinking stemmed from the sudden availability of no-fault divorce in Australia, in 1975. It burst a bubble of pent-up demand from intellectuals with money to get divorced. Among our intellectual friends, it was rife.

Mary would come back on the charter flight with us to Perth, and we would leave her there. I did not want her to return to Melbourne with me. I needed a clean break to concentrate on Jolyon and Guy.

Leaving Cocos on that November day, I saw the dawn rise through the clouds and Christmas Island from above. The boys were well behaved, but I was quiet with my own thoughts. Mary and I did not speak.

While the boys slept at the Perth hotel, I arranged the tickets for the flight to Melbourne for the boys and me. By now it was Wednesday and our choices were fly that night or wait until Saturday. Saturday meant three wasted days in Perth. Eager to put the miles between Mary and I, I booked to leave that night at 10.40pm.

That day, Mary and I lay on the bed crying a lot, both about different things.

Before I left Perth, I called Cocos and spoke to Wal Young, the island's secretary. I broke down when he told me how respected and liked I was.

Mary and I told the boys about the separation. They did not yet understand its meaning, but they were mildly disturbed as Mary was sobbing piteously. Then I wrenched away onto the 10.40pm flight home with two sleepy boys.

A month after our flight from Cocos, the administrator Charles Buffett called Chris in and sacked him as an air-traffic controller. He told Chris to get off the islands. Having heard about the affair, Charles told Chris that they had lost the best doctor the islands had ever had.

Mary waited for Chris in Perth, with his arrival presumably expedited by the sacking. When they were finally together, she became confused about what she wanted – Chris or the boys and me – and she said she could not make up her mind. She wanted to work as an ABC journalist, but really it was just a dream. I wasn't holding her back from that, I encouraged her. She had got on the grog on the islands, convincing herself that her family held her career back. Well, her career went nowhere without us too. She and Chris ended up living in Brisbane. Things were pretty mucky at this stage, but the boys were my only priority now.

Chapter 25
Treating the Medics

After two years at the Melbourne State College, a terrific job came up as the in-house doctor to the Royal Women's Hospital staff. Doctors, nurses and admin staff get sick and need a doctor too.

When I started in 1983, the clinic was next to the pharmacy department but soon moved to opposite the hospital in Cardigan Street. Along with running the clinic for appointments, I screened both men and women for rubella and ran breast screening clinics for staff twice a week. I would vaccinate staff too, although fewer than 100 would take the influenza jab back then.

Over settling in, two things became apparent. Firstly, nurses were continuously getting back injuries from lifting patients. Having experienced my own back operation in 1983 after years of lumping in my youth in WA, I knew preventative measures were needed urgently.

And secondly, staff were underreporting needlestick injuries. They felt a report would lead nowhere, so fewer than 10 were reported in 1983. It would not be long before staff would begin reporting needle stick injuries with alarm. There was also a viral timebomb ticking – by July, 1983, Australia would have its first death from AIDS. (Four years later, the federal government would launch its "Grim Reaper" AIDS-awareness campaign.)

Aware that stray needles were now an even greater workplace hazard, I vowed to improve the reporting of needlestick injuries. To get the word out that I would be investigating each case, I promoted it in the *Royal Examiner*, the in-house newsletter, and spoke to heads of nursing and unit managers. It was a relentless campaign. As the reports came in, I looked at the circumstances: What were the conditions at the time? What was the state of the floor? How were the racks positioned? Where and how was the needle disposed of?

Over time, I could get a picture of what was happening. The vast majority of injuries occurred in the handling of the needles after they were used.

Nurses would put the syringe and needle into a dish and walk with it to the disposal bin. Nearly all the injuries occurred between fishing it out of the dish and disconnecting the syringe before disposal.

My suggestion to staff was that they bring a sharps disposal bin with them on their rounds, which began in about 1988. That way, once the injection was complete, the needle could be removed while they were still holding the syringe securely, rather than double-handing it. I also impressed upon the nurses the dangers of leaving needles in sheets, trolleys and shelves by the bedside.

In 1988, there were 86 needlestick injuries reported. But the following year, that figure fell to 24, with fewer people getting injured.

Still, in 1989, the risk of HIV at the Royal Women's was not as high as at other hospitals. Fewer than 50 women were diagnosed with HIV in Australia to October that year (seven in Victoria), while men made up 1481 cases (317 in Victoria). Needle and syringe exchange and disposal programs were said to have helped contain the virus.

Nurses' backs remained my other big concern. At that time, an adult woman was supposed to lift no more than 16 kilograms, yet the nurses were often hoisting much more. Even the lightest person was too much weight for two nurses to lift. I did think briefly that the nurses could have used my old wheat lumping hook to pick up patients by the scruff of their collar, but instead I suggested "donkey ropes" – a rope that hung at the bottom of the bed so that patients could pull themselves up. It was a short-lived solution, later replaced by Jacob's ladders for patients to hall themselves up. This too has gone by the wayside.

Up until the 1980s, nurses transferring a patient from one bed to another would have to grab the sheet and pull the patient over. It took so much energy. Instead, I suggested sliding a board between the two beds, so the patient could be rolled or shuffled across.

Strike

As often happens where I work, there was a strike. In October, 1986, the Royal Australian Nursing Federation (Victorian Branch) went on strike, and RWH nurses joined them. It was an incredible time. A 50-day strike was sparked when negotiations broke down with the Cain government and Health Minister David White. It was a powerful moment for nurses because, up until then, the general population believed nurses would not abandon their jobs to force improved conditions and wages. But there they were on picket lines with tents set up, standing their ground, with only a skeleton staff for emergencies in hospitals.

During the strike, I was required to stand up for a diagnosis and stick by it. At this time, the medical services director at the Women's had closed the theatres. No elective surgery could be done as the theatres could not be staffed. Feelings were running high.

As I was the staff doctor, a nurse came to see me with abdominal pain. I was initially worried it might be her right ovary. A gynaecologist had checked her pelvis that morning and reassured her that there was no pathology in the pelvis. I knew the nurse. I went over her history about three times. I gave a rectal examination, which, I believe, along with other medical signs, showed an acute attack of appendicitis had occurred, and her appendix had subsequently ruptured. The released pus had become walled off behind the bowel, leaving her with a retrocaecal appendicular abscess.

The medical director was none too pleased that a nurse would need an immediate operation in the middle of a nurses' strike. He questioned my diagnosis, given the patient had seen a gynaecologist that morning.

At once I recalled Rudyard Kipling's poem *If –*. (Albeit an imperialist call to arms, the poem thrilled me as a child, as I was in awe of British culture.) A line from the poem rang out as clear as a bell while I was standing with the director:

If you can trust yourself when all men doubt you,
But make allowance for their doubting too.

My resolve was there. I stood firm – this nurse had to be operated on. A very fine surgeon removed the abscess.

"And who in the hell is this Percy?" the surgeon was heard to say. I could never find out whether he posed the question before the operation as a criticism, or after, as a compliment.

During the strike, I supported other nurses in other ways. My neighbours, Di Earl and Laurel Guymer, were both nurses and I helped them in whatever way I could. Usually, I gave them a hot meal so they could make their savings stretch further as the strike dragged on. They became great friends of mine.

When the strike ended on December 20, 1986, the nurses had won. The state government offered a $30-million package, providing wage rises, the return of qualifications allowances and a new career structure.

Fuming cabinets

At the Royal Women's I developed a habit of sitting with the pharmacy staff at their lunch table in the staff cafeteria. They were a raucous bunch, due entirely to a lovely woman from the Scottish Highlands called Edna Macchi, who used to threaten to trim my unruly eyebrows with scissors. (I never did find out how she got that Italian-sounding surname though.) While I was not initially doctor to all 13 of the pharmacy staff, before too long they were all coming to my clinic at Cardigan Street.

When I started at the clinic, I decided to investigate the viruses and bacteria at the hospital by swabbing the noses and throats of my first 50 patients. Most of them carried some form of bacteria – usually streptococcus and staphylococcu. Some tested positive to a virus. Of these, few had any thought of taking time off work. In my experience, it's nurses in particular who have a heightened sense of duty and tend to carry on regardless of illness. The only way to get them to take time off from work to get better was to tell them they were transmitting their infections to their patients.

Over the first couple of years, I noticed that all the older pharmacy staff – about five of them aged in their late 40s and 50s – appeared to constantly have low-grade virus-like symptoms – colds and fevers, mostly. It was odd.

By the end of 1984, these symptoms had amounted to a bizarre cluster. A couple of the older pharmacy staff came to me saying that their regular doctor had diagnosed them with glandular fever, a virus virtually unheard of outside your early 20s – so much so that by the time we reach maturity, most people have had it without noticing it and are, therefore, immune. (The symptoms are similar to chronic fatigue syndrome and, based on my observations, I believe glandular fever may be a precursor to chronic fatigue.) I refused to believe a cluster of 40 to 59-year-olds had glandular fever.

After interviewing all the pharmacy staff, I realised the older ones also shared a common workplace role – they all prepared cytotoxic drugs ("cyto" as in cells, "toxic" as in poison) for the treatment of cancer patients. These powerful chemotherapy drugs are effective in killing cancer cells but are dangerous to healthy cells too. Precautions were taken because, even back then, it was known that working with cytotoxic drugs posed a risk of altering normal cell counts in the handler. Other risks have since come to light, including abnormalities and mutagenic activity; abdominal pain; hair loss; nasal sores; vomiting; liver damage; fertility changes; miscarriages;

and deformities in unborn children. The drugs can even be excreted in the urine of exposed workers.

At the RWH, to protect workers, the drugs were prepared in a fume cabinet – a laboratory cupboard with its own ventilation system. Handlers also need other protective equipment, such as masks.

The younger, relatively healthy staff did not work in the cabinet. This was a presumptive measure to protect women planning a family and their unborn children. The older pharmacists were initially rostered to work some 20 hours in the cabinet each week, with a changing of the guard every three months. For the most part, the work was shared among the older five pharmacists.

Puzzled, I began full blood screens for all hospital staff working with cytotoxic drugs every six months. This was Peter MacCallum Cancer Centre's protocol, and I felt it prudent to follow the leader on cancer drugs.

About the time I recognised the cluster, I read an article by a former university colleague, Professor Alex Morley, in Adelaide, who was working with lymphocytes – part of the white blood cell system. He suggested I speak with Dr Judy Ford, head of the genetics department at the Queen Elizabeth Hospital in Adelaide. She was looking into whether disease could cause chromosomal changes. She was also investigating whether handling hazardous chemicals could alter cells, leading to abnormalities in birth and the development of cancer. After explaining the situation, I sent her bloods from all the pharmacy staff. All 13 staff members agreed to have their blood tested as part of the investigation.

In blind testing, Dr Ford found that only the five pharmacists who handled the drugs had chromosomal abnormalities which were mutagenic (able to change DNA) and teratogenic (able to cause abnormalities in gestating fetuses). Among those five, Dr Ford found that all but one had a marked neutropenia (lower than normal levels of neutrophils, a type of white blood cell). This condition is often found in leukaemia patients receiving cytotoxic treatment, and makes those patients suspectable to infection.

Then I contacted Dr Neil Boyce, the Monash Medical Centre's head of clinical immunology. He found that the five pharmacy patients all had an inversion of the CD4/C08 ratio of the T helper cells – meaning they had low immunity. Typically, this is found in a person suffering from HIV, tuberculosis and (now we know) coronavirus. The findings were pointing to toxicity to the bone marrow.

I alerted the hospital administration. The fume cabinet's filters were checked and found to be clear and working. Despite this, I remained convinced the fume cabinet was the root cause of the cell abnormalities.

I continued to test the pharmacists' blood to look for changes. But about six months after the first results came in, the hospital administration ordered me to stop: the results were alarming the staff. No wonder! Meanwhile, I had other staff writing to me, asking me to continue my tests.

Of the five affected staff in the pharmacy, Joseph "George" Landers was by far the worst off. Having worked in the RWH pharmacy since 1973, George had begun preparing cytotoxic drugs for chemotherapy patients in 1983.

By February 1986, he developed shingles, which affected the 7th cranial nerve in his face and caused a Bell's palsy paralysis. Along with an iron deficiency and anaemia, he acquired pancytopenia, a condition where all three blood cell types – red, white and platelets – were low.

In June 1989, worryingly, he also had gastrointestinal bleeding. I immediately sent George to surgeon Mr Donald Kemp at The Alfred Hospital, with a presumptive diagnosis of carcinoma of his gastrointestinal tract. A thorough examination found a significant malignant tumour of the duodenum invading the pancreas. The second part of the duodenum is an extremely rare location for cancer: so rare that Mr Kemp investigated its incidence worldwide. He found just five other cases – three of whom had been involved in handling the same type of cancer-treating drugs.

George was forced to stop working in 1989, before his surgery. By November that year, he was forced to give up work altogether. He was 59. Forced into early retirement, George took his case to arbitration. Both Mr Kemp and I were witnesses.

The pressure was enormous during this period of 1988 to 1990. The staff were anxious and the hospital administration tetchy. A senior administrator wrote to me to tell me he disagreed with my diagnosis, saying the blood changes were the result of viruses. I ignored him.

About a fortnight before George's case went to arbitration, I was called into a meeting with my boss, the director of clinical services, Clive Wellington. When we arrived, there were more than a dozen "suits" lined up, including the hospital's lawyers, the heads of pharmacy from Monash Medical Centre and RWH, and the hospital chief executive, Gary Henry. They addressed Clive, not me.

"Now Clive," one fellow began, "what you've got to do, the minute they refuse to go into that fume cabinet to do the analysis of the drugs, is sack them."

"You shit," I thought.

Next, the head of the pharmacy department for RWH spoke. He was more conciliatory.

"Perce has been looking at this for a while," he said. "And I must say, the staff are worried." But we haven't seen anything definitive yet."

"You rotten bastard," I thought.

They kept talking as if there was a virus problem. I don't often get cross, but I did this time, and I carried on like a pork chop.

"Look," I said, "I think we'd better stop this talk of viruses. We've got a patient with cancer. Now you don't get that from mucking around. You get that from something – a cancerous agent. And this talk of sacking, you can forget that. These people have got a legitimate case."

I then pointed out Mr Kemp's research about the other rare cases.

In the end, it was Gary Henry who stepped in. "I think we'd better stop talking about viruses," he said. "The evidence is that people have got cancer."

I left and they thanked me for my time.

George took his case to the Accident Compensation Tribunal (now the WorkCover List in the County Court) in September 1989. On March 14, 1990, Judge John Bowman found the hospital and the Accident Compensation Commission (now WorkSafe) had the burden of proof to show the preparation of the cytotoxic drugs had not caused George's cancer. Judge Bowman found that while there was a possibility that the drugs had not caused George's cancer, the defence had not proved it was not the cause.

Judge Bowman found the fume cabinet was a biohazard cabinet, rather than one specifically designed for cytotoxic drug preparation. Its construction and location made it unsafe. Hearing evidence that the hospital was warned of this in 1984, he also found that the masks that George (and other staff) wore left staff more exposed to the fumes than other available masks.

The cabinet was finally removed in 1989.

The George Landers case transformed the way drugs were handled in hospitals throughout Australia. Word spread rapidly in hospitals about inadequate fume cupboards, leading to a general revision and tightening of conditions in the preparation of cytotoxic drugs. The Royal Women's had all its cytotoxic drugs prepared off-site after this case.

A senior doctor working in a field related to cells and immunity contacted me to say the dangers were known among hospitals. One senior specialist in immunology told me that his wife, a nurse, was preparing the same drugs as George Landers beside patients' beds, without protection. Not long after, I heard that this nurse had a carcinoma of the breast. A few months after that, her other breast had a lump too. I could not dismiss from my mind the possibility that the cause was the result of preparing cytotoxic drugs.

In 1993, with a new administration at the helm, I was called in. I was told the hospital would be advertising my position. I was welcome to apply. In anyone's books, that was the sack. I chose to resign rather than suffer the potential indignity of being overlooked for my own job.

The last time I heard from George, he was in Crete, working at archaeological digs, in the fresh air – well away from cytotoxic drugs.

Chapter 26
The one that almost got away

Just before the fume cabinet court case in September 1989, a woman had come to see me at my surgery at the Royal Women's Hospital. Although she was not a staff member, a nursing friend had suggested she come to see me anyway. I was at once struck by how alive, alert and interested she was in what was going on in the world. With a good sense of humour, she shone bright.

In the course of our lively chat, she asked me where I came from.

"I'm a boy from the bush," I said.

She too was from Western Australia. We discussed mutual experiences, friends and feelings arising from our common upbringing in WA.

While we eventually got to discussing her symptoms, she did not take any diagnosis without question. She said someone she knew had had that same diagnosis and was in a wheelchair. As a rehabilitation therapist she was not happy with my diagnosis at all. She made it clear this could not be the case, as it was not happening to her. We did not make a follow-up appointment.

I wondered about her for many weeks but, as I have already mentioned, as a doctor you cannot date a patient romantically.

Going nuts over Roz

By 1990, Jolyon and Guy were aged 12 and 14 and becoming independent. Although they were still my focus, like all budding teenagers, their focus was beginning to shift. It was around this time they decided they did not want to go to the farm anymore as their interests now lay in the city. With them in mind, I put the farm on the market and got no bids.

When, after the auction, I met Sue and Ken Ophel, two locals, I was delighted to hear Ken had been the federal secretary of the Australian Theatricals and Amusement Employees' Association (now part of the Media Entertainment and Arts Alliance). I employed him to help me with the farm and he became like a farm manager and a friend. Together we planted nut trees continuing on from the plantings I had done in what I called the Nut Birthing Centre.

When I started the Nut Birthing Centre, I planted a few chestnut, hazelnut and walnut trees. The chestnuts just went mad. I planted more – 100 in the top paddock – until I ran out of space and planted another 100 in the bottom paddock. (I would later buy up more land, from the adjoining property, to end up with two parcels of 65 acres and 79 acres, covered in 2500 chestnut trees.)

Back in town, my friendship with nurses Di and Laurel continued (although Laurel had moved to Clifton Hill by this stage). They often pondered my non-existent love life, thinking of matches for me. Laurel kept telling me about a single mother who lived opposite her in Dally Street, Clifton Hill – she was apparently really lovely and shared my opinions on politics. Laurel told me how the woman's first husband was a Russian who had done his honours thesis on the Mensheviks, the opposition to the Bolsheviks in the 1917 revolution. She said the woman was a feisty and committed left-winger, ready to take up a battle for a cause. As I was forever fighting for causes, I could hardly say no. I suggested Laurel and Di bring this mystery woman up to the farm and we could see how we got on.

The love-match responded with a counter offer – she invited me over for dinner. But I stuck to my guns, insisting on the farm visit. (It has long been my practice not to go for private dinner at other people's homes where someone is always rushing off to the kitchen. It distorts relationships too much and disrupts conversation flow. In my view, it is only acceptable if everyone brings something to eat, so that nobody is rushing back and forth.)

We decided to head up on the Labour Day weekend, March 10-12, 1990. As Di and Laurel would be travelling up with friends, they asked me to pick up the mystery woman and drive her to the farm.

Knocking on an unfamiliar door at Dally Street, Clifton Hill, I stood on the threshold in more ways than one. To my shock and delight, I was greeted by a familiar face. It was the same woman who had come to my clinic six months earlier!

"You're coming with me," were my first words to Roz Lensky that day.

All the way there, Roz and I talked. I hardly noticed the drive. It turned out that Roz's daughter, Anna, was just a little younger than Guy. And, although I had just entered my 60s and she had just finished her 40s, we had lots to talk about.

We chatted again about growing up in Western Australia, and how she had then gone to work on a farm in Wagin, which was close to my hometown of Narrogin. As a kid, I had played football against Wagin. Roz, as a young folk singer, had toured the areas I had worked in – Corrigin and Wickepin – staying at farmhouses and performing recitals in whatever halls were available.

I learnt that Roz's artistic talents ranged far and wide. She had travelled to England in 1968, where she studied painting and fine art at London's prestigious Byam Shaw School of Art (now part of Central Saint Martins). In later years, as a dancer, she had started a dance school at the Clifton Hill Presbyterian Church.

Her politics came from her father, who seemed a very decent man. He was ahead of his time in many ways. Very passionate about the environment, he was interested in the value of food and the sorts of foods we should eat. He was also a runner.

Roz's maiden name was Smart. At some point, I realised it was her Russian married name that I had noticed on the UMFAG telephone list.

Arriving at the farm, I could tell immediately that she loved it. (At that time, I had 79 acres with a bit over 1000 trees.)

Di and Laurel and a bunch of others arrived and we had a party at the farm with people sleeping in the house, in tents and in the cowshed I had converted as a sleep out.

That night, I took the cad's way and got her drunk. We talked all night. After a little sleep, I was up at 6am, slashing blackberries on a path, to show Roz the natural water spring on the property.

Court finding

Days after the visit to the farm, the judgment in the George Landers' case was complete. On or about Wednesday, March 14, 1990, I was so immersed in reading Judge Bowman's findings and the nuances of opinions throughout the case, that I did not notice all my evidence and clippings falling from my arms as I walked down Bourke Street. A kind person ran up behind me and handed them back to me.

On the Saturday, I went around to Roz's house, taking the findings with me. She was hanging out washing and I offered to help. I'd been hanging out the boys' washing for 10 years, and I figured showing my peg prowess could go in my favour.

"Are you OK hanging out women's washing? There are no men here," Roz replied and, of course, I obliged.

Within a fortnight, I asked her to marry me. I thought we made quite a good pair.

"It's too early," she replied. She felt she hardly knew me and it was too early to ask. My feeling was instantly that she was the one for me. While I would have to bide my time, I set out to woo her.

I quickly adapted to the conditions of a romantic life again. Roz and I established a very good working relationship on the farm, and a loving relation elsewhere. She loved to get out and do things on the property.

Roz's daughter Anna loved the idea of Jolyon, Guy and myself living together as an all-male household, and she loved the idea of mixing in with two boys and the man of the house. Anna insisted she and Roz come live with us, and Roz did not need much encouragement. They moved into Arnold Street in mid-1990.

Anna was so very beautiful, and still is. I claim her as my own daughter. I remember she would sit up on the edge of the couch, in the back room, above Jolyon and Guy and their friends, holding court. She loved it, and so did they. (Anna works in publishing now and I'm very proud of her.)

Up until that point, I would say that looking after Jolyon and Guy had been the single most personally satisfying part of my life. I cherished every moment of tending to their needs and guiding them to manhood. When Roz and Anna arrived on the scene, my life filled out all the more beautifully.

At the end of 1990, with Anna, Guy and Jolyon being looked after by Roz's parents, Billie and Johnny Smart, who were over from Perth, Roz and I had some alone time on our hands. So, I asked her if she would like to come to Cocos (Keeling) Islands. Despite everything that had occurred with Mary, the islands were still a paradise that I wanted to share with Roz. She jumped at the idea.

On the islands, Roz got to meet some of the children I had helped deliver. My Cocos Malayan friends were especially welcoming. There was James Jamaludin, who wouldn't stop hugging me, and Capstan (which was the only name I ever knew him by, so I don't know if it was his given or surname) demanded that we come to stay on Home Island.

Capstan and James shared a wife, and it looked like it was Capstan's month on. Still, Capstan vied for Roz's attention. He tried to test my manhood when he took us out on a reef and issued me with a challenge: "Down there is an octopus, can you pull it up?"

Having caught many octopuses in the past, I was aware that their beaks carry a poison, which can turn very nasty. The tentacles never bothered me, though. So, I put my hand into the cracks in the reef and got hold of a tentacle. I pulled it up, being careful of the beak. It was quite a big one. I asked Capstan whether he wanted it for food. He said he didn't want it but wanted to see if I was "man" enough. I returned it to the reef.

After a wonderful stay on the islands, we returned to our home life and, on December 14, 1991, Roz and I got married on the top farm at Fumina. Roz's parents, Billie and Johnny Smart, her brother, Roger, and his then-wife, Andy, came up to the farm for the wedding. Roger is a professor of surface physics. Jolyon, Anna and Guy all came too. We were married by a forward-thinking Presbyterian reverend that Roz knew and I liked. After the wedding, we went to the nearby hamlet of Hillend, where I had booked a dinner at a local domestic reception place. Roz asked for a bottle of Champagne to toast the wedding, but there was no alcohol on the premises, so afterwards we returned to the farm for some Champagne.

Growing pains

I knew my boys were maturing fast, but I had chanced upon an added reminder in the months before Roz and Anna moved in with us. Hidden under the air conditioning vents, I had found salacious newspapers and magazines with nude women on them. Unsure what to do, I approached my neighbour, Bloss Robertson. Bloss was a very sensible and enthusiastic educator at RMIT, but importantly, she understood boys, having a son of her own. I asked her if she would speak to Jolyon and Guy about women and femineity. At the time, I was wary of asking too much of Roz as a mother figure to the boys.

Bloss called Guy into the room first and he acknowledged the material was his and Jolyon's. Bloss started by saying that there were men around who did not like women very much, but that the Carlton men we knew were not like that. She told Guy he needed to be strong like they were to fight against that kind of sexism, and to respect women. It sunk in, and I think the boys' attitude to women has remained terrific.

It was not long after this that I became unhappy with the boys' school, Princes Hill Secondary College. Jolyon was falling behind and Guy was miserable there.

"You can go to whatever school you like because I've insisted you go to a public secondary school and it has not worked out too well," I said.

Jolyon had a friend at Wesley College and wanted to go there, so Guy and Anna, who was going into Year 7, joined him. At Wesley, Jolyon just bombed on, going from strength to strength. But Guy hated it. Though he was good at English, and a very good writer, at one point his teacher refused to accept that Guy had written an excellent piece, because Guy played the fool in the classroom. I had to ring the teacher and explain that my son was not the "wolf twerp" he presented. Guy never liked the "very clever" persona, and hid it.

These were tumultuous times, particularly for Guy. He quit school and, at 16, ran away to South Australia to live with a friend of ours for 10 days. He got the bus back.

"No, you don't come back to live at home unless you are studying or working," I told him.

In response, Guy went out that afternoon and got five jobs. One of his jobs was at Barkly Square, the nearby shopping mall in Brunswick. He was underpaid, so I went down to remonstrate with his employers. He received $300 in back pay.

In this messy year, Guy took on a great saviour mission when he moved into a share house with a mate, Urch, who was a heroin addict. When Guy tried to help him, he had everything he owned stolen. It was a great, if tough, lesson. There was also an online girlfriend in Queensland.

After a year away from school, he got sick of the job he had taken folding sheets in a hospital.

"Dad, if I don't get an education, I'm going to be folding sheets until after I'm 30," he told me. "And you don't get much older than 30."

When Guy asked to return home so he could go back to school, I welcomed him back. I offered to pay him an allowance each week and to help him study. Thanks to support again from Bloss Robertson, Guy went to RMIT to complete Year 12 and loved it. His scores were sufficient to get him into arts at La Trobe University.

He is now a member of the police force, and treats everyone fairly. He has a particular rapport with Aboriginal and Sudanese kids. In 2016, at the Melbourne Youth Justice Centre in Parkville, inmates were rioting on the roof and they only agreed to come down if it was Guy who cuffed them. I would say he is a pretty good police officer, not a "bash 'em" type. I like to tell him that if he sees me on a sit-in protest line, he needs to help me get up off the ground, rather than arrest me.

Jolyon had his struggles, too. He felt his mother's absence a great deal, although he never spoke to me about it other than in an oblique way, and I was always careful not to discuss her in the boys' presence.

After excelling at Wesley, Jolyon became a corporate lawyer. He handles himself very well. Now a father of boys himself, his little boys are always around his neck, holding him close. It's clear he loves them back. He and his wife have an unusual way of bringing up their boys; everything is a positive and he rarely disciplines them. It is hard to take, but it does seem to be the fashion. We spend time with them at their holiday house in Cape Paterson on the Bass Coast. The family noise factor is unbelievable. There is a special place in heaven for women who give birth to three boys!

I take great proud in seeing my two boys grown into great men now. I'm delighted with them.

Farming down

Back in 1991, I joined the Chestnut Growers of Australia (now Chestnuts Australia). Its members were enormously helpful with advice for putting in a cool store and processing plant. I later joined a breakaway group of larger growers, called Premier Chestnuts Australia. While we worked to increase the quality of our nuts, and were successful in doing so, and commanding an extra $1000 a tonne, our stated ambition to enter the lucrative Japanese market came to nought.

Roz and I continued to develop the farm at weekends, pruning and getting out on the tractor as needed.

In 2000, working on the farm suddenly got a lot harder. Walking into the tractor shed one day, I failed to notice a patch of oil on the ground. I slipped, and my right leg went straight out in front of me, but my left leg remained locked. As I lurched backwards, all my quad muscles in my left leg were torn away, and I hit the floor, knocked out. Eventually, I awoke and used a nail bar as a crutch to get back to the house.

Roz organised an orthopaedic surgeon in Melbourne to repair my leg, stitching my muscles back onto the kneecap. Although I did everything I could, I could not return to running. Unfortunately, the surgeon seems not to have repaired the nerves and the leg does not function properly, making my knee wobbly. It worked well enough for some years, but I now require a mobility walker to assist me.

Even so, the farm continued to give us great joy. On a trip to Europe in

1998, Roz and I went to Spain to check out a chestnut peeling machine for the farm. By then, the Nut Birthing Centre was quite well advanced and I was getting quite a few tonnes of chestnuts. I found the owner's wife, an English literature lecturer at a Spanish university, was much more interesting than her husband. At dinner we spoke for hours about English literatures, but I never did buy that chestnut peeler.

Without a peeler I continued in my practice of employing a team of 14 Thai pickers, whom I paid a bit over the going rate to pick up the fallen chestnuts. For eight hours a day, they would pick them up and when the season was over, we would give them a great party to celebrate and thank them. I did this for a few years until I bought a harvester made by a couple in Newcastle. The harvester had brushes that drew up the nuts from the ground and combed the husks away.

We continued with the farm as it was until 2008. We then sold all but five acres, and the house. It is a perfect retreat, but age has meant that even that has become too much.

Chapter 27
China

In 2011, Roz and I took a trip to China. Having for decades been fascinated by the Chinese Communist Party's struggle for leadership and the exploits of the Red Army, I was excited by the prospect of finally experiencing the spirit of the Chinese people firsthand.

The political alliances between the rulers and the communists during the civil war in China was the source of hours of study for me. One of my favourite stories involved the communists' Red Army fleeing the advancing Nationalist Army in the Long March up to the city of Yan'an in the 1930s. This was at a time when the nobility of the Red Army had been fighting a Japanese invasion in 1931 while the National Army, instead of fighting the foreign aggressors, was fighting the communists. While academics may have since disputed the sequence of events, it wasn't until the communists captured National Army leader Chiang Kai-shek in 1936 that the communists forced an alliance with the National Army to fight the Japanese invasion. This alliance continued until 1945, when Japan was forced to retire from World War II and the Japanese were defeated in China. From here, the Communists defeated the Nationalists and the People's Republic of China was declared on October 1, 1949. With that sort of history in mind, I wanted to see for myself how well the country was coping under communist rule.

Enthralled as I was, I was well aware of China's harmful stupidity towards its people. The Great Famine of 1959 to 1961, which was responsible for the deaths of up to 55 million people, was a largely man-made disaster caused by the Great Leap Forward. During this time, the ruling communists, led by Chairman Mao Zedong, forbade farm ownership and cultivation of private plots. Instead, people's communes were created, and the harvest they reaped was appropriated by the state. The people starved. It was just stupidity.

I also followed the exploits of the Cultural Revolution (from 1966 to 1976), during which Chairman Mao closed schools and mobilised students into the Red Guard to purge the elderly and intellectuals for their lack of revolutionary spirit. An estimated 1.5 million were killed, while millions more suffered humiliation, property loss, imprisonment and torture.

Not all of China's troubles were self-inflicted. Over the centuries, many Western countries had sunk their financial claws into China, trying to extract as much wealth as they could from the country. Britain started it in the 1830s, when it tried to force China to take its Indian opium. (Since the 18th century, British traders had been illegally exporting opium from India to China, with the trade hitting new heights of scale and addiction by 1820.) When China refused, Britain sent in warships (eventually claiming the strategic port of Hong Kong) and the first of the Opium Wars began. Other countries followed – Germany, Japan, Holland, America and Italy. They treated the Chinese like slaves.

Roz and I spent three months in China. I found the people were very friendly, well-dressed, well-nourished and fairly affluent, particularly in the cities. In Beijing especially, I was surprised by the high price of clothing and the preponderance of exclusive labels like Max Mara.

Though we didn't see much of the countryside, we did get to the Great Wall, and took a boat trip up the Yangtze River to Chongqing. Walking up to the Great Wall, I had a local stand in front of me and ask, "How old are you?" I told him approximately. He wanted to know if I was all right to make the walk. I told him I'd have no trouble.

After the trip to the Great Wall, we stopped at a silk factory, which was interesting. We bought Roz silk pyjamas and all manner of other silk items.

On a side trip during our cruise up the Yangtze, I nearly got drawn into a Buddhist monastery. We had taken a bus up a hill, where a monk saw me and beckoned me to follow him. Up in the hill face, if you had an extreme imagination, he showed me how you might be able to see the face of Buddha. (Roz likes to say that my physical characteristics – my round face, my bald head, long ears and especially my bushy eyebrows – all embody the image of wise men in China.) We visited the monastery and continued on with our journey.

While on the boat trip, we also met the grandson of US Rear-Admiral Matthew Perry, who opened up trade with Japan in the Perry Expedition from 1852.

Out and about in the Chinese cities, we heard bicycles all the time. The riders liked to aim at you. The traffic lights did help in slowing the traffic, but I couldn't say they stopped the traffic completely.

I found people in China were very appreciative when they realised you could speak and understand a little bit of Mandarin. I have always been fascinated by Mandarin, and learnt a smattering with my old uni housemate Siew in Carlton, but I also took lessons for two years before going to China. Once there, I was able to make myself understood when I ordered a bottle of wine, although the fellow said he could only understand the word for wine in my pronunciation.

In a Shanghai market, my attempts to bargain for a silk shirt became a piece of theatre. I drew many onlookers as I threw back my head at the price, saying, "*Tai gui le! Tai gui le!*" ("Too expensive!"). As the store was up a flight of stairs, and packed with highly flammable silk, it was a good thing no one struck a match – with the milling crowd we would have struggled to get out!

It was in Shanghai that I tried the local whisky. It was clear, like water. I found it a bit strong, so I added some water from the tap. For the next two days I was violently ill – from the water, I suspect.

In Beijing, we saw where the Communist Party was formed in Shanghai in 1921, with mannequins set around a table to represent Mao Zedong with two members of the Soviet-Comintern, who were trying to get China to adopt the Stalinist method of revolution as Russia. It called for China to get the working class to rise up. The problem was there were not enough working-class people and Mao ended up relying on the peasants.

It was also in Beijing that we were done like a dinner by four grifters. In front of the Gate of Heavenly Peace at Tiananmen Square, there were four Chinese girls all practising their English. They asked us if we would like to have a cup of tea so they could try out their language skills on us. I thought this was a great opportunity to get to know the people of China. Less enthusiastic, Roz tried to convince me otherwise, but I was full of the hope of friendship with the locals. We followed them down a series of laneways until we got to an incredibly seedy place, with a curtain into a small room. The girls began pouring tea and telling me of their aspirations for their future and their English studies. I'm afraid to say that my hope for the future of China blinded my judgment. The bill then arrived for our six cups of tea and some buns – we had been charged the equivalent of $A1000.

I paid up. To be honest, I thought we were going to be attacked. Seeing that outrageous amount on the bill, I had looked for the nearest escape and realised there was no easy way out. For all we knew, there was an enforcer at the ready if we did try to make a dash for it.

When we left that seedy place, there was a crowd outside, laughing – although Roz and I dispute the source of their mirth.

Ireland

On another overseas trip, in 1998, I had my wallet stolen. We were in Palermo, Sicily, where Roz's nephew was having a significant birthday. As in China, I had let my guard down. But occasional disappointments aside, I would prefer to live this way, as I believe that most people are good.

During these travels, Roz and I also went to Ireland. Though my father had rejected his Irish family, and with them Catholics, I felt immediately at home here. I felt an affinity with the pubs and the people. I knew about the insurrection in 1916, and I knew the songs of the Uprising against the British, like the *Foggy Dew* and *The Ballad of Kevin Barry*.

We went to see where the bullet holes went into Dublin's General Post Office during the Easter Monday, in 1916, when rebel leaders held the British at bay before Irish language activist Padraig Pearse proclaimed Ireland a republic. We then went on to Galway, and enjoyed the pubs along the way.

But it was in 2018 that I got to fully embrace my Irish ancestry, at the anniversary of the landing of the last transported convicts to Australia – among them a man I believe to be my distant relative, Thomas Hassett. He was one of the Fenian and Irish Republican Army dissidents aboard the *Hougoumont*, which docked in Western Australia in 1868.

One hundred and fifty years later to the day, I proudly carried the flag towards the Fremantle prison to mark the anniversary. But sadly, my legs could not take me all the way. I asked my cousin Annette to take the flag for me, saying that if she could not walk the distance, she could hand it on to the next person.

"Death is the only thing that will part me from this flag," Annette replied.

Chapter 28
Fly-in Doctor

After leaving the Royal Women's in 1993, I worked in clinics in Carlton and Kensington for 16 years. Both clinics are now gone.

At Kensington, when I refused to charge a gap fee beyond what Medicare paid, nearly all the patients wanted to come to see me. It wasn't that popular with the other staff, but there was nothing they could do about it, and the other doctors ended up dropping the gap fee as well.

At Kensington, we doctors built up a rather large practice, each with good personal followings. Although it was run-of-the-mill medicine, the patients and staff I met were reward enough.

There are two main patient cohorts in medicine: the well and worried; and the unwell and unworried. The well and worried see a doctor for every ailment – real and imagined – and want every test to allay their fears. The unwell and unworried are the patients who need most of your attention as they are unconcerned by the gravity of their own health situation. I decided I could do the most good by treating the unwell and unworried. I considered the different groups and Indigenous Australians were much more likely to be in the unwell and unworried, than middle-class Melburnians. I felt they were the group of Australians most likely to ignore symptoms or not realise their significance.

I turned my attention to Indigenous Australians, well aware that they had some of the poorest health outcomes in the country and a much lower life expectancy than others in Australia. My earlier research dispelling myths about poor Indigenous intelligence was valuable, and I was a long-time supporter of the Victorian Council for Aboriginal Rights. I had met Indigenous activists Sir Douglas Nicholls, Harold Blair and Bill Onus. But it was time to do more than talk.

I approached the Northern Territory Department of Health to offer my services as a locum doctor. I would fly into communities and work there, filling in for a doctor who needed a holiday or, in some cases, be the stop-gap doctor for a town or settlement that could not attract a permanent doctor.

From my perspective I could live in Indigenous communities and see a different side of medicine by working in remote communities. Both Roz and I were keen to see the land up close. Roz, being an artist, could paint the vivid landscapes of the Top End. We would both also relish an opportunity to meet Indigenous artists.

The health department was thrilled to have such an experienced doctor as a locum. The money was much more than I had ever imagined – $6000 a week. I could have done that job forever, and I nearly did. I was in my 80s when I signed up, so I was a little older than your typical locum, but people were very kind to me.

Oenpelli

In January 2010, to try out the lifestyle and the work, I took leave from my clinic duties at Kensington for my first posting – a six-week stint at Oenpelli, at the Gunbalanya Community Health Centre, 300km east of Darwin in Arnhem Land. Known for its rock and bark art, Oenpelli was the perfect Top End starting point for Roz and me.

One of the first things I had to learn as a locum was the computer system, which was incredibly complex to get my head around at first. I was well-versed in Victoria's computer system. I used to ring the help desk number and say, "It's Percy Rogers here, now don't hang up." I'm sure they got sick of me, but I did get the hang of it in the end.

The thing that struck me was that the staff – nurses and health workers – all knew their patients so well. They knew where they had been upcountry. They knew who had been on sorry business (the traditional ceremonies and practices for bereavement). They knew who was in Darwin and who had come back. They knew who had been "in long grass" in Darwin, which was code for being drunk all the time. They knew how everyone was related to each other. This was an incredible resource in medicine.

Every morning we had a staff meeting to discuss what was likely to come up that day. Other than emergencies, the staff with their local knowledge could just about predict what was likely to happen on the day.

The staff worked hard to ensure people were healthy. Their work made a mockery of the federal government's Northern Territory National Emergency Response, also known as The Intervention. This was introduced in the dying days of the Howard government by Indigenous affairs minister Mal Brough, in 2007. The Intervention was a series of measures introduced after the *Little Children are Sacred* report, which alleged widespread child and sexual abuse in remote NT Aboriginal communities. The government placed restrictions and bans on alcohol and pornography. Sweeping changes were made to welfare payments and health, employment and education services.

By the time I arrived, The Intervention was in full swing. There were members of the Australian Defence Forces and teams of health specialists, who were living in these remote communities, with nothing to do. I saw neglected children but never once a case of child sexual abuse. I saw plenty of sexually transmitted diseases in adults in settlements but never with children. The Intervention was a messy and unnecessary breach of human rights.

With all the patients well documented and well treated, the Top End health services were very good to excellent. The nursing staff were the key to it all; the doctors were a back-up service. I confirmed, consulted and organised conveyance out of the settlement to Darwin where necessary. The locums I met fully deserved the acclaim they got from the locals. In 2012, The Intervention legislation was repealed after successive Labor governments introduced several changes.

That is not to say that there was not then or now a series of crises in health in Aboriginal settlements. While I was at Oenpelli, the son of an Indigenous health worker took his own life, casting a pall of sadness over the entire community. Unfortunately, it would not be the only case of suicide I would see in my locum work.

The lay of the land

At Oenpelli, Roz and I stayed in the locum house opposite a three-mile-long billabong. Seeing the billabong with logs floating in it, I wondered where the timber came from. Then I realised the logs had eyes and teeth – crocodiles. There was no swimming in that billabong.

Roz was keen to climb onto rocks and paint in and around Oenpelli, but it soon became clear that doing so wasn't as straightforward as we expected. Having gone for a drive and then walked along a dry riverbed, we came to a pool of water with a cascading waterfall. Here, a mother and son were fishing. It turned out that the woman was a custodian of the land. She told Roz she couldn't paint the land without permission.

Gaining permission was made more complicated because there were three areas, based around three mountains, with different custodians. One of the custodians said she did not want "whities" depicting the land in ways that didn't suit the locals. In the end, Roz got permission to paint some areas but not others. She painted a wonderful picture of Injalak Hill, near Oenpelli, with permission.

Roz also tried her dexterous hands at weaving pandanus fibres with the local women but found it far from easy. We bought some baskets from the experts instead.

One of the highlights of that first trip was a walk up Injalak Hill to view several cave paintings. These were more meaningful than any gallery trip in Europe. About halfway up, we found Mimi, the ancestral Earth Mother, carbon-dated to 40,000 years ago. I felt insignificant in the face of it, especially when I realised the baskets we had bought were the same style that the woman was carrying in the painting.

Roz and I enjoyed the whole Oenpelli experience so much. I loved the work. After a month back at Kensington, I quit my clinic job. I told the NT Health Department it could call on me for other stints in remote communities.

By June, I was back in Oenpelli for another stint, staying for a month, while Roz stayed on in Melbourne to attend an exhibition. On arrival, I discovered that dozens of green frogs had made themselves at home on the toilet seat at the locum house. When flushed away, the amphibians re-emerged from their refreshing dive.

Hermannsburg

The second community I was posted to was Hermannsburg. As Roz had an exhibition in Melbourne, she would join me later.

Also known as Ntaria, Hermannsburg is 125km south-west of Alice Springs, in the MacDonnell Ranges. The first whites there were Lutheran missionaries who tried to convert the locals. Whether they made them Christian or not, they did succeed in protecting many of them from a notorious policeman and killer, Mounted Constable William Wiltshire. As Officer in Charge of Native Police, Willshire was moved from Hermannsburg in 1891 when three cuffed Aboriginal prisoners were shot in the back trying to escape. The villain policeman was the first in Australia to be tried for an Indigenous murder. Although several Aboriginal witnesses gave evidence at the murder trial, Willshire was acquitted (his defence lawyer was Sir John Downer, grandfather of Alexander Downer).

I had previously been to Hermannsburg for a fly-in fly-out clinic, literally, with the Royal Flying Doctor Service, in December 1983.

To get to there in August 2010, I booked a Tiger Air flight to Alice Springs. But the ground crew closed the doors early and I was forced to book a new flight, at a cost of $700. Apart from the outrageous price, the flight up was pretty standard until the hostess asked me about the chestnut logo on my blazer. Although I had planned on using the flight to finish reading *One Hundred Days of Summer* – Bob Ellis' take on Australia's changing political landscape – I was happily distracted. We spoke about the grove and Roz and my plan to start milling chestnuts. Then we spoke about remote settlements. Before I knew it, the flight was over, with just pages of my book to go.

I stayed for a night at the Crowne Plaza Alice Springs Lasseters hotel and casino. The place stank of smoke, and the food was appalling. The whole place was dark. My lesson learnt.

After that, I was keener than ever to get the Hermannsburg's Ntaria Health Clinic. When I got there, the staff asked me what I would like to be called: "Dr Rogers", "Dr Percy" or just "Doctor"? I told them they could cut all the doctor nonsense – "Percy" would do. I find that people never tell the truth when they use a person's title. They rarefy and relate to the title rather than the person. Any reading of the books about the British monarchy and the toadies surrounding them is testament to that.

On my first clinic I saw a five-month-old who was fat as mud and very healthy, as well as a man with the kidney disorder nephrotic syndrome. He weighed 170 kilograms and had a suspected broken patella (kneecap).

While on this posting I also saw the white, scarring after effects of trachoma, a bacterial eye infection never seen in suburban Melbourne. It can cause blindness, yet simple good hygiene prevents it. I saw plenty of young people with sexually transmitted diseases, but they got transferred to the health clinic in Darwin. There was syphilis in the township, but I never saw it myself.

On the first night, I was asked to attend the anger management men's group, where I met a man who was dealing with his anger by riding a horse from Yirrkala in East Arnhem to Port Augusta, South Australia – a distance of more than 3000km down the middle of the country. I encouraged him to write a book about his journey. I later heard he published his book, but I am yet to find a copy.

I loved to hear about the lives of the patients, like the man who had been waiting to join the police. On the day he was accepted, he came to me with sacroiliac pain (back) that immobilised him. I told him to rest up and he would recover. I also told him to fess up to the police academy that he wouldn't be able to join them just yet.

Some stories were less heartwarming, but a silver lining could be found. There was the 17-year-old boy who had been a drug user since the age of 12. He came to me after smashing a guitar over his sister's head. We agreed he needed to see someone in Darwin for expert anger management counselling.

While at the Hermannsburg clinic, I was also presented with a boy, aged 10, who felt feverish and nauseous. His symptoms convinced me he had the early stages of meningitis. An ambulance was over an hour away in Alice Springs. Getting him there meant a two-hour trip, as well as a delay in treatment. Without the right equipment, I couldn't tell if the boy's meningitis was viral or bacterial, but waiting for a definitive diagnosis could spell death. I put a drip line into him and took a punt that it was bacterial. Dexamethasone can treat inflammation generally, so I gave him some to treat the swelling in his brain, and some antibiotics. If my hunch was right, I could save him. If I was wrong and it was viral, there would at least be no harm in the medication. By the time the ambulance arrived, the boy was unconscious. When he arrived at Alice Springs, I got a blast from the resident paediatrician. He demanded to know why treatment had begun when the causative agent was unknown. I could tell he was very used to bossing underlings around. I pointed out the dangers of delaying treatment. Even if the causative agent did turn out to be a virus, we had covered the more sinister bacterial agent. I ended up putting the irate doctor through to the clinic manager, who knew how to deal with doctors with no experience of remote-area medicine. The pathology tests showed the causative agent was bacterial. There was great rejoicing at the clinic. The boy made a full recovery and was back in the community after a week.

While I was at Hermannsburg, an older teenage boy nearly added to the already alarming suicide statistics among young Indigenous males. Luckily, a health worker cut down the hanging boy who, nonetheless, had a serious jolt to the neck. Surrounded by distressed relatives, we resuscitated the boy at the clinic. We then sent him to Alice Springs Hospital.

I later discovered the boy's back story. He had been seeing a girl who was not the same "skin" as him. They were not meant to be together. Skin is a very complicated area and I cannot begin to explain it, except to say it is a kinship system and certain skins don't mix. The girl had told the boy she was calling it off because they were of the wrong skin. After this conversation she came to see me with a broken forearm. It is a common injury among women in Indigenous communities – defending themselves from a blow to the head. This particular blow was from an iron pole. Stricken with remorse and sadness, the boy was driven to attempt suicide.

When the boy was sent home from Alice Springs Hospital, tempers were still high in Hermannsburg. The boy's family blamed the girl, and she needed to be taken to a safe house. (She was still there when I left.)

Travelling to Wallace Rockhole, about 50km from Hermannsburg, I found this community to be spotlessly clean, with lovely lawns fed by the nearby gorge. Along with its tidy appearance, it seemed the locals here took greater care of their health. While there, I saw only the occasional trauma, coughs and colds and, once, an unconfirmed case of influenza. The town was also blessed with many terrific artists. I particularly remember one woman painting a "sugar ant dreaming", depicting, with amazing accuracy, thousands of very small ants.

While at Wallace Rockhole I was reminded of my time as a Melbourne University psychology tutor. There, I had once suggested to an ambitious new SRC representative that a good cause might be to introduce scholarships to bring smart and studious Indigenous teenagers to the university.

It was a good idea, but working at the Wallace Rockhole clinic made me realise a flaw in my good intention. I met an Aboriginal man working behind the supermarket counter. He was the first Indigenous man to win a scholarship to Geelong Grammar. He passed and enrolled in arts at Adelaide University. Though he was doing well there, he left when he became homesick. I heard a similar story from Rachel, the nurse at Wallace Rockhole. She described how she had enrolled in arts at Sydney University but quit her degree when the draw of home got too great.

It is a common problem and is seen with footballers too. Aboriginal people in their own country are surrounded and supported by family. Taking kids and young adults away from their family for educational purposes simply may not work. I looked out for another way that might work.

When I had been at Hermannsburg for a couple of weeks, the federal election was held, on August 21, 2010. I found the polling place and volunteered to help out the Greens candidate, William Warren. Even though the Greens candidate did not get up, I was glad to see Julia Gillard and the ALP scrape back into power in place of the divisive Liberal government.

Topping off my posting, Roz and I took a trip to Kings Canyon, a spectacular destination after a 200km scenic drive.

East Arnhem Land

Of all the places I've been to, East Arnhem Land is the most intriguing, and possibly contains some of the most beautiful scenery anywhere in the world.

From April 2011 to May 2013, I was offered locum stints at three East Arnhem clinics – at Miwatj Aboriginal Health Corporation in Nhulunbuy, the Yirrkala Health Centre and Elcho Island's Ngalkanbuy Health Service.

Roz and I had a great time during these postings – visiting the sights, and particularly shopping for art at the Buku-Larrnggay Mulka art centre in Yirrkala.

Yirrkala had always been on my list of places to see as it was the home of the first Bark Petition sent to Federal Parliament, in 1963. Signed by the Yolngu people of Arnhem land, the petition was against the declaration that a parcel of their land be sold to a bauxite mining company. Though the petition marked the first documentary recognition of Indigenous people in Australian law, native title was denied – the courts ruled that the mining leases were valid.

In the clinic one day, I was impressed when one of my patients said his father's mark was on that petition.

The work that the local communities were doing cooperatively impressed me enormously. A prime example of this is the Gumatj Corporation – representing the 13 Yolngu clans – which owns a cattle station and abattoir about 90km from Nhulunbuy. As a result, the community has access to fresh food, jobs and income. I saw how fresh meat was delivered to places like Gunyangara, 13km from Nhulunbuy, where the shop was also trying to assist with healthy eating and truancy by selling ice cream only outside school hours.

The Gumatj model is something I feel could work for other communities.

I was there when the then Prime Minister Julia Gillard attended the signing of an historic agreement between Gumatj Corporation and mining giant Rio Tinto Alcan in 2011. The handover was a magnificent day. The Aboriginal men did a corroboree with a sand dance and would dance up fiercely to Julia Gillard, but she didn't turn a hair. The beauty of it was that the little kids were doing the dance too and kicking the dust up.

Adelaide River, Batchelor and Pine Creek

In June 2012, I went to Adelaide River, about 100km south of Darwin on the Stuart Highway. Adelaide River is much like a suburb in Darwin with well-established homes, an excellent pub and a World War II cemetery. Some locals even commute to work in Darwin. It is not an Aboriginal settlement.

One day a week I would go Batchelor to work at the town's medical clinic. There I saw the Batchelor Institute, which is working on ways to keep families together while their bright child or parent is studying. Its system seemed to me to be the most successful form of educating Indigenous students. Universities in major cities should look at the Batchelor model to improve retention of Indigenous students, in my opinion.

About 100km south of Adelaide River, on the Stuart Highway, was a little medical clinic at Pine Creek. Pine Creek was an old gold mining town and it used lead to make gold ingot moulds. One young man came to me with constant headaches for which I could find no good cause. It turned out his job was to create the lead mould. He was not too particular with the handling of the lead, especially the fumes. I felt he had a mild lead encephalopathy. Years later, I heard his lead reading was consistent with low-grade lead poisoning. I understand he changed jobs and towns, hopefully for a healthier occupation.

Timber Creek

Timber Creek is a settlement roughly halfway between Kununurra and Katherine, on the Victoria Highway. I arrived there on October 1, 2012, and after four weeks, I was asked to stay for a further two weeks. I stayed on for the extra fortnight, but Roz had to return for other commitments at home.

While locums fill in for doctors on leave, in some communities there is no doctor. This was the case at Timber Creek. In places like this, the Northern Territory Health Department does what it can to fill the gap. Until they can get a doctor to stay, it is appalling for continuity of care.

In my time here, I certainly felt appreciated. The Aboriginal people gave me a special name: "Ya-ya". I was told it means "uncle."

From Timber Creek township, I needed to go to Yarralin Health Clinic. As I didn't know where it was, I called into the Timber Creek police station and the seven-foot-tall officer told me it was only 150 metres south and then gave me a tour of the station. He showed me the local police station museum, with manacles on the walls. Then he showed me the boab tree that had been used in the past as a whipping post for Aboriginal people.

When I arrived at Yarralin, the head nurse introduced me to two Aboriginal health workers, one of whom had written a book on the therapeutic and medicinal properties of all the plants in the area. I have since unsuccessfully tried to get a copy.

Aboriginal health workers are incredibly valuable in these communities. If there is a need for a translator they will translate; if there is an anxiety question, they will be there to assist and often throw in useful anecdotes, which may help support the person or help with the diagnosis and treatment of a patient. I found their incidental knowledge was always helpful in treating patients.

Roz was at Timber Creek with me most of the time. Every morning we would wake up around 6am, and sometimes have a cup of tea, before climbing up one of the mountains. Invariably, we would meet Greg, one of the male nurses from the clinic, as he went up and down the mountain four times every morning. He was an incredible bloke. He gave away being a stockbroker to study nursing. He wanted to study medicine but was hesitating because he was already 50 years old.

"Enrol next year," I said. "Don't fool around. If you want to do it – do it. It's a five-year course. You've got the money. Those five years are going to pass whether you do it or not, so you may as well do it."

The last I heard, Greg was going into his fourth year of medicine in Adelaide.

It was during my time at this clinic that a patient came to see me coughing up blood. He was convinced he had carcinoma of the lung. I was forceful in my response: "Stop smoking now!" He stopped smoking that night. It wasn't a carcinoma but an abscess on the lungs. I put him on a course of antibiotics and it cleared up.

"Where are you going next time?" he asked me. "Because I'm coming to see you wherever you are."

While I was there a young man had a schizophrenic episode. He was cursing and saying he wanted to go to "Cubby", which is the colloquial name of the psychiatric ward in Royal Darwin Hospital. I told him we would arrange for him to go. He continued to be gruff and upset, so I asked him to come in and lie down while we organised everything.

Up to this point, I had thought the head nurse was unflappable. But this patient got her upset and anxious. She was suddenly bossing everyone around, and trying to remove every potential danger from the room "in case he turns violent". Later, she was upset that the other staff were critical of her reaction. I told her not to worry as I was not in the business of saying "next time". She dealt with the situation and that was that.

While in Timber Creek I also met a well-travelled Spanish patient. She told me about her time in India, where she had seen women use whistles to stop wife abuse. If a woman felt threatened, she would blow the whistle and all the other women would come to the house banging pots and pans to shame the man into stopping. And if that didn't stop him, they would give him a biff with a pot. At the staff meeting we considered whether this might work for Indigenous communities, but decided the kids would play with the whistles and it would lose all its power to draw a crowd.

From Timber Creek I had two other clinics. One was at Kildurk, also known as Mialuni, on an Indigenous-owned property, managed by a white man. To get there, I drove about 100km from Timber Creek and turned onto a dirt road. From there it was a lazy 60km, with about 20 paddock gates to open and close.

The other clinic I went to was at Bulla, about 60km from Timber Creek. Here I met Jack Little from the Northern Land Council, a most dignified man, who, despite the means to move to a bigger town with more conveniences, refused to leave his homeland. It was a privilege to meet him. I have since discovered the Bulla clinic has been renamed in Jack Little's honour.

Elcho Island

In January 2013, I went to the fascinating Elcho Island, known to the locals as Galiwin'ku. It is part of a series of islands along the north coast of East Arnhem. These islands made up part of the bridge from New Guinea to Australia during the last Ice Age, when the sea level dropped and these islands were exposed.

While on Elcho Island, Roz and I walked along South Beach and met a man who claimed to be a traditional owner, although we later discovered this was hotly contested. He showed us columns of exposed rock which were just magnificent. Each outcrop of rock had its own vivid colours.

Mostly they were randomly scattered, but some were arranged into circles. You could imagine the corroborees that could have happened there.

Part of my interest in Elcho Island lay just north, on the larger Marchinbar Island. It was here, in 1945, that RAAF radar operator Morry Isenberg found nine copper coins in the sand. He collected them, put them in a cigarette tin and left them in his garage for decades. In 1979, he took them out, believing they might be worth something. A numismatist identified four of the coins as Dutch doits dated from the 1690s to the 1780s. Five were identified as from the Kilwa Sultanate of Zanzibar in East Africa. As the Kilwa dynasty was overtaken by the Portuguese in the 16th century, it was thought that it was shipwrecked Portuguese sailors who brought the coins to the island.

One of my patients, Schelley, from Trieste in Italy, had married an Aboriginal man and was planning an expedition to find more coins on the island. In 2018, another coin from the Kilwa Sultanate was found, this time on Elcho Island – though unfortunately not by Schelley.

My other interest in these islands was sociological. Alcohol is forbidden on Elcho Island, and I soon noticed that there were very few signs of domestic violence coming through the doors at Elcho's Ngalkanbuy Health Service. Teenagers turned to dance instead of booze to fill their time. The island became famous in 2007 when the local Djuki Mala dancers choreographed and performed a dance routine to *Zorba the Greek*. It became immensely popular via YouTube and it led to tours for the dancers. The island was also the inspiration for the song *My Island Home* (after the Warumpi Band's lead singer and Elcho Islander George Rrurrambu Burarrwanga), made famous by Christine Anu at the closing of the 2000 Sydney Olympics.

The island was not without its health problems.

One man claimed he was a doctor. Given his shabby attire, I was surprised. He had come for a repeat on his schizophrenia tablets. One of the saddest sights was a 12-month-old child who weighed only six kilograms. The mother claimed to be breastfeeding her baby, but I was told she cared more about the gambling cards than the food in her babe's mouth. I made arrangements for her to be supervised.

It was on Elcho Island that I saw one of the world's rarest genetic disorders – Machado-Joseph disease. At the time it was found in only three places in the Northern Territory – Elcho Island, Groote Eylandt and Yirrkala – but has now spread further afield in the NT. It is found in other parts of the world, but numbers are small. This inherited degenerative disease can leave a person in a wheelchair and eventually unable to swallow food. It affects the nervous system and a part of the brain called the hindbrain. Previously known as Groote Eylandt Syndrome, it was thought to have come from Portuguese sailors in the 16th century, but DNA haplotyping has since hypothesised that it came from Asia. It is hard to leave behind the romance of Portuguese sailors.

My time at the Elcho Island clinic was not without tragedy. A 12-year-old boy hanged himself down on the beach. Another life needlessly lost.

My feeling about Aboriginal suicide is that after fighting and being displaced from their land, being whipped by police and shot in the back, it is no wonder this historical backdrop makes Indigenous people angry and causes alienation. They are dispirited. They may reject the authority of their family and the elders. They may hold white law in contempt, which leads to incarceration and sometimes death. Getting drunk at least alleviates this feeling, but not for long enough. Despair grips far too many of these young Indigenous people.

It is no accident that the suicide rate in most Aboriginal communities is among the highest in the world – 24 for every 100,000 the Kimberley, that figure rises to 70. There is one community near Kings Canyon where I understand there are no Indigenous males left over the age of 30. Suicide was not known in Aboriginal culture before the arrival of Europeans.

As a priority, a treaty of acknowledgement needs to be enacted between the federal government and a body of Aboriginal leaders – an extension of the Uluru Statement from the Heart – that commits the nation to recognising Indigenous people in the constitution, to truth telling and agreement making. It needs to enshrine no more humiliating interventions, or projected amendments to the Racial Discrimination Act that allow for further discrimination. It is time the government ceased the rhetoric and acted in the interests of the Aboriginal people instead of the interests of those whites who simply make money out of Aboriginal people or their land. Some of Australia's richest people need to show more respect for Aboriginal people and their land. Only then, when Aboriginal people are afforded this respect, will we see young boys grow to be old men in Indigenous Australia.

Borroloola

In mid-June 2013 I went to Borroloola, land of the Yanyuwa people, on the west coast of the Gulf of Carpentaria. I had read about its sorry history, of cattlemen droving their herds across Aboriginal land only to claim it as their own. These "overlanders", as they are called, would shoot Aboriginal people who had the affront to walk on their own custodial lands. (A great friend of Roz and mine, Professor Lyndall Ryan, is collating all the massacres that occurred in Australia from 1788 through to 1960. The overlanders were responsible for many of them.)

While in Borroloola, we attended a rodeo where, to my astonishment, no injuries were sustained – except maybe pride in a fall.

The diseases of Borroloola, like most locum clinics I worked at, followed the same pattern: Too little fresh food and too much processed foods, leading to poor diet and health.

At Borroloola and Elcho Island, like many parts of the Northern Territory, it was clear that people were behind the eight-ball in getting fresh fruit and vegetables. The first difficulty was the distance. When you took into account travel time, the freshness of food was often in question, and it was often quite dear. You cannot blame someone for thinking twice about "fresh" food when it is days old by the time you get it.

I often thought it would be much better to subsidise and teach people how to cultivate the land to grow food locally rather than waste fossil fuels getting the food to them.

As part of my duties in Borroloola, I was rostered to visit Robinson settlement. During the wet season, this small community is only accessible by plane. Flying in for the day, I found it was neat as a pin, without any rubbish lying around. While there, I worked with a medical student whose speed with computing more than made up for the time taken in seeing each patient. The nurse with us was unsure about her obstetrical skills, and I helped her with examinations. I'm fairly sure I saw every pregnant woman in the community that day.

With some rare time off, I was invited to join some of the staff on their way to see the "lost city" rock formations of the Caranbirini Conservation Reserve, about 50km south of Borroloola. Along the way, I went searching for the McArthur River crossing used by the German explorer and naturalist Ludwig Leichhardt on his 1844 expedition from Moreton Bay (Brisbane) to Port Essington, north of Darwin. At McArthur River I saw a lilypond to rival Claude Monet's garden at Giverny in France. It is unclear how the lilies arrived.

Bowing out

In 2014, after essentially being addicted to life as a locum, I gave it away. This was around the time that Roz's mother, Billie Smart, was ailing. Roz's father, Johnny, had moved across from Western Australia in 1991, but he had died a short time later.

Billie and I had always got along very well. Well into her 90s, in a Melbourne nursing home, she was tough as old boots. Jolyon would always get her going, teasing her and giving her a slap on the bottom.

"Oh Jolyon, you are a fool," she would say.

There was one day when Roz and I had come back from visiting Billie in hospital. We both realised Billie, aged 97, was dying. We sat and drank a whisky each. I got up to get a glass of water in the kitchen and fell back – bang. I don't know why, but I lost consciousness while standing, and then had to spend a few days in the Royal Melbourne Hospital. Roz had to contend with her mum dying and me being in hospital.

I knew then that I had to call time on my locum days. It was too much pressure on Roz to have to hold the family fort, care for her mother and worry about me off in outback towns. With my last locum trip already under my belt – my second trip to Elcho Island in 2014 – I decided it was time to settle down. The Northern Territory health department retained me as an advisor to assist with the selection of overseas doctor candidates who wished to work with Indigenous communities. In 2019, I ended that role. So, ending a 59-year love affair with medicine.

A farm farewell

In 2021, Roz and I realised we could no longer keep the farm. We sold it to a younger couple. It was heart-wrenching because we loved the place so, but we could no longer maintain it. But our most pressing problem was what to do with the farm's book collection.

After a childhood with just five books in the house, I had amassed a massive library – four tonnes of books, all kept in a shipping container at the farm. There were more than 500 biographies as well as history books, an extensive spy collection, medical books, and the complete works of Stalin, Lenin and Marx. It took months to find the collection a new home, but one, fittingly, came up at the New International Bookshop, at the Victorian Trades Hall in Carlton. The shop will sell the books – and they are welcome to anything they make.

I hope someone finds a book of great inspiration, as I did from that arcade in Perth all those years ago.

Chapter 29
Cases and Comments about General Practice

After nearly six decades of active medical practice, I would never claim to know more medicine than the next doctor, but I have found that everyday common decency has always got results for patients. Throughout my career I have tried to translate the science of medicine through the prism of humanism. To me, this is the true function of a general practitioner. A practitioner's interest and inquiry should, as far as possible, include the history and culture of patients and their societies. This is relatively easy when doctors are practicing in their place of birth, or where the population is stable, but worldwide multiculturalism makes this increasingly rare.

Empathy was my first lesson in medicine. Emotional and intellectual empathy goes beyond sympathy. It seeks to understand and feel a patient's culture and history.

In my first private practice in 1960s Coburg, the society was made up of pensioners serving out their days in the south and to the north, with a burgeoning influx of migrants from all over the world. They came from countries I had only ever read about. I knew little of their country's health and experiences.

White faces were the norm in my first home in Western Australia. Growing up, I saw the Aboriginal faces of those whose ancestors had survived the murderous white invasion and had not died from the despair of losing their home country.

In my early years, the only migrant community I was aware of was the Italian Prisoners of War camp in Kalgoorlie and the Italian farm hands. I had briefly come into contact with them, with Jack, during my wheat-lumping youth. Back then, empathy for other nationalities was not part of my personality. While growing up in Western Australia taught me prejudices, working in and around Coburg provided me with a rich opportunity to dispel those prejudices. I empathetically treated Turkish people in Merlynston, and Italians and Serbians living in Fawkner.

When a new patient came to me, I would try to make an immediate assessment. I would take note of their age and ethnic origin while scrutinising their face. Not only is the face the window to the soul, it also reflects the passage of the years. A face can show hard survival years, which often result in a face of kindness and compassion. Cruel and vicious times can also show little evidence of kindness. Hands, too, have their own voice in pathology. Rough, gnarled or calloused hands can be signs of physical labour and missing fingers the sign of a workplace accident. Gentle or soft hands are usually owned by those working intellectually. Pale hands might show anaemia; while red hands could indicate a number of conditions, from too many red blood cells to excessive heat retention. Blue hands could be a sign of oxygen deprivation. Ridges in nails can be a sign of a vitamin or mineral deficiency. Swollen joints might be an indication of arthritis, and palms that will not flatten out, the sign of a Dupuytren's contracture.

My initial patient questions would be both medical and empathetic, with mixed success.

A patient once came to see me about the acne vulgaris covering her face. She was seeking relief from depression. Distressed and downcast, she did not like to appear in public. I wondered at the circumstances of her life that allowed the acne to take such a hold. From my empathetic questions I discovered she worked as a night receptionist in a brothel. This job allowed her to avoid public exposure for most of the day. But in our chats, she told me she loved writing. That was something we could work on to raise her opinion of her herself, I thought. I asked to see some of her writing, and she brought some examples in. They were rather good. I encouraged her to enrol in a creative writing course at RMIT. Despite her initial self-doubt, she did just that. To her amazement, she topped her year. She sent me a photo of herself in her graduation gown with two tongue studs in pride of place. No antidepressants were given, just some antibiotics to clear the initial acne flair up, along with support, encouragement and interest.

Careful watching of how a story is told is an imperative skill for a doctor. One patient came to see me quite irate. A colleague of mine had not deigned to look up at this patient when she presented with a persistent headache.

"Ah, migraine," he had responded as he typed the script.

According to this patient, an intelligent woman, the doctor barely looked up. By the time she saw me, another doctor had diagnosed her with a degenerative neurological disease. She had never been prone to migraines before seeing the first doctor. She wondered if her prognosis would have been better had the first doctor looked upon her with empathy.

Also, a little bit of knowledge can be a dangerous thing. In the late 1970s, when nurses were wanting to see some patients who might otherwise have been seen by a doctor, I could understand their logic. The nurses wanted to have a greater role in patient treatment. But there were dangers in this. While working at a Kensington health centre (not the one I finished my practice with), I treated a patient for bronchitis and was keeping a close eye on him. I soon found a nurse slapping a stethoscope on this patient and, not hearing anything, telling him: "You can go. No need to see you any more." She had failed to check the left apical region, or apex, of the lung. I stepped in. This man was still very sick, and continued observation was necessary.

Another nurse came to a staff meeting around this time, and told us about a patient she was looking after: "He's an elderly man. He's very happy, but he can't sleep at night because he's vomiting. I'm sure that it's the result of loneliness. So, I go to see him quite often."

I was horrified.

"You get that man down here tomorrow morning," I said, forcefully. "You're sitting on a carcinoma of the stomach until proven otherwise."

The nurses were quite upset with me in instances such as this. I felt a chill from the staff. But the nurses simply didn't have the insight or training for these cases. I felt they were putting lives at risk.

Examining the elderly man who had been vomiting, I found that he had a fulminated carcinoma of the stomach.

Still, the nurses remained upset with me. I suggested that they come in while doctors were consulting. I told them they could do some consulting if there were prepared to be semi-directed. It seemed to work, but I was soon off to Cocos (Keeling) Islands, so was never sure whether the consulting continued.

Diagnosing the bizarre

Bizarre stories are difficult to diagnose, as I found when a 17-year-old girl came to see me with an odd complaint. She had been falling on the floor, seemingly without any warning. It was puzzling and frightening for her. Other doctors she had seen had found her blood pressure to be normal. A neurologist had ruled out epilepsy. Through conversational questioning, I found that the girl had no real passions, but she did have a sweet tooth. I arranged an immediate glucose tolerance test and, sure enough, the results were abnormally low. An endocrinologist agreed with my suggested diagnosis of a beta cell adenoma. Beta cells of the pancreas pump out insulin, which, if not controlled, leads to states of hypoglycaemia can lead to the patient fainting. The endocrinologist arranged further testing, but the girl disappeared before they were done. Neither of us have heard from her since.

While not all patients tell the truth in consultations, my attitude is always to believe a patient until proven otherwise. On one occasion, two men – strangers to each other, working in different parts of Melbourne – came in to see me with the same complaint. Both had back pain following workplace accidents.

The first man, who worked on the wharves, had been struck on the back by a loaded sling. He was able to walk but when he bent over or put pressure on his right side, he felt pain in his lumber region.

Unbelievably, a young doctor at a major hospital sent him home with a Disprin, clearly dispensing medicine commensurate with his prejudices against "wharfie bludgers". By the time the wharfie saw me a week later, his pain was obvious. His X-ray revealed an appalling oversight by the young doctor. The patient had transverse fractures of the lateral processes (the part of the vertebrae that connects bone to muscle and ligaments) in his first four lumbar vertebrae. Although the patient healed well with standard treatment, I remained livid at the doctor's dismissal of this man's back pain. I contacted the hospital's medical director, demanding that he tell his trainee doctors to leave their prejudices at the front entrance.

The second man came to me with back pain a week later. He worked on a car assembly line, where a component part had struck him. His workplace doctor prescribed two days' rest, believing it was a muscle injury. Yet, when the man saw me, he complained about severe pain. Again, I ordered an X-ray. This showed an identical series of fractures like those of the first man. It was an incredible coincidence.

Nurses like to say that injuries come in threes. Alas, I could only muster two. Though I had another back injury patient at this time, this third case was a very different fracture. The patient was a schoolteacher who had stepped off the dais next to the blackboard and landed flat on his back. He had to wait for help before he could move. After the fall, despite the ongoing pain, the X-rays revealed nothing. The pain was so intense that, for a time, he gave up teaching as he could not stand for long periods without severe pain. As it was a workplace injury, he was receiving workers' compensation, but the compensation doctors (paid penny-pinchers) accused him of malingering, as repeated X-rays showed no pathology.

By the time this hobbled schoolteacher came to me, he was distraught. I made it clear that I believed him from the outset. When new X-rays revealed no pathology, I suggested we do magnetic resonance imaging (MRI) – a much more powerful investigation. This revealed a fracture of a vertebrae. The patient's pain was stopped when an orthopaedic surgeon performed a spinal fusion. The teacher went back to work. Another stark reminder: The onus of proof should never be on the patient to prove the symptoms but on the doctor to show the pathology behind the symptoms.

Back injuries are debilitating and have a poor reputation generally. But if the pathology is not apparent at the initial examination, doctors must exhaust the investigations until a definitive conclusion can be reached.

Privilege and gambling

Doctors in one sense play the odds. When they make an initial diagnosis, they cannot be certain they are right until the decision plays out. Using their training and knowledge, they do their best to glean a patient's history and perform a clinical examination. Frequently, there is an area of doubt.

When a doctor makes a decision and is faced by doubters, the doubters must be respected, but doctors must stick to their decision.

I had not long been in practice when I was consulted by a young woman who told me she had started bleeding in the middle of her menstrual cycle. She was not on the contraceptive pill, nor had she had any sexual experience. She and her family were quite religious, and I braced myself for push-back on the course of action I would suggest.

After examining the young woman and her history, I said that until it was proved otherwise, I believed she had a carcinoma of the endometrium – the lining of the uterus. The girl would require a dilation and curettage, which would mean rupturing her hymen. The family was strongly opposed to this. The patient's outraged mother believed it would ruin her daughter's chances of marriage. I recall pointing out that not doing the procedure could well reduce her chances of living. The daughter insisted on being investigated, which she was by a leading Melbourne gynaecologist. The biopsy confirmed my diagnosis. The discovery was lifesaving. The daughter was grateful and the mother apologetic for being so angry. We all ended up friends.

In Perth in 2001, I attended a Royal College of General Practitioners' conference, where a discussion about the role of GPs ensued. Some speakers were critical of the differential fee structure between consultants and general practitioners. Others argued that the role of a general practitioner should be considered specialist in its own right. I agreed with the latter speaker and argued that GPs had a crucial role to integrate all the signs and symptoms in a patient. Consultants specialised and provided valuable opinions on one system, but GPs focused on integrating all we heard and observed of a patient's conditions. Patients' total care was best left in the care of general practitioners, I argued.

To illustrate this, I told the story of a Royal Women's Hospital nurse who came to me as the staff doctor. She had a bleeding nose, which was oozing at the time. The nurse told me on one occasion she had vomited blood. She had seen an ear, nose and throat specialist, who reassured her that everything was fine with her nose and throat. A gastroenterologist had performed a gastroscopy and found her oesophagus and stomach were clear. Still, I smelled a rat in her system somewhere, and I continued looking for clues. The patient's periods were heavy, but a gynaecologist had reassured her that her reproductive system was fine. She had been given the same story after finding blood in her urine. As a GP, with all the information before me, I diagnosed blood dyscrasia (a blood disorder). The nurse finally received appropriate treatment.

About six months before I left metropolitan clinical work to treat remote communities, I was asked to see a man who wanted a check-up. I won't name him in deference to his family. We chatted and I warmed to him easily. He was extremely fit from regular running. He told me he was quite well apart from feeling a bit more tired than usual. He had been a Jesuit Catholic priest, but had left to marry the woman he loved. His family were displeased. His two brothers were Jesuit priests who now refused to speak to him. Their only communication was at Collingwood football matches, when they sat together. The patient had been a Catholic schoolteacher and was very active in the fight for proper pay for teaching staff.

He was also a writer, penning stories about ordinary people he met in his neighbourhood of Flemington. Curious about the former priest's bloods, I sent a sample off for examination. The results came back showing a prostate-specific antigen, an indication of carcinoma of the prostate. The antigen was far too high. I referred him to a urologist. The man endured a series of painful injections without a murmur. He found great solace in prayer, praying every day until his death. Through it all, he frequently expressed great sorrow at the grief he was causing his family. About 100 people came to his wake. I am sorry to say I was too upset to speak, but speaker after speaker spoke of him in glowing terms. I thought that night that the practice of medicine was a rare privilege.

The power of women

After years of campaigning as a GP obstetrician for the rights of women in childbirth, I found that in the end it was women themselves who ended their appalling treatment. They used their fiscal power to turn away from hospital births, which forced hospitals and obstetricians to take notice. In response to hospital and obstetrician brutality, women began opting for homebirths to gain more control of their child's birth and their own bodies. Hospitals could not tolerate the financial loss. They had to change – and money was the great persuader. By bringing the home-style setting into the hospital, through family birth centres, the trend towards homebirths was reversed and the hospitals' financial haemorrhaging was staunched.

While the Royal Women's Hospital lays claim to Australia's first family birth centre baby, in 1979, these centres are now found in every major hospital across the nation. I wish I could report a decrease in medical or surgical interventions without an obstetrical reason, but I cannot. In 2004, the caesarean rate for women giving birth for the first time was 25.1 per cent and in 2018 that figure had climbed to 30.1 per cent. Too often, parents want to time their child's birth to suit their social calendar, or to suit their doctor.

On one particular day, I was reminded of how far we have come. One of my midwifery patients, Jenny, asked if her mother could come into her appointment. The mother was frail looking, quite small, and seemed nervous. When I explained to them that I did not expect any trouble or complications, Jenny's mother said that having a baby was quite different in her day. I asked her to tell Jenny what it was like. The older woman burst into tears, sobbing as though her heart would break. She had never told Jenny because she did not want to upset her. Uninformed by her doctor, she had been left alone with terrible pains and did not know why. Jenny kept hugging her mother, pacifying her until she stopped sobbing.

To bring some joy to the situation, I offered to let Jenny's mother listen to the baby's heart. She was thrilled. Then I asked, if Jenny wouldn't mind, whether her mother would like to feel the baby's head? I assured the mother she would not hurt the baby. Her smile was more than ample reward for the time spent talking and reassuring her. Jenny had an uncomplicated birth and a lovely baby girl.

When I worked at the University of Technology at Lae, in Papua New Guinea, an Australian woman and talented painter, Margaret Phillips, came to see me late one Saturday morning, just as I was preparing to knock off. She sat down abruptly in a chair and said, "I am pregnant."

Her displeasure was apparent. I asked her how many weeks she was.

"About 20," she said. "I was violated with the first one so I don't want to go through that again." She told her previous birth story and it was horrendous. I understood her attitude. After a long chat, I explained that she was too far along to do anything but have the baby. She and her baby were in good health. I invited her to my antenatal classes. She learnt the breathing techniques but maintained a distinct air of cynicism. When the woman's husband rang to say his wife was in labour at Lae's ANGAU Hospital, I hurried along to see her. From the doorway I could tell she was in strong labour, but she said nothing was happening. Surprised, I examined her perineum and found the head of the baby was on view. She would not believe me, so I shined the back of a kidney dish to show her. With a couple of pushes her baby would be out, I told her. The transformation in her attitude was dramatic.

The baby was delivered after one push. The mother was ecstatic. Later, she moved to North Queensland and I returned to Melbourne. She fell pregnant again and asked me to come to North Queensland to deliver her baby. I told her she knew what to do. This empowered her. She was so confident that after that baby was born, she started running antenatal classes in her town. Her painting of a breastfeeding Highland New Guinea women has pride of place on the wall in my front room.

Even though a solution and preventions may be obvious, nothing happens quickly in medicine. While working in the Northern Territory, I could see how the outback conditions led to some disease processes and how a minor alteration could prevent some diseases. This was the case with melioidosis, a disease caused by a very active bacteria that lives in the water and soil. The organism can be transmitted by coughing or breathing, but the most common mode of transmission is through skin cuts and abrasions. Like everyone in the bush, Aboriginal people love sitting around a fire yarning. Unfortunately, any abrasion on their legs that comes into contact with the soil is an entry point for bacterium *Burkholderia pseudomallei* – the cause of melioidosis. If people were to use a chair or a blanket, rather than sitting directly on the ground, this would stop a lot of infections. Change was slowly happening when I was last in the Northern Territory, but only with a few families.

Early in my Indigenous locum career at Hermannsburg, I once treated a relative of the famed Australian artist, Albert Namatjira. She was a woman of 49, with stage-four renal failure – her options to prolong life were a kidney transplant or dialysis. She had generalised oedema (fluid retention), and a sugar reading that was through the roof. I was dismayed to think how she got to this level of disease. I sent her in to Alice Springs for stabilisation with dialysis.

As I went to other postings, it was clear this woman was not alone. Her condition was the result of other factors but was chiefly due to the poor diet found in the outback settlements and towns up north.

The British invasion brought many profound changes to the Aboriginal way of life, but one of the most diabolical and long-lasting was the change in diet. Pushed from their homelands where they hunted and foraged, Indigenous people were exposed to refined foods, high in sugar and fat.

Today, packaged foods filled with sugar, salt and preservatives are actively preventing successive federal government from achieving their goal of "closing the gap". Having such fast foods readily available in community stores only promotes the disconnect from bush tucker. It means Aboriginal people are still developing illnesses that are caused by poor diet and sugary drinks. As I discovered in remote communities, fresh food is all too often expensive, and less than fresh.

Most alarming is children's consumption of sugary soft drinks, even in remote communities where the water supply is quite good. Some children I saw seemed glued to the soft drink bottle. The federal government has toyed with the idea of altering glucose content in sugary drinks, but elsewhere far more has been done. In the UK and Mexico, they have introduced taxes on sugary drinks to combat the problem, with some reduced demand, particularly in lower socioeconomic groups. It is promising.

Legislation is needed to ban sugar, in all its forms, from Indigenous community trade stores. It will be a battle to wean the community off sugar. Witness the struggle to ban sweets in school canteens and lower the sugar content of supermarket products. Yet, organisations like Rethink Sugary Drink – a coalition of cancer, health, parent and Indigenous groups – have banded together to apply pressure on government, manufacturers and communities for change.

I believe sugar plays a major role in forming cancers. I gleaned this after reading the research of Otto Heinrich Warburg, the 1931 Nobel Prize winner and outstanding German chemist, who discovered that cancer cells require glucose (sugar) to survive. Without sugar, cancer cells die. Only now are some cancer clinics recognising this profound finding, and using it as a basis for therapeutic regimes.

In the US, Boston College's Professor Thomas Seyfried and his colleagues are showing that by restricting carbohydrates and lowering a person's glucose level, the blood will enter a state of ketosis. This is a natural state in which the body, lacking glucose, must rely on ketones for energy – and ketones do not fuel cancer cells. This provides a gateway to inhibiting or even eliminating cancers.

The arguments against sugar have concentrated on the waistlines of children, but it is my hope that sugar's role in cancer growth may soon be raised in the community's consciousness.

Worldwide, we spend billions on cancer drug treatments, yet an estimated 26,000 people die each day from cancer. While global cancer mortality has fallen by 22 per cent over the last 25 years across almost all ages, the incidence of cancer has risen by the same amount across almost all ages.

Back in 1971, the then US president Richard Nixon declared a war on cancer. More than 50 years later, it is clear that we won't see an overall reduction in the incidence of cancer until we win the battle against sugar.

As seen with smoking, prevention may be the only real solution. For decades in the US, lung cancer was the most prevalent cancer, and the deadliest. With fewer people taking up smoking, we have finally seen an overall reduction in the percentage of US residents dying from cancer. Breast cancer is now the most common form of cancer.

Telling cancer patients to cut out sugar and limit carbohydrates in the face of expensive anti-cancer drugs might seem ridiculous. But I believe –

like not smoking – it may be the best cancer prevention advice we have. The dietary regime is rigorous and demanding but – combined with hyperbaric therapy in some cases, or mild radiotherapy in others – it may be an effective treatment of this stubborn frontier in medicine.

Chapter 30
Musing on Ageing

Ageing is rapidly becoming a major health problem in Australia. Doctors are heroically prolonging life by finding new ways to replace worn-out body parts and prevent degeneration. These endeavours raise philosophical questions, mostly involving wealthy societies trying to stave off the inevitable. Some people have had themselves frozen in the hope that they may rise again. They take heart from the scientific success of freezing embryonic plant and other lifeforms – a process designed in the event of a catastrophic world disaster. Meanwhile, enormous health dollars are spent on chronic illnesses suffered by those in aged facilities, retirement complexes and hospitals, yet there is often little hope of a cure.

Different communities deal with the inevitability of death differently and make little attempt to resuscitate the dying. They simply ensure death is not painful.

In 2019, I gave a series of lectures about the ageing brain, at the University of the Third Age in Melbourne. Preparing for it, I realised how little I knew, but I was able to study up, and the lectures were well attended. I'm sure I drew a crowd in part because of my audience's interest in dementia – perhaps the most distressing ageing illness. The pathology is most likely due to the tangled fibres in the brain and the deposition of amyloid-like proteins or possibly myelin-like substance proteins throughout the brain. The meaning of these proteins and protein substances to Alzheimer's patients is not clear, but they may play a profound part. The jury is still out, but some very interesting research involving Catholic nuns – The Nun Study of Ageing and Alzheimer's Disease – show that biochemical changes in the bloodstream may not be the predictor of dementia that we might think.

In this longitudinal study of 678 nuns living a convent life in the US, epidemiologist and professor of neurology David Snowdon found that even though a nun's brain post-mortem might contain all the tangles and proteins indicative of Alzheimer's, not all suffered from the affliction. One nun,

Sister Mary, lived to be 101 and worked until she was 84. She kept active in her reading, her convent and her outdoor activity. Her brain had all the traits of dementia at her death, but in life she passed cognitive tests easily. This study has looked further into reasons for dementia, with protective factors including physical exercise and an early education.

My view is that the social brain and the production of dopamine are the keys. Dopamine is a neurotransmitter which comes from an amino acid called tyrosine. Tyrosine is found in foods like seaweed, soybeans and egg whites. Dopamine plays a role in how we think, plan and take pleasure. Dopamine is also a powerful motivator and mood changer. In the body, dopamine latches onto receptors in the brain, and when it does it has the most powerful effect on mood and activity. Unfortunately, when we age, our dopamine production decreases, as do the cells in those parts of the brain which can accept the dopamine. The neural circuits powered by dopamine also decrease as we age. Parkinson's disease occurs when a part of the brain called the substantia nigra is deprived of dopamine. The answer might seem to be to administer L Dopa, an analogue of dopamine, but this can only be used for a limited time as it can induce hallucinations and even full psychosis.

Dopamine can assist, but how we live our lives can impact on our social brain. It is vital for the ageing to remain positively engaged in the life around them to ward off dementia. Research into communities who have documented evidence of longevity – up to and over 100 years – show a number of interesting features. In Japan, the Okinawans eat very little meat, if any at all. But I believe the longevity clincher is that they continue to be actively involved in work and the community. They don't know the meaning of retirement. They laugh at work and play. They appear to enjoy simple and hard life.

They drink awamori – a strong, rice-based liquor. Those Okinawans who follow the US diet, however, do not appear to live as long. We have much to learn from Okinawa. Whether education, diet, blood proteins or exercise have the greatest influence on dementia is not clear, but without doubt, social isolation, or loneliness, is strongly correlated with dementia. My time at Coburg could tell me that.

The hippocampus and stress are the last pieces of the memory puzzle. The main job of the hippocampus is to forge a memory between an external stress and its cause. This is absolutely essential to survival in the wild, but perhaps not so crucial in modern-day living. After the stress connection is made, and the stress has passed, it deactivates cortisol, the stress hormone. If cortisol accumulates in the blood stream, it can trigger anxiety and cause diseases such as diabetes, hypertension and osteoporosis. Not a happy prospect, but old age is not for the faint-hearted. So, avoid prolonged stress, for not only does the function of the hippocampus diminish but research also shows the actual brain tissue itself can decrease in size under high cortisol levels.

Euthanasia

I had not been in practice very long in Coburg when my friend Jack came to see me. He was a detailer for a pharmaceutical firm – a kind of spruiker for drug companies – always putting on lunches to describe new drugs to doctors. I would say to him, "What are you bribing us with today, Jack?"

He was a smoker and travelled around Victoria for work. He came to me with a persistent cough and some chest pain. He was bringing up copious amounts of phlegm. He had no blood coming up, but after an X-ray I diagnosed him with carcinoma of the lung. I sent him to a specialist, but Jack was too far advanced. Little could be done. Within a few weeks, I had him into Sacred Heart Hospital, in Coburg. I would go in and chat to him, ensuring he was as comfortable as possible. He was in a lot of pain, losing strength and found it hard to eat.

One night I got a call to say he was unwell. When I arrived he was on the edge of the bed, gasping in agony.

"Can you do something about the pain?" he pleaded.

I felt he was dying.

"He's in pain," I told the nurse, and prescribed a high dose of morphine. She was a nun.

"But, doctor, that wi–"

I cut her off: "See how he goes."

At 3am, I got a call to say Jack had died. It was an unintended consequence of relieving pain.

When it looked as though the Australian Medical Association was going to ban euthanasia campaigner Dr Rod Syme for assisting a terminally ill patient with his death, I thought I should speak out. He asked me whether I would be in an article for *The Age*. I thought, "I've done the same for my patients. I'm going to support him."

These days, though I have difficulty walking, I'm fortunately not in any pain. If I was in pain and I became dependent on anyone, I would not want that.

Roz looks after me in all sorts of ways, with cooking and driving. It's not my legs that stop me from driving; it's my eyes. That boy who hated to wear his glasses has lost his sight in one eye, and the other eye is not too good either. My ophthalmologist said I may well look out with my good eye and not see a car or a pedestrian. I thought it best to give it away.

Continuing the good fight

Marx analysed emerging capitalism in *Das Kapital*. Lenin took the study further to say that imperial capitalism – capitalism exported to other countries – was the highest form of capitalism for the greatest profit. But now, I think we've gone a stage further, with the multinationals and the commodity economies threatening the existence of the world. They are not only using the resources of the world and destroying them, but also creating such abuse and byproducts with that commodification that it's affecting the climate. I'm more concerned now by climate change than by class conflicts, because nothing is more important than the health of our planet. I will never understand why Prime Minister Scott Morrison accepts the science of COVID-19 but not the science of climate change. The evidence is piling up in front of politicians, and they are denying that climate change exists. It makes me so angry.

Politicians are the only ones protecting the fossil fuel industry in the face of the climate emergency. One cannot help but wonder whether they are getting backhanded payments to continue propping them up.

Politics has been so important in my life, and now I spend my time supporting those who tell the truth, like the ABC and those who protest against fossil fuels.

I have a Twitter account but don't use it to agitate for climate change. I cannot bring myself to use it. They don't pay money to distribute the news, so why should I support them? When Twitter starts paying appropriate fees to news outlets, I might start using my account.

Now we have sold the farm, we will sell our big diesel car and buy an electric car. We have tried a couple on for size, and they aren't that comfortable for me to get into. The larger ones are expensive but we will get one as soon as we can.

Roz and I were early adopters of solar panel and battery technology and have not paid a bill in years. Every so often, we get a cheque for the power we have added to the grid. We put the limited money we have into companies that are supporting renewable energy. We invest in companies so we can vote at general meetings. We give our proxies to Market Forces, an off-shoot of the Friends of the Earth Australia. We have even invested in two coalmining companies, just to have a say.

Millions of people have taken to the streets to call for climate action, and I've joined them. After I took part in a protest in 2019, the ABC's 7.30 program interviewed me and other seniors as unlikely climate-change warriors. Many are surprised at the number of older people who want to see an end to fossil fuels and real action on climate change.

While the politicians may ignore our rallying voices, the business world is taking notice. Even the polluters are refusing to pollute any longer – Rio Tinto, BHP and AGL are all pulling back from polluting, and the banks are refusing to lend money for polluting projects.

I feel that, just as women did with childbirth, people are seeing the need to take the lead and force the changes to save the planet.

In my own way, I would like to think I too have helped make the world a better place. I know I have saved lives, and not just with medicine but also with a listening ear. Of this, I am most proud. I have worked hard but I have been rewarded with some of life's great experiences. The people I have met and known have enriched my life beyond measure. While class struggle preoccupied my early life, the overriding lesson from that time was that people must fight injustice and be wary of incursions into their rights. I have had two saviours in my life: medicine, which fulfilled my intellectual and humanist soul; and my soulmate, Roz, whose love I could not bear to be without. Looking back at my life and at where I am now, I feel remarkably fortunate. While I have had many barriers put in my way, for a lonely boy who grew up with five books in the house, I am content in my life and look forward to many more years (and protests) to come.

www.ingramcontent.com/pod-product-compliance
Lightning Source LLC
Chambersburg PA
CBHW071933090426
42811CB00042B/2427/J